Steven Van Wolputte (Ed.)

Borderlands and Frontiers in Africa

Afrikanische Studien
African Studies

Band/Volume 40

LIT

Borderlands and Frontiers in Africa

edited by

Steven Van Wolputte

LIT

Cover Image: Werda Checkpoint, Northern Namibia, July 2002.
Photo by Steven Van Wolputte

Made possible through the financial support by the Research Foundation – Flanders and the Belgian Association of Africanists

Belgische Vereniging van Afrikanisten BVA Association Belge des Africanistes

FWO VLAANDEREN
Fonds Wetenschappelijk Onderzoek
Research Foundation – Flanders

This book is printed on acid-free paper.

Bibliographic information published by the Deutsche Nationalbibliothek
The Deutsche Nationalbibliothek lists this publication in the Deutsche Nationalbibliografie; detailed bibliographic data are available in the Internet at http://dnb.d-nb.de.

ISBN 978-3-643-90333-4

A catalogue record for this book is available from the British Library

Zweigniederlassung Zürich 2013
Klosbachstr. 107
CH-8032 Zürich
Tel. +41 (0) 44-251 75 05
Fax +41 (0) 44-251 75 06
E-Mail: zuerich@lit-verlag.ch
http://www.lit-verlag.ch

LIT VERLAG Dr. W. Hopf
Berlin 2013
Fresnostr. 2
D-48159 Münster
Tel. +49 (0) 2 51-62 03 20
Fax +49 (0) 2 51-23 19 72
E-Mail: lit@lit-verlag.de
http://www.lit-verlag.de

Distribution:
In Germany: LIT Verlag Fresnostr. 2, D-48159 Münster
Tel. +49 (0) 2 51-620 32 22, Fax +49 (0) 2 51-922 60 99, E-mail: vertrieb@lit-verlag.de
In Austria: Medienlogistik Pichler-ÖBZ, e-mail: mlo@medien-logistik.at
In Switzerland: B + M Buch- und Medienvertrieb, e-mail: order@buch-medien.ch
In the UK: Global Book Marketing, e-mail: mo@centralbooks.com
In North America: International Specialized Book Services, e-mail: orders@isbs.com
e-books are available at www.litwebshop.de

CONTENTS

LIST OF ILLUSTRATIONS

LIST OF CONTRIBUTORS

Laura E. Bleckmann (Institute for Anthropological Research in Africa, IARA, University of Leuven) recently defended her Ph.D. on the performance of memories and identities in southern Kaoko. She previously published on the poetics of Herero praise songs.

Mark Breusers teaches economic anthropology at the University of Leuven and works as a food security manager with Caritas International in Brussels. His current research interest is in borderland encounters in Burkina Faso and Côte d'Ivoire.

Ira Dworkin is assistant professor of English and comparative literature at the American University in Cairo, and associate director of the Prince Alwaleed Bin Talal Bin Abdulaziz Alsaud Center for American Studies and Research.

Paul Enzlin is associate professor at the Faculty of Medicine of the University of Leuven, and Programme Director of the Master in Human Sexuality Studies.

Tammary Esho recently finished her Ph.D. at the Faculty of Medical Sciences of the University of Leuven on the psychosocial experiences of women who have undergone female genital cutting among the Maasai of Kenya. She works as a family therapist and a clinical sexologist in Nairobi, Kenya.

Els Hoorelbeke (IARA, University of Leuven) is currently finishing her Ph.D. on the border region between Namibia and Angola, more in particular on the processes of identification among the Dhimba living there.

Gillian Mathys is affiliated to the Department of Contemporary History of the University of Ghent, Belgium, and a Ph.D. fellow of the Research Foundation–Flanders. Her Ph.D research focuses on the borderland around Lake Kivu.

Ana Cristina Roque is researcher of the Centre of History (HIST) at the Tropical Research Institute in Lisbon, Portugal. Her current research interest is in border processes in Mozambican history.

Steven Van Wolputte is associate professor of social and cultural anthropology at the University of Leuven, and a fellow of the Morphomata Center for Advanced Studies of the Universität zu Köln, Germany.

Eline Versluys holds a Ph.D in linguistics from the University of Antwerp, Belgium. Her current research interests include: discursive identity construction, urban multilingualism in Africa, and social constructionism.

PREFACE

Somewhere in the beginning of 2006 the administrative board of the Belgian Association of Africanists decided to organize its next biannual colloquium on the theme "borderlands and frontiers in Africa." This event was scheduled as a one-day event, to take place on November 23, 2007, in the Okapi-room of the Royal Museum for Central Africa, Tervuren (Belgium). As the then chair of the Association, I was charged with the the colloquium's organization. But in the weeks before the event, while on a symposium in Leiden, The Netherlands, my spine gave up on me. I was out for several months. In a very literal sense, then, neither the conference nor this volume would have been possible without the friends and colleagues who came to the rescue: while I was lying on my couch, they took care of all the small and bigger issues that pop up in the last weeks before such an event. So a very special word of gratitude goes out to Anne Mélice, Filip De Boeck, Knut Graw, Ann Cassiman, Michael Meeuwis, Danielle de Lame, and Wolfgang Zeller.

Many people —a mix of junior and seasoned researchers, from Belgian and international institutions— presented their findings on November 23. Circumstances and time constraints, however, made that a number of them dropped out or had to withdraw in the long process that eventually led to this collection. Timothy Raeymaekers, Wangui Wa Goro,

Camille Lefebvre, Petra Vervust, Sarah Whiteford, Wolfgang Zeller, Oliver Bakewell, Kristof Titeca, Koen Vlassenroot, Clemens Zobel, Véronique Bragard, and Christiana Panella, they all expressed ideas, explained concepts, and highlighted perspectives that somehow made their way into this volume.

Also, I would also like to express my gratitude to a number of people whose contribution was essential: Kathleen Geens took care of administrative matters, and Ann Weemaes of the financial aspects of this project. Hugo Plowdeen copy-edited the manuscript. The latter was completed while enjoying a fellowship by the Morphomata Center for Advanced Studies of the Universität zu Köln. Finally, the conference and this book would have been impossible without the kind support of the Royal Museum for Central Africa and its Director, Guidy Gryseels, or without the funding provided by the Research Foundation–Flanders.

The editor

1
INTRODUCTION: LIVING THE BORDER

Steven Van Wolputte

This volume is on borders, and concentrates on the marked influence borders and boundaries, whether "real" or "imaginary," have on the lives of those who happen to live near them or are involved in making them. As Filip De Boeck pointed out in his keynote address to the conference on *Borders and Frontiers in Africa* —the event that led to this book:

> The notion of frontier is increasingly used to convey the post-colonial cosmogonies of the interstitial, the fold (*le pli*). The world of the frontier is currently portrayed as one of fluid margins rather than fixed boundaries. In this interpretation, the notion of frontier as "spatial boundary" becomes one of "borderlands." As such it deconstructs and dissolves the clearcut center/periphery or the local/global binarism embodied in the traditional border fetishism of the nation state ideology and its imperialist extension in the colony. [De Boeck 2007:1]

This perspective is the point of departure for the seven contributions collected here, whether they look at how political and symbolic borders took concrete form or at how borders and boundaries shape life in the city, mould the experience of "state," or morph the relations between those in power and the not-so-powerful. Important is that from the outset this volume argues that borders and boundaries do more than simply indicate where one territory stops and another begins. They are much more than spatial designations, and more than simple markers of "otherness" (see Das and Poole 2004:8). Therefore, the contributors to this volume see borders and borderlands in line with what Ana Tsing (1994:279) has argued with regard to the notion of margins, "the zones of unpredictability at the edges of discursive stability, where contradictory discourses overlap, or where discrepant kinds of meaning-making converge." In Tsing's understanding, then, margins appear as an "analytical placement that makes evident both the constraining, oppressive quality of cultural exclusion and the creative potential of rearticulating, enlivening, and rearranging the very social categories that peripheralize a group's existence" (Tsing 1994:279).

A view "from the margins" (Tsing 1994) thus, first of all, implies a simultaneous focus on the boundaries of social discourse, on the one hand, and on the hybridities and ambivalences social discourse creates, on the other hand (Van Wolputte and Fumanti 2010:8; Tsing 1993). Secondly, such a perspective implies going beyond discourse and forces us to look at what people do when received boundaries between "us" and "them," citizen and state, modern and traditional, public and private become blurred or suddenly seem not that sharp. Therefore, this understanding of margins comes close to what Victor Turner (1969, 1974) referred to as liminal or liminoid, or Michel Foucault (1986) as heterotopic. These liminal or liminoid and heterotopic places, and the dynamic of challenging, making and unmaking boundaries that characterizes them, are not confined to the political periphery. One finds them everywhere. One example are bars, pubs, and other drinking places, where revellers are allowed, even encouraged, to experiment with received categories (see Van Wolputte and Fumanti 2010:8–10; Argenti 2005; De Boeck 2004; Van Wolputte 2010:82–83).

It is in this sense of marginal that the contributors to this volume use the term borderland: as a shifting place, time or domain where competing discourses and regimes of power overlap, characterized by overt contradictions and paradox, by a simultaneous presence (or absence), often imagined at the "outside" but pertaining to and defining the core (Abinett 1995; Kopytoff 1987). Therefore, a borderland is a concept, an analytical tool to think "lived" ambiguity, paradox, and uncertainty not as an unwanted outcome of social processes, but as their "state" and precondition (see, in this regard, Friedman 2011; Gluckman 1955). Yet, at the same time, a borderland also is something real, something concrete: it refers to a space (whether geographical, physical, social, and so on) characterized by the presence of a dividing line between "this" and "that," between "here" and "there," or between "self" and "other," a distinction that, paradoxically perhaps, calls into being the hazy and ambiguous (Bolt 2012; Bryceson and Potts 2006; Flynn 1997).

Such a dividing line may take the form of a sign, a line of white paint on the road, or another symbolic marker such as passports, identity cards, passes or other travel documents. Often these demarcations take on a more compelling form, such as border control posts, a concrete wall, roadblocks, an increased police and military presence, sometimes even minefields. These signs serve as a marker (*limes*) of the state's acclaimed monopoly on violence and its sovereignty over a particular territory and its subjects, or to the perceived limits of citizenship. A borderland, in contrast, refers to the more or less gradual transition towards this *terminus* (to use the ancient

Latin expression): a grey zone in which "this" side always already implies the presence of the opposite side, to a context of mutual implication or overlap between different political, economic, and social structures.

In this volume, then, a borderland may refer to the overlapping margins between the Portuguese and British/ South African imperial project (Roque); to the discursive grid imposed on Burkina Fasso's past and present by French administrators-cum-ethnographers (Breusers); on the strategic bordering (Linde-Laursen 2010; Newman 2006a:183) youngsters in suburban Dakar deploy in the narrative making and unmaking of identity (Versluys); to the mobility of African actors in navigating the (shifting) border between Belgian Congo and Rwanda (Mathijs); to the political and ethnographic gerrymandering —fencing— along Namibia's border with Angola (Van Wolputte, Hoorelbeke and Bleckmann); to the fading distinction between churches and state in Belgian Congo due to U.S. racial politics (Dworkin); or to the embodied boundaries between child and adult, non-Maasai and Maasai in Kenya (Esho, Enzlin and Van Wolputte).

BORDERS MATTER

A border or borderland, in short, is both an analytical tool, and a locality defined by the physical (or meta-physical) presence of one or more divides. This also means that each border(land) is characterized by a particular history, a local (political, economic, cultural, ...) context, a specific constellation of structures, actors, and a tangible dynamic of all of these (see De Boeck 2000). As the booming literature on the topic illustrates, one of the consequences of this particularity of borders and borderlands is a staggering variety of theoretical vantage points, methodological approaches and analytic themes (for a recent overview, see Donnan and Wilson 2010; Newman 2006; Wastl-Walter 2011; Wilson and Donnan 2012). In its turn, this variety is the product of, and the rationale behind, the comparative and interdisciplinary character of the domain of boder studies, as political scientists turn towards ethnography, anthropologists indulge in the intricacies of concepts such as sovereignty or nation-state, linguists borrow from economic theory, and lawyers develop a keen interest in culture. This multi- and interdisciplinary orientation is also reflected in this volume.

The study of borders and borderlands is, indeed, booming ever since the 1990s. The reasons for this expansion seem rather obvious: the fall of the Iron Curtain in 1989 and the implosion of communist regimes in Eastern Europe sparked off an unbridled neoliberal belief in the possibility of an earth gone flat without barriers to hinder the free, global traffic of people, goods, and capital. "Reaganomics" and Thatcherism resonated with a popular reading of Francis Fukuyama's "end of history" (in which Fukuyama proposed liberal democracy as the synthesis of human evolution) culminating in a firm belief that free enterprise was not only desirable, but was the only way forward, and in efforts to deregulate societies and economies. Paradoxically, however, the waning of boundaries (or, at least, the ideologically inspired idea that boundaries were disappearing) worldwide only seemed to inspire a resurgence of ethnicity and nationalism (eg, in the former communist states in Eastern Europe). Moreover, the euphoria that dominated much of Euro-American political and economic thought during the 1990s, came to a grinding halt on September 11, 2001.

Obviously, the scholarly interest in borders and boundaries was not only inspired by a changing political climate and ideology. More importantly, scholars witnessed that the globe was characterized by more boundaries, not less; that existing tensions were exacerbated by an ideology of unbridled growth; and that new inequalities resulted from economic globalization. Given these social and political concerns, then, and given the increasing and intensifying flows of people, technologies, images, ideas, resources, and finance across the globe, the renewed scholarly interest in the making and unmaking of boundaries may come as no surprise. As testified to by the recent publication of two important textbooks (Wastl-Walter 2011; Wilson and Donnan 2012), the interest in borders and borderlands also results from a growing scholarly fascination for the in-between, in flows rather than states-of-being, and the salient questions the border paradox —the presence of a border creates the possibility of its transgression—raises with regard to sovereignty, state, citizenship, identity, marginalization, mobility, power, ecological concerns, and so on (Wilson and Donnan 2012:15; Donnan and Wilson 1999, 2010).[1]

This volume, then, ambitions to add to the growing "postdisciplinary" (Wilson and Donnan 2012:20) body of border studies by bringing together seven case studies from Africa. These cases on the western (chapters three and four), central (five and seven), eastern (two and eight) and southern part of the continent (two and six) have in common that they, first of all, resolutely opt for an actor-oriented (or "bottom-up") perspective on the making and unmaking of borders and boundaries; that, secondly, they draw attention to the "physicality" of the borderscape; and that, thirdly, they place question marks behind the idea that states and other anonymized institutions are the principal actors in border-making. Let me hasten to qualify this by adding that the seven contributions here prefer to see the state in terms of what Timothy Mitchell (1999) coined the state effect: the practices, routines, discourses, imaginings, and experiences of local actors (whether administrators, surveyors, officers, colonial ethnographers, missionaries, laborers, chiefs, villagers, urbanites) in their dealings with what is commonly referred to or understood as "government," "state," or "bureaucracy." When studying borders the state is, indeed, never far away. It is, however, important to note that in the cases presented here states function rather as a backdrop to the ongoing negotiation and bargaining in their borderlands than as actors in and of themselves. The remainder of this introduction will elucidate how these three perspectives have informed the seven cases collected here.

ARE STATES DEFINED BY THEIR BORDERS?

It is obvious that states and state or international institutions do play an important role in the making and unmaking of borders. As obvious is the observation that borders (as Van Schendel [2005:332] circumscribes them, "zones of national concern [that] demarcate a nation's imagined homeland and a state's territorial jurisdiction" have always been problematic.

The most well-documented example is probably the border between Mexico and the USA, which according to Alvarez (1995:452) was "the model for border studies and borderlands genre throughout the world." First of all, states are often very present at their borders. Away from its centre, the state is often more tangible, controls are usually tighter, and officials, policemen and the (para-)military often more present. As such, borders then exemplify the state (and the nation) itself, that needs to be safeguarded against foreign threats.

Borders, however, are not only there to keep aliens out, but also to keep citizens (and subjects) in. They remind them of the power of their sovereign. From this perspective, international borders then also exemplify the state's panoptical pretence, and its claim to control the life of its subjects. For instance, Veena Das and Deborah Poole (2004:7–8) circumscribe margins with reference to an omnipresent (albeit an often illegible) state: first, they see margins as "containers for people considered insufficiently socialized into the law"; secondly as "the spaces, forms, and practices through which the state is continually both experienced and undone through the illegibility of its own practices, documents, and words"; and thirdly as "the space between bodies, law, and discipline" (see, in contrast, the quotation from Tsing 1994, above).

Still, however, the common use of notions such as nation, state, citizenship and even culture presupposes that national or state borders are unambiguously defined, and this despite the fact that this powerful modernist equation has been under scrutiny for over a decade (see Comaroff and Comaroff 2000). It is indeed no coincidence that in this globalizing and transnational age scholars across various disciplines have been looking at borders in order to scrutinize received notions of culture, state, and even space (Ingold 2011; for an introduction to the role of border studies in the social sciences, see Wilson and Donnan 1998:3–12). These studies distinguish different actors (agencies, officials, administrators, elites, interest groups, politicians, and so on) who decide or otherwise weigh upon processes of inclusion and exclusion; so doing, they offer a more practical (as opposed to institutional) approach of the state (see for instance Comaroff and Comaroff 1997). Such a perspective approaches the state from the point of view of the actors affected by, or making part of, governance; it, in other words, focuses more on the effects of state (Mitchell 1999). Such a vantage point moves beyond questions of mere territoriality or sovereignty. In the words of Aradhana Sharma and Akhil Gupta:

> The boundary between state and non-state realms is thus drawn through the contested practices of bureaucracies, and people's encounters with, and negotiations of, these practices. Everyday statist encounters not only shape people's imagination of what the state is and how it is demarcated, but also enable people to devise strategies of resistance to this imagined state. Those who are the subjects or targets of state programs, and thus "outside"

> bureaucracies, learn to use the very same techniques that lower-level state agents use to sabotage official mandates and orders. (...) they use these practices in their everyday interactions with officials to gain institutional access or to subvert official scrutiny; they also use them when interacting with non-officials in order to establish their authority over others. [Sharma and Gupta 2006:17]

Therefore, Ana Roque and Mark Breusers look at border-making practices and routines of state-affiliated actors regarding, respectively, the geodesic demarcation of the colonial boundaries decided upon in Berlin or Lisbon, or the discursive demarcation of ethnic and administrative divides in Burkina Faso.

In examining this negotiated character of borders and boundaries, processes of power come to the fore: power relationships shape the course of borders, and, conversely, borders and boundaries shape policy and the exertion of power. As a brief glimpse at the geopolitical map suggests, Africa is a case in point and in postcolonial discourse the artificial and seemingly arbitrary division of the continent between foreign empires and states is a recurrent theme. It is, however, important to understand what power relations are involved in the making and unmaking of borders and boundaries. In chapter five, for instance, Gillian Mathys argues that the role of local chiefs in the making and unmaking of colonial boundaries is much larger than commonly assumed. In general, colonial (or colonizing) boundaries were highly ambivalent, and in chapter six Van Wolputte, Hoorelbeke and Bleckmann subscribe to Mathys' argument that borders affected local actors (whether chiefs or commoners, administrators, policemen, and so forth) differently, depending on their social position, hopes, and expectations. These two chapters warn against overestimating the role of state in Africa's colonial past, and against too strong an emphasis on institutions. A similar actor-oriented perspective is adopted by Ira Dworkin when investigating the effect of racial boundaries in the USA on the boundaries between mission and state in Belgian Congo.

Finally, the state also functions as a backdrop in the sense that it functions as a frame of reference to think, discuss and "feel" modernity and tradition, urban and rural identity, whether in the context of symbolic demarcations in sub-urban Dakar (Versluys), or in that of female circumcision in Kenya (Esho, Enzlin and Van Wolputte). In Senegal, state, colonialism and "modern" government are firmly linked with the use of French, whereas in Kenya state and government are strongly associated with the efforts aimed at the eradication of Female Genital Cutting (FGC).

BORDERSCAPES

A second important theme that runs throughout this volume then is that boundaries do have a profound, often physical, effect on those inhabiting the borderland. Borders are more than just symbols: they exert a tangible influence on the landscape, and on how people move through it.

The landscape shapes the border: whereas the meandering boundaries in, say, Europe create an illusion of "natural" or "organic" growth, their shape and location in many of the more recent nations in, say, Africa, explicitly confront us with their artificial character and violent origin. One common misconception, though, is that regions were divided arbitrarily: it is no coincidence that these international borders were located far away from the then centres of colonial power or that they often cross-cut the more arid regions of the African continent. With the explicit intention of creating buffer zones, borders were located in regions that were considered "empty" or without resources or, which amounts to the same, people.

One of the consequences is for instance that pastoralists groups in Africa were, quite literally, marginalized and that they nowadays find themselves in those often dry and violence-prone border regions (Azarya 1996; Van Wolputte and Verswijver 2004:3–5). In these border zones, often characterized by low and erratic rainfall, global warming is resulting in a higher mobility of people and animals, thereby increasing the risk of Transborder Animal Diseases (TADs, such as Contagious Bovine Pleuropneumonia or Foot and Mouth Disease), which in its turn requires a closer surveillance and stricter control of the border.

But borders also shape the landscape: colonial authorities were not too keen to invest in the development of infrastructures in these buffer zones or in those regions they considered as "marginal" or "empty." In chapter two, Roque demonstrates, moreover, that the construction of the Mozambican-South African border drastically changed the local landscape as the demarcation of the intended border implied the destruction of local resources (the clearing of a 27 kilometre-wide stretch of woodland to ensure full visibility). The more general point Roque is making here is that the demarcation of a border needs to be negotiated not only between local actors, but also between these local actors and the material conditions of the technology they possessed and the landscape they encountered. A similar observation is that in Opuwo, a small city in northwest Namibia, the boundaries of the city have shifted in recent years because of the availability of mobile communication: being in the city nowadays means to be able to connect to the cell phone network. More pervasive contemporary examples, perhaps, include the tendency to construct hydropower or nuclear power plants near borders, thus to minimize political risk at home and exporting any political fallout to neighbouring countries.

Such borderscapes, however, do not only provide threats; they also offer opportunities. Borderlanders in the

Horn of Africa, for instance, move through the different "political, legal, and economic spaces with their respective opportunity structures" to escape violence, exploit resources such as pasture or water, or to engage in cross-border traffic of commodities (Feyissa and Hoehne 2010:12; Long and Villareal 2003; Lentz 2003; Love 2012; Nugent 2002; Titeca 2012; Talle 1999). Likewise, the inhabitants of the Namibian-Angolan borderland were, to some extent at least, able to use the presence of the border as a means to escape violence, look for labour opportunities, or augment their herds (see the chapters by Mathys and by Van Wolputte, Hoorelbeke and Bleckmann). Also the recent literature on boomtowns, for instance, testifies to the creativity and opportunism of traders exploiting the differences in political and economical regimes on either side of the border (Bryceson and Mwaipopo 2010; Dobler 2008, 2009).

While borders can be symbolical (a white line on the road, or a designation in your passport) or even immaterial (such as between identities, or races), they —or their effects— can at the same time also be painfully tangible (and the very same examples can be cited here). As the chapter on Female Genital Cutting (FGC) among the Maasai in Kenya suggests, the distinction between circumcised and non-circumcised marks socially constructed differences (such as adult and child, Maasai and non-Maasai), but also connects and interrelates across these divides. This paradox complicates the efforts by the Kenyan government and international organizations striving for eradication of the practice. As also the chapter by Ira Dworkin makes clear, to an important extent borders and boundaries are negotiated through and on the body of local actors.

STATES OF AMBIGUITY

This emphasis on an actor-oriented approach is the third theme that binds all seven contributions together, and one of the merits of the contributions collected here certainly is that their study of borders and borderlands offers us offer a prism through which to refract the dynamics between local actors, structures and contingencies, or between state officials, elites and "common people" (Baud and Van Schendel 1997:219). Admittedly, these dynamics are found everywhere. But as Wilson and Donnan (2012:1) remark, it is often in borderlands that such processes and performances are found in sharper relief.

Such a vantage point "from below," however, also implies one must account for the ambivalences, paradoxes and contradictions that characterize life in a borderland. Indeed, what makes borders and boundaries fascinating to study is the fact that they are geographical and political, discrete and hybrid, fixed and malleable, physical and social, empowering and disempowering. They may appear as impediment and as opportunity, as limit and as resource, as challenge and condition for identity, all this usually at the same time. These paradoxes are not contingent or coincidental, nor the result of opposing claims, hopes, and expectation. They are at the heart of what borders mean, and quintessential to what they are —as a concept, and as a tangible reality. Borders, in short, are defined by the paradoxes they create. Writing about 19th-century urban London, Stallybrass and White circumscribe the most fundamental paradox as follows (also see McClintock 1996).

> The point is that the *exclusion* necessary to the formation of social identity at level one is simultaneously a *production* at the level of the Imaginary, and a production, what is more, of a complex hybrid fantasy emerging out of the very attempt to demarcate boundaries, to unite and purify the social collectivity. [Stallybrass and White 1986:193]

Even if this citation relates to the role of boundaries in defining "Self" and "Other," it also applies to, for instance, political or administrative boundaries: borders divide, but also relate, and rather than containing people, they create new, and often unanticipated, forms of mobility (Raeymaekers 2010, 2012). As the opening sections to this introduction suggested: each border creates a borderland, zones of overlap between political and economic regimes, systems of value, and local histories (see Guyer 2005).

Hence the seven case studies presented here focus on what in a different context has been labeled the "problems of meaning" (Flax 1990:222) associated with the experience and execution of political and semantic power, with, so to speak, the politics and poetics of inclusion and exclusion. These problems of meaning, for instance, surface in the linguistic practices of youngsters in Dakar as they try to draw ethnic distinctions, distinguish between city and village or construct their "Africanness" (see chapter four), or in the efforts by Maasai women in Kenya to construct the boundaries of sociability, respectability, and womanhood (see chapter eight). With regard to the first example, Versluys notes in her conclusion that whereas the identities claimed by youngsters in Dakar seem to be rather clear-cut in discourse, in practice they overlap and contradict, as ethnic identities come in degrees, people seem to continuously move between city and village, and identify both as "assimilated" and "authentic." Likewise, Maasai women "navigate the borderlands" as the boundaries between circumcised and non-circumcised, Maasai and non-Maasai, old and new, or adult and child do mark socially constructed differences, but also connect and interrelate. As Tammary Esho (2012) noted elsewhere, most Maasai women in her study experienced FGC not as an impediment, but as a precondition to become adult, sexualized beings. But also in the chapters focussing on Africa's colonial past, ambiguities move to the centre stage of analysis —if only because these analyses demonstrate there was a huge discrepancy between what was said and done in offices in Berlin, Paris, Brussels, London or Pretoria and what happened "in the field," and between colonial discourse and colonizing practice. Therefore, problems of meaning are central to Ana Roque's investigation of the demarcation of the Mozambican border with South Africa, as –for instance– African agents held completely different views regarding the meaning of borders (or of treaties) when compared to their European counterparts. In similar vein, Mark Breusers points towards the inability of a sedentary worldview to deal with the mobility (both in terms of geography and in terms of semantics) of Fulbe herders. Part of his argument is that a modernist worldview was (or is, see Van Wolputte and Verswijver 2004) is unable to harbour hybridity and multiplicity. Important to note, however, is that the symbolic violence inherent to colonizing categories also had a marked influence on down-to-earth political reality, as is demonstrated by Gillian Mathys when discussing how the efforts by representatives of the Belgian colonial administration to impose a labour migration scheme undermined their attempts to tap the flow of labourers from the Rwandese-Congolese borderland. A similar argument is made in the chapter by Van Wolputte, Hoorelbeke and Bleckmann. This sixth chapter focuses explicitly on the ambivalences of colonial rule by probing into two case studies set in northern Namibia; a first one illustrates the uncertainties of the colonial, "ethnogracizing" (Wilmsen 1989:vii) grid by taking up the case of a group that fell in between categories; the second case these authors develop looks at the ambivalence that characterizes the way inhabitants of northern Namibia experienced colonial gerrymandering. Finally, Ira Dworkin analyses the early history of the American Presbyterian Church in Congo Free State. This mission, pioneered by William Sheppard, an African American graduate, was founded in the interstice created by US racial politics, religion and state power, and the first decade of its existence was dominated by the ambivalences and contradictions of being a black- (and American-) headed mission station in a racially polarized society in Congo, supposed to exemplify Leopold II's civilizing mission while being highly critical of the violence and exploitation of the then colonial regime.

Like the six other case studies presented in this volume, Dworkin's analysis refuses to take received borders and boundaries for granted. That also is why the contributors to this volume took up an actor-oriented perspective "from the margins" (Tsing 1994). Such a vantage point requires a case-by-case approach to elucidate the many ways borders and boundaries are made and unmade, negotiated, crossed, rendered obsolete and re-invented. Such an approach, moreover, forces us to look at the problems of meaning that define people's lives in today's world —and this interest in ambiguity and flow, in fluid identities and fluctuating constellations of power certainly are among the reasons why border studies have proven to be such a fruitful domain of study. At the same time, borders are more than just categories of thought or classification, as they do have a material impact on people's lives. After all, and despite neo-liberal rhetorics, the world has not "flattened," on the contrary.

ACKNOWLEDGEMENTS

This introduction profited from discussions with and remarks by Katrijn Asselberg, Michael Bollig, Filip De Boeck, Larissa Förster, Mattia Fumanti, John Friedman, Fatima Müller-Friedman, Anne Mélice, Katrien Pype, Wolfgang Zeller, and many others, and was made possible by successive research grants by the Research Foundation Flanders and the project *Beyond the border: a political ecology of the Kunene Frontier* (G.0251.07N) funded by the same institution. At the time of writing, the author enjoyed a fellowship from the Morphomata

Center for Advanced Studies at the University of Cologne. The *Freiraum* and the interdisciplinary exchange I enjoyed there greatly contributed to the ideas expressed here, as did the relentless questions and remarks by the students in the course on political anthropology at the University of Leuven. All shortcomings, however, are entirely mine.

NOTE

[1] Two recent volumes, one with an emphasis on political geography (Wastl-Walter 2011), the other leaning more heavily on anthropological approaches (Wilson and Donnan 2012) offer an excellent review and cross-section of current themes and approaches in border studies. Also see, for instance, Alvarez 1995; Baud and Van Schendel 1997; Chalfin 2001; De Boeck 2000; Donnan and Wilson 1999, 2010; Linde-Laursen 2010; Love 2012; Martin and Ayimpam 2012; Newman 2006a,b; Nugent 2002; Wilson and Donnan 1998). An elaborate bibliography on borders and boundaries in Africa is found at the website of the African Borderlands Research Network (ABORNE, see http://www.aborne.org. accessed Nov.7, 2012).

REFERENCES

Abbinnett, R. 1995. The phenomenon of shifting frontiers. The Kenya-Somalia case in the Horn of Africa, 1880s-1970s. Journal of Asian and African Studies 30(1–2):1–40.

Alvarez, R. R. 1995. The Mexican-US border: the making of an anthropology of borderlands. Annual Review of Anthropology, 24, 447–470.

Argenti, N. 2005. Dancing in the borderlands. The forbidden masquerade of Oku youth and women, Cameroon. *In* A. Honwana and F. De Boeck, eds. Makers and breakers. Children and youth in postcolonial Africa Pp. 121–149. Oxford: James Currey.

Azarya, V. 1996. Nomads and the state in Africa. The political roots of marginality. Leiden: African Studies Centre.

Baud, M., and W. Van Schendel. 1997. Towards a comparative study of borderlands. Journal of World History, 8(2):211–242.

Bolt, M. 2012. Waged entrepreneurs, policed informality: work, the regulation of space and the economy of the Zimbabwean-South African border. Africa: Journal of the International African Institute 82(1):111–

130.
Bryceson, D. F. and R. Mwaipopo. 2010. Rural-urban transitions in Tanzania's northwest mining frontier. *In* Rural-urban dynamics. Livelihoods, mobility and markets in African and Asian frontiers. J. Agergaard, N. Fold and K.V. Gough, eds. Pp. 158–173. New York: Routledge.

Bryceson, D. F. and D. Potts, eds. 2006. African urban economies. Viability, vitality or vitiation. Houndmills: Palgrave MacMillan.

Chalfin, B. 2001. Border zone trade and the economic boundaries if the state in north-east Ghana. Africa 71(2):202–224.

Comaroff, J.and J. Comaroff. 2000. Milennial capitalism: first thoughts on a second coming. Public Culture 12(2):291–343.

——— 1997. Of revelation and revolution, volume two. The dialectics of modernity on a South African frontier. Chicago: University of Chicago Press.

Das, V. and D. Poole. 2004. State and its margins. Comparative ethnographies. *In* V. Das and D. Poole, eds. Anthropology in the margins of the state. Pp. 3–33). New Delhi: Oxford University Press.

De Boeck, F. 2007. Keynote address. Paper presented at the conference Borderlands and Frontiers in Africa, Tervuren, Nov 23.

——— 2004. La frontière diamantifère angolaise et son héros mutant. *In* Matière à politique. Le pouvoir, les corps et les choses J.-F. Bayart and J.-P. Warnier, eds. Pp. 93–128. Paris: Karthala.

——— 2000. Borderland Breccia. The mutant hero and the historical imagination of a Central-African diamond frontier. Journal of Colonialism and Colonial History 1(2):1–44.

Dobler, G. 2009. Oshikango: the dynamics of growth and regulation in a Namibian boom town. Journal of Southern African Studies 35(1): 115-131.

——— 2008. From Scotch whisky to Chinese sneakers: international commodity flows and new trade networks in Oshikango, Namibia. Africa: Journal of the International African Institute 78(3):410–432.

Donnan, H. and T.M. Wilson. 1999. Borders: frontiers of identity, nation and state. Oxford: Berg.

——— eds. 2010. Borderlands: ethnographic approaches to security, power, and identity. Lanham: University Press of America.

Esho, T. C. 2012. An exploration of the psycho-social experiences of women who have undergone female genital cutting. A case of the Maasai in Kenya. Unpublished Ph.D. Dissertation, Faculty of Medical Sciences, University of Leuven.

Feyissa, D. and M. V. Hoehne, eds. 2010. Borders and borderlands as resources in the Horn of Africa. Woodbridge: James Currey.

Flax, J. 1990. Thinking fragments. Psychoanalysis, feminism and postmodernism in the contemporary West. Berkeley: University of California

Press.
Flynn, D. K. 1997. "We are the border": identity, exchange and the state along the Benin-Nigeria border. American Ethnologist 24(2):311–330.
Foucault, M. 1986. Of other spaces. Diacritics 16(1):22–27.
Friedman, J. T. 2011. Imagining the post-apartheid state. An ethnographic account of Namibia. New York: Berghahn Publishers.
Gluckman, M. 1955. The judicial process among the Barotse of northern Rhodesia. Manchester: Rhodes-Livingstone Institute Northern Rhodesia.
Guyer, J. 2005. Marginal gains. Monetary transactions in Atlantic Africa. Chicago: University of Chicago Press.
Ingold, T. 2011. Against space: place, movement, knowledge. *In* Boundless worlds. An anthropological approach to movement. P. W. Kirby, ed. Pp. 29–44. New York: Berghahn Books.
Kopytoff, I. 1987. The internal African frontier: the making of African political culture. *In* The African frontier: the reproduction of traditional African societies. I. Kopytoff, ed. Pp. 3–84. Bloomington: Indiana University Press.
Lentz, C. 2003. "This is Ghanaian territory!": land conflicts on a West African border. American Ethnologist 30(2): 273–289.
Linde-Laursen, A. 2010. Bordering. Identity processes between the national and personal. Farnham: Ashgate.
Long, N. and M. Villareal. 2003. Small product, big issues: value contestations and cultural identities in cross-border commodity networks. *In* Globalization and identity: dialectics of flow and closure. B. Meyer and P. Geschiere, eds. Pp. 125–150. Oxford: Blackwell Publishing.
Love, R. 2012. Borders and borderlands as resources in the Horn of Africa. Review of African Political Economy 39(132): 396–398.
McClintock, A. 1996. Imperial leather. Race, gender, and sexuality in the colonial contest. New York: Routledge.
Mitchell, T. 1999. Society, economy and the state effect. *In* State/ Culture: state formation after the cultural turn. G. Steinmetz, ed. Pp. 76–97. Ithaca: Cornell University Press.
Newman, D. 2006b. The lines that continue to separate us. borders in our "borderless" world. Progress in Human Geography 30(2):143–161.
Newman, D. 2006a. Borders and bordering. Towards an interdisciplinary dialogue. European Journal of Social Theory 9(2):171–186.
Nugent, P. 2002. Smugglers, secessionist, and loyal citizens on the Ghana-Togo frontier. The lie of the borderlands since 1914. Athens, OH: Ohio University Press.
Raeymaekers, T. 2012. African boundaries and the new capitalist frontier. *In* A companion to border studies. T. M. Wilson and H. Donnan, eds. Pp. 318–331. Malden: Blackwell Publishing.

——— 2010. Protection for sale? War and the transformation of regulation on the Congo-Ugandan border. Development and Change, 41(4):563–587.

Sharma, A. and A. Gupta. 2006. Introduction: Rethinking theories of the state in an age of globalization. *In* The anthropology of the state. A reader. A. Sharma and A. Gupta, ed. Pp. 1–42. Malden: Blackwell Publishing.

Stallybrass, P. and A. White. 1986. The politics and poetics of transgression. London: Methuen.

Talle, A. 1999. Pastoralists at the border: Maasai poverty and the development discourse in Tanzania. *In* The poor are not us. Poverty and pastoralism in eastern Africa. D. M. Anderson and V. Broch-Due, eds. Pp. 106–124. Oxford: James Currey.

Titeca, K. 2012. Tycoons and contraband: informal cross-border trade in West Nile, north-western Uganda. Journal of Eastern African Studies, 6(1):47–63.

Tsing, A. L. 1994. From the margins. Cultural Anthropology 9(3):279–297.

——— 1993. In the realm of the diamond queen. Princeton: Princeton University Press.

Turner, V. 1974. Liminal to liminoid, in play, flow and ritual: an essay in comparative symbology. Rive University Studies 60(3):53–92.

——— 1969. The Ritual Process. Structure and anti-structure. London: Routledge and Kegan Paul.

Van Schendel, W. 2005. The Bengal borderland. Beyond state and nation in South Asia. London: Anthem Press.

Van Wolputte, S. 2010. Beers and Bullets, Beads and bulls. Drink and the making of margins in a small Namibian town. *In* Beer in Africa. Drinking spaces, states and selves. S. Van Wolputte and M. Fumanti, eds. Pp. 79–105). Münster: LIT Verlag.

Van Wolputte, S. and M. Fumanti. 2010. Beer and the making of boundaries: An introduction. In Beer in Africa. Drinking spaces, states and selves. S. Van Wolputte and M. Fumanti, eds. Pp. 1–25. Münster: LIT Verlag.

Van Wolputte, S. and G. Verswijver. 2004. Introduction: border lands, border people. *In* At the fringes of modernity: people, animals, transitions. African Pastoralists Studies 2. S. Van Wolputte and G. Verswijver, eds. Pp. 10–37. Tervuren: RMCA.

Wastl-Walter, D. 2011. Introduction. *In* The Ashgate research companion to border studies. D. Wastl-Walter, ed. Pp. 1–8. Surrey: Ashgate Publishing Limited.

Wilmsen, E. N. 1989. Land filled with flies. A political economy of the Kalahari. Chicago: University of Chicago Press.

Wilson, T. M. and H. Donnan, eds. 2012. A companion to border studies. Malden: Blackwell.
——— eds. 1998. Border identities. Nation and state at international frontiers. Cambridge: Cambridge University Press.

2
A HISTORY OF MOZAMBIQUE'S SOUTHERN BORDER: THE ARCHIVES OF THE PORTUGUESE COMMISSION OF CARTOGRAPHY

Ana Cristina Roque

INTRODUCTION

Created in 1883 under the instruction of the Geographical Society of Lisbon, the Portuguese Commission of Cartography (PCC) was assigned to produce a collection of credible and accurate maps of all of Portugal's overseas territories.[1] Its subsequent scope, however, extended far beyond this initial purpose. Today, the PCC's legacy has become an important corpus of information on Portuguese colonial policy and on Portugal's former overseas territories. Yet, it is only recently that the highly diverse collection of the PCC has become the object of systematic scrutiny.

However, there has been no overall assessment of the importance of the PCC archives. First of all, until recently most of them remained unknown —with only very few exceptions. Second, the PCC archives were dispersed across several research units in the Tropical Research Institute (*Instituto de Investigação Científica Tropical*, IICT) in Lisbon.

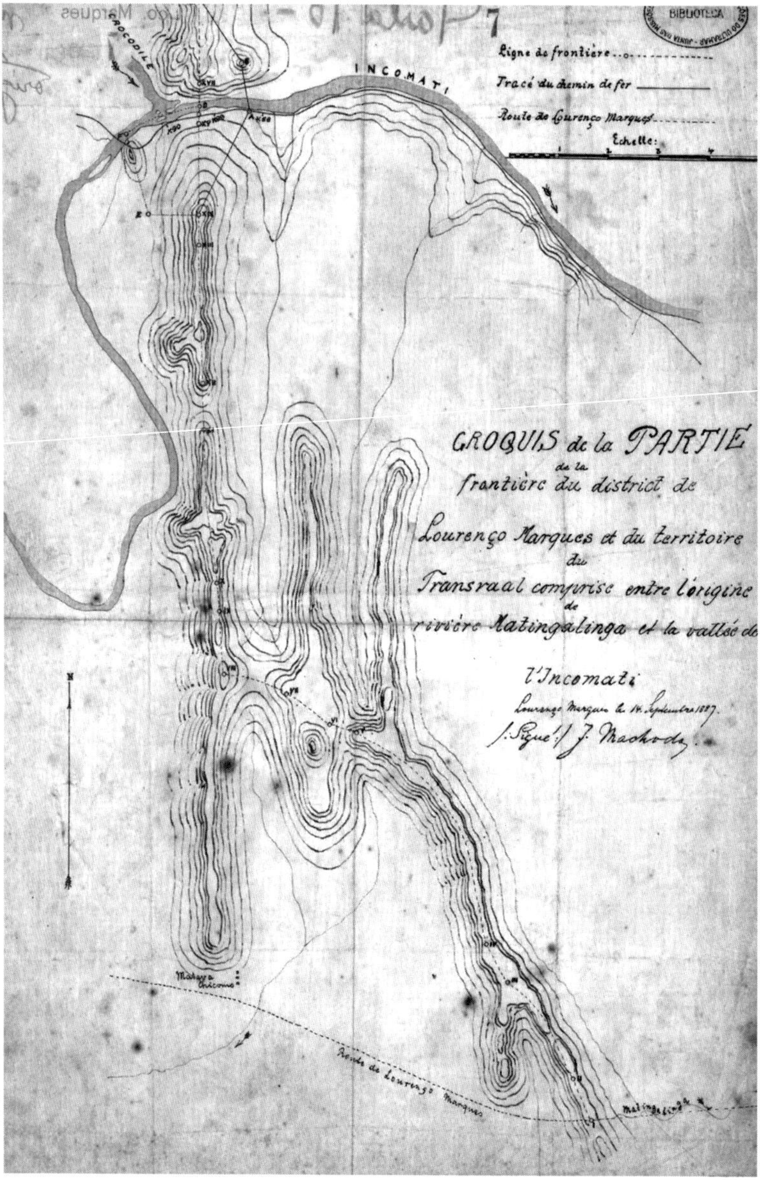

Fig. 2.1. Joaquim José Machado (1887), Croquis de la partie du District de Lourenço Marques et du territoire du Transvaal. IICT — GeoDes Archive of the Frontiers

A third element is that what we now call the archives of the Portuguese Commission of Cartography is a wide and heterogeneous collection of documents and equipment produced or used by the PCC between 1883 and 1936, when it was abolished. These documents concern all former Portuguese colonies, and along with equipment used during the PCC's survey missions, they include: scientific findings, official and diplomatic documents, correspondence, proceedings of the meetings held by the joint commissions, reports, field notes, geographic coordinates, topographic and geodesic works, sketches, maps, photographs, and detailed descriptions of the various landscapes and beacons. These materials can be grouped under three headings. These are: first, the *Map Collection* (10 folders with 481 manuscript maps and sketches on Mozambique as well as some printed copies and a few maps used but not produced by the PCC); second, the *Archive of the Frontiers* (the record of the daily works of the commissions involved in the demarcation and delimitation of the frontiers); and third, the *Geographic Registries* (relating to the fieldwork by members of the Geographic Survey Mission).[2]

For more than half a century, this collection was only accessible via old catalogues. These, however, were not kept as part of the IICT's central archive but, instead, entrusted to the *Centro de Estudos de Historia e Cartografia Antiga*, Centre for the study of History and Antique Cartography, CEHCA), one of the research centres of the Institute.[3] Researchers here and at the Department of Human Sciences made sporadic use of this collection,[4] but a systematic scrutiny of these materials did not take place until there was a recent reorganization of the IICT. The need for such a critical examination resulted in —amongst other things— the project on *Political Cartography and Colonial Territories*. This and other projects[5] reflect the strategic objectives of the IICT with regard to the members of the Community of Portuguese Language Countries (CPLP), namely to "[facilitate] access of CPLP

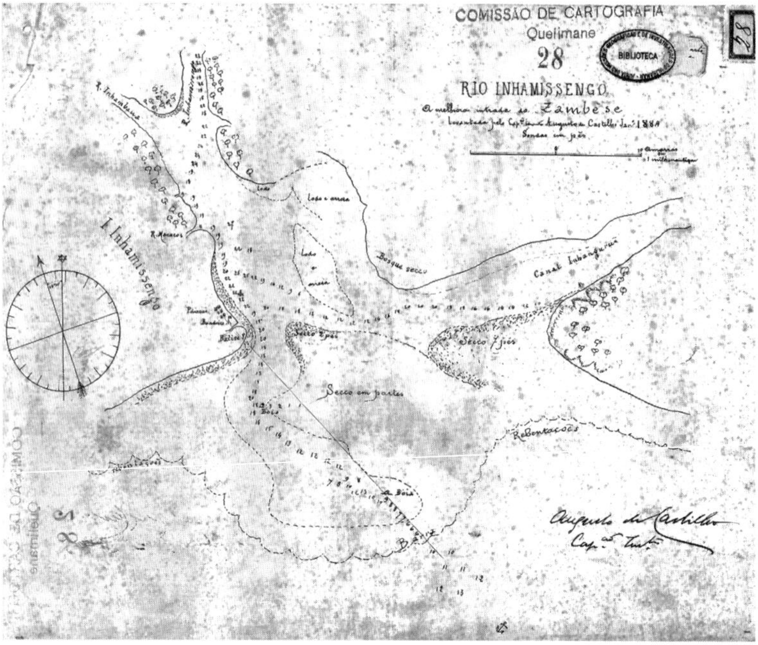

Fig. 2.2. Augusto de Castilho (1884), Rio Inhamissengo. IICT —Centro de História P04CO28.

countries to its vast historic and scientific heritage, as recommended by the CPLP Ministers of Science and Technology in 2003."[6] Also, these projects are a response to the recent demand of the Portuguese-Speaking African Countries (*Países Africanos de Língua Oficial Portuguesa*, PALOP)[7] to access the official documents on borders and provide the necessary support to the border demarcation process which is presently in progress, in order to observe the resolutions of the African Union Border Declaration Programme.[8] A recent report by *the Instituto do Mar e das Fronteiras* from Mozambique (IMAF 2009) indeed states, with regard to Mozambique, that the lack of these documents has been a major restriction in settling the country's international boundaries: Mozambique has 2,685 kilometres of terrestrial and 2,700 kilometres of maritime borders, which it shares, respectively, with six and four other countries.[9] Therefore, the project on political cartography also became a starting point from which to address the PALOP's concerns. Maps and other documents were scanned to create a cartographic database that was subsequently cross-referenced with the reports, photographs, and other materials, whether within the PCC collection or not. That way, the collection was made available for future studies (Santos 2006).

Creating this database and adapting it to the specific history and situation of each country constituted the bulk of the work. In the case of Cape Verde, Angola and Mozambique, it immediately began to function as a base for further research and ensuing deployment studies. In Mozambique, the project began with a study of the PCC maps, in order to evaluate their importance in understanding the physical evolution of the coastal areas and its consequences (Roque and Ferrão 2006a, 2006b, 2007). The results suggested that climate change, for instance, was already affecting the Mozambican coast long before the impact of humanity in the late 20th century. This resulted in an ensuing research project that broadened our scope to include the more inland areas of Mozambique.[10]

THE PCC AND THE DEFINITION OF THE MOZAMBICAN BORDER

In the past, the PCC documents relating to border delimitation and demarcation were classified under the title *Archive of the Frontiers*. Apart from the maps, this archive contains hundreds of photos and thousands of handwritten entries.[11] For central and southern Mozambique, most of these materials were produced in the late 19th century, following the Berlin Conference of 1885. These documents shed new light on the particular history of this region: they demonstrate that, in some cases, the occupation and demarcation of territories did not necessarily occur in accordance with the decisions taken in Berlin.

The Mozambique–Transvaal borderline, for instance, was already laid down some 15 years before the conference, and, in 1885, the Governments of Lourenço Marques and the Transvaal were setting up commissions to carry out the fieldwork needed for its physical demarcation. As José Machado's sketch illustrates, negotiations and construction works for the road and railway connection between Pretoria and Lourenço Marques were already well on their way on the eve of the Berlin Conference (see figure 1). Defining this border (and having it recognized), however, was dependent upon finding an agreement with regard to all the southern borders of Mozambique, which, at the time, corresponded to the area of the Lourenço Marques District, regardless of any international decision. Indeed, while it solved the question of the Mozambique–Transvaal border, this particular demarcation process created a problem elsewhere —where Mozambique bordered Swaziland and Thongaland (Roque 2010; see below).

Nevertheless, the process of dividing and occupying Africa must be considered within the broader scope of European presence and interest. By the end of the 19th century, in the full scramble for Africa, Portugal felt pushed to define the borders of the African territories it had claimed since the 1500s. The possibility of a new, redesigned, map of Africa — following the decisions made in Berlin— combined with the need for an effective occupation of the claimed territory, fuelled the Portuguese fear that the small and scattered Portuguese settlements along the Mozambican coast (from Lourenço Marques Bay up to Cape Delgado) would not suffice to substantiate the pretence of Portuguese sovereignty over a wider territory of which nobody knew its true extent (Botelho 1936:269).

For more than three centuries, the Portuguese had not given consideration to any border other than the Indian Ocean. This was the only frontier separating the known and the unknown, dividing between "two states of the geographical

Fig. 2.3. Portuguese caravan crossing the river Sabié (1890-91). IICT — AHU Photo *Archive of the Portuguese Commission of Cartography*, Album 10-3264.

space" (Gadal and Jeansoulin 2000:14). This distinction is crucial for the understanding of Portuguese expansion and settlement: the coastal area was the borderland that could (and, in view of Portugal's pretence to mediate between Africa and the Orient, *should*) be occupied, regardless of the existing Muslim settlements along the coast, and regardless of any African political or territorial division at the time. For the Portuguese administration, any borders except the so-called natural barriers, were temporary: every itinerary brought another *limen*, and any new border that might result from these travels was just an adjustment to a changing reality.

During this period, Portuguese explorers, missionaries, travellers, and traders were travelling across Africa, from Mozambique to Angola, entering into the interior and extending their contacts and commercial influence.[12] Establishing trade networks and influence, though, was completely different from exerting political control. The acceptance of Portuguese authority was laid down in agreements and treaties with the local authorities, but they meant different things to the various actors involved —even if these treaties included the payment of tribute. Like the Portuguese, African rulers were quick to identify the benefits of commercial relations but, unlike them, they did not consider such relations to be a political compromise of any kind, and felt free to rule their subjects and territories as they had always done. As Landow (2001) suggests, these African agents perceived the border in a completely different way than did the Portuguese: African rulers were concerned with people, not with territories, and the basis for prosperity, political power and stability was networks of kinship. In this sense, the state as a bounded, well-defined geographical entity was an alien concept: borders were useless and meaningless, as power was negotiated between people. As Landow (2001:1) writes: "where the people went, there the state went." No wonder then that the colonial history of Mozambique is rife with reports of broken treaties, conventions or agreements between Portugal and the local chieftaincies: the different parties differed considerably in their understanding of the relationship between people, state, and territory (Roque 2012). We will probably never know to what extent the Portuguese authorities were conscious of this situation or to what extent Portuguese officials even cared —as long as the crown could continue to collect taxes and the Portuguese explorers and merchants could keep safely travelling in the interior whilst expanding their trading networks.

These diverging perceptions are reflected in the maps from this period. The African ideas on political space and shifting borders, and the sheer multitude of local chieftaincies, were impossible to graphically represent on European maps. This resulted in a lack of descriptions and graphic representations of the interior. This lack, however, also reflected Portuguese ideas on political control and colonial rule (see above). By the middle of the 19th century, however, the Portuguese Government was compelled to invest in cartographical, geographical and hydrographical surveys (Fig.2.2) or to go ahead with a military occupation of the territories it claimed (Santos

Border Area		Date	Fieldwork
Transvaal-Mozambique (Lourenço Marques District)	Incomáti-Metinga tinga	1887	Border delimitation
	Singuedézi-Incomáti	1890	Border delimitation
	Singuedézi-Pafúri	1894	Borderline definition (agreement)
	Singuedézi-Pafúri	1894	Border demarcation
Swaziland-Mozambique		1894–1900	Border delimitation and demarcation
		1898	Border demarcation (readjustments)
	Namaacha	1900	Border demarcation
Thongaland-Mozambique	Confluence of the Rivers Pongolo and Maputo	1894	Determination of the geographic position of the point of confluence
		1895	Delimitation (confirmation of the borderline)
		1896–1897	Border delimitation and demarcation
		1898	Border demarcation (readjustments)

Table 1. Southern Mozambique: Portuguese Commission of Cartography / Commission of Delimitation of Frontiers (late 19th century).

Fig.2.4. Wagon with supplies: Caravan of the Portuguese Commission for the Delimitation of the Mozambique-Transvaal Border (1890-91). IICT – AHU Photo *Archive of the Portuguese Commission of Cartography*, Album 10-3280.

1997): an effective territorial presence was the only criterion by which one's political claims on a given territory could be internationally recognized, and by which one might ward off rivals in the scramble for Africa. Maps like the one by Augusto de Castilho were indispensible in substantiating Portuguese claims in Africa.

Created in 1883 under the rule of the State Department for the Navy and Overseas Affairs, and closely connected to the Portuguese Geographic Society, the PCC was charged with drawing up an atlas of the Portuguese colonial territories as well as with developing a cartographical discipline to support the creation of maps. PCC members were carefully chosen. Most of them were reputed military or naval officers with long experience of survey missions in the area. The first five members chosen for the PCC included Hermenegildo Capelo and Roberto Yvens, the first Portuguese explorers to cross the interior of Africa from Angola to Mozambique in 1884–85 (Capelo and Ivens 1886). Their knowledge and experience justified their involvement in the most important operations in the region and their participation in the special commissions dealing with the definition of the borders of the Portuguese territories in Africa. Between 1887 and 1900 PCC members were not only instrumental in carrying out several cartographic surveys, they were also directly involved in the commissions which had been created for the purpose of delimitating and demarcating the southern borders of Mozambique with the territories of Transvaal,[13] Swaziland,[14] and Thongaland[15] (see Table 1). In this, the PCC was either directly involved (through conducting fieldwork and negotiations), or indirectly (through its role as an expert body on cartographic and geographic issues). Therefore, PCC members turned out to be of crucial importance not only for increasing the knowledge on Portuguese colonial territories and the progressive recognition of Portugal's claims to them, but also for the implementation of Portuguese colonial policy there.

THE ARCHIVE OF THE FRONTIERS: AN OVERVIEW

The *Archive of the Frontiers* is a collection of the daily accounts of several Portuguese commissions created for the purpose of border delimitation and demarcation of Portuguese overseas territories in Africa and Timor, and of their dealings with a range of European and African commissions involved in the same process, such as the British Commission (Thongaland-Mozambique), the Boer Commission of Transvaal (Transvaal-Mozambique), or the British Commission representing the Protectorate of Swaziland (Mussuate-Mozambique). The work of these joint commissions operating all over southeastern Africa in the late 19th century resulted in a considerable corpus of documents that provides ample information on the region and on the particulars of the border-making process that established the boundaries of present-day Mozambique, Swaziland, and part of South Africa. The facticity of these particular borders may lead us to forget that, prior to their final demarcation, long discussions and negotiations had to take place, and that the outcome of these negotiations had a profound impact on European policy —not to mention their influence on local kingdoms and chieftaincies, which were not involved in the talks. Still, the sheer number of subjects, the specific information on the technical and scientific aspects of fieldwork or on the nature of the discussions and negotiations, and the amount of detail on the surveyed territories and their populations (including their attitudes towards the division of their lands) contained within these documents is astonishing.

Fieldwork: logistic, technical and scientific work

The *Archive of the Frontiers* testifies to the number of people, scientific instruments, groceries, cattle, transportation (see Fig.2.3) and equipment that needed to be mobilized in order to get the work done. Survey missions also required camping facilities in the areas under surveillance, requiring additional logistics.[16] Conversely, these logistics often required additional surveys of the region to be undertaken, in order to locate local resources (namely water, wood, and game) in order to maintain each commission's caravan (see Fig. 2.4). Details on the composition of each caravan, or on what it carried, inform us about: its capacity to move through the region, on the specific needs of each camp, or (even) on each commission's particular attitude toward the region they were traversing. According, for instance, to a preliminary report by Freire de Andrade, the different composition of the Boer and Portuguese caravans reflected the capacity for quick movement of the Boers compared to the Portuguese, but imposed special condi-

Fig. 2.5. Topographic works. Lourenço Marques District (1907-1910) IICT –AHU Photo *Archive of the Portuguese Commission of Cartography*, Álbum 4-2801.

tions that their camping area needed to be near good hunting ground.[17] A daily hunting trip guaranteed them their food, and this was also the reason why one of the Boer commissioners was a reputed hunter. This, however, also meant that they could not venture for long in areas without game (Roque 2009).

The need for rigorous and systematic work to update the topographic and geodetic registries, to determine the coordinates of the beacons to be built, or to draw precise maps, compelled the use of accurate instruments and techniques, and the presence of experts in using them (see Fig. 2.5). Both were indispensable, and the work often needed to be interrupted or postponed because one or other of them was unavailable.[18] The extensive notes on procedures used and on the technicalities of the instruments deployed, and on the way they met the requirements (or not) of the different situations encountered in the field, resulted in a better understanding of their possibilities, but also necessitated new experiments.[19] Hence, the border process became a *campus* for the development and application of new scientific methods: the border was also a scientific frontier.

The definition of the borderlines: discussions, agreements and impositions

One of the most revealing aspects of the information provided by the *Archive of the Frontiers* concerns details of the discussions and previous agreements on the definition of the borders of Mozambique. Final decisions often came as a result of a long period of meetings involving the commissions officially appointed to discuss the technical problems related to the delimitation and demarcation of the African territories. For southern Mozambique these commissions involved two European colonial powers (Britain and Portugal), and one Afrikaner (Transvaal) working together in joint commissions (Fig. 2.6) As already mentioned, African rulers were never considered as partners in these discussions, and their petitions or their will were always disregarded. The notes on the proceedings of these joint commissions clarify what were the real interests at stake. Predefined lines (rectilinear or not) were not always possible to apply in the field, and readjustments had to be made. Also, individual interests sometimes interfered. These adjustments, indeed, constitute an important part of the work of the joint commissions.

The long discussion on the borderline along the Libombo's mountain crest clearly illustrates these difficulties. This border was agreed upon in a treaty between the Governments of Portugal and the Transvaal in 1869, and ratified in 1871, but it turned out to be the most difficult one to settle.[20] Its negotiation and implementation also affected the negotiation process on the rest of southern Mozambique's borders with the Transvaal and Swaziland.

For a start, there was no agreement on exactly where the mountain crest was on the Mozambican side, nor on the position of some of the hills mentioned. Also, it was almost impossible to reconcile the existent definition of the border with the very geographic orientation of these mountains and the toponymy of the most relevant geographic features considered —even after the 1869 treaty had been corrected in 1875 with, among other things, a more precise circumscription of the borderline.[21] And if this problem (the location of the mountain range) could be solved with new observations and a registration of the precise geographic coordinates, the problem of the toponymy, was even more difficult to solve as it depended upon information given by local people as well as upon local knowledge.

Local toponymy reflected the social organization of local societies, which was largely unknown to the PCC. This discrepancy reflected the lack of cognisance of the region and exposed deficiencies in the way that information had been collected. This necessitated the importance of verifying all the data *in situ*, as it was the only way to have the border accepted by the parties involved in the negotiation process.

Moreover, after the borderline was defined, in 1887, it had direct implications for the demarcation of the Mozambique-Swaziland border, as it was going to divide land areas that the Swazi king had recently granted to individuals and industrial companies. The petitions presented to the Luso-Swazi Commission in 1899 clearly illustrate this situation. Also, they highlight the position of both the Transvaal and Swaziland commissioners towards the owners of the concessions.[22]

On the one hand, there were the missionaries and inhabitants of "Lebombo Portuguese South East Africa."[23] They defended the position that the area under discussion "always has been recognized as Portuguese territory," and expressed the hope that the joint commission "will not consent to the

Fig. 2.6. Transvaal Border (1890-91), IICT —AHU Photo Archive of the Portuguese Commission of Cartography, Álbum 3–3991.

present boundary being altered" as they had all built their houses there, "expended much money and opened up the country to trade" and that even the local population, "a mixture of all types of *kaffirs* with some *kaffir* refugees,"[24] considered themselves not Swazi but to be under Portuguese sovereignty. On the other hand, there were the petitions asking that the land between the two countries not be divided. These requests were filed by industrial and commercial enterprises[25] and by important farmers who owned vast stretches of land in the region, most of them recently acquired by concession in an area they knew was disputed.[26] Several meetings to solve this dispute were organized between 1897 and 1899. In October 1899, however, the war between the British and the Boers broke out. As a result, negotiations were suspended, and at the beginning of the 20th century the borderline remained undefined.[27]

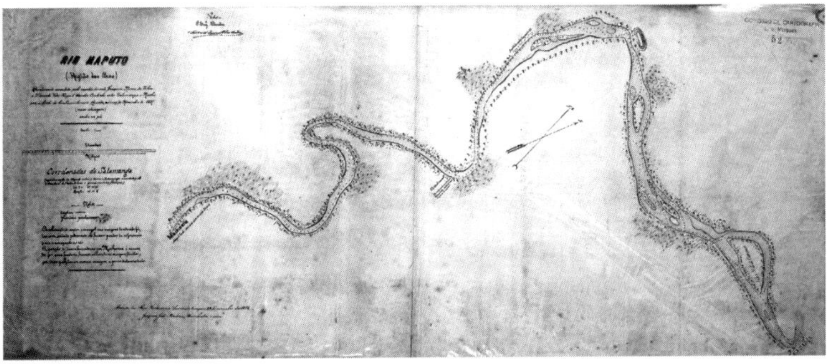

Fig. 2.7. Joaquim Nunes da Silva (1897) Rio Maputo. IICT- Centro de História P10CO53

These demarcation problems resulted from the conflicts between colonizing powers, and their strategies to expand and consolidate their possessions in Africa. Nevertheless, the border-making process also affected local, African, kingdoms and chieftaincies, at least indirectly. Even though information on land disputes involving local communities is relatively scarce in the PCC archives, the few exceptions in southern Mozambique concern areas (Thongaland and some areas located in today's Kruger Park) that were considered crucial for British claims in the region, and it probably is no coincidence that these cases are documented in the reports and minutes by members of the Commission (Roque 2009).

Northern Thongaland bordered southern Lourenço Marques Bay (Delagoa Bay) and was historically coveted by the British. The possibility of creating a British Thonga Protectorate would have provided Britain with the opportunity to define a buffer zone that stretched from the coast to the Transvaal, thus preventing the Boers from accessing the Portuguese port of Lourenço Marques and the English port of Durban. Also, such a protectorate would have resulted in the possibility of creating new alternative seaports to facilitate British-controlled exports from Swaziland (Machado 1889b:28–29; Gibbs 1889:53).

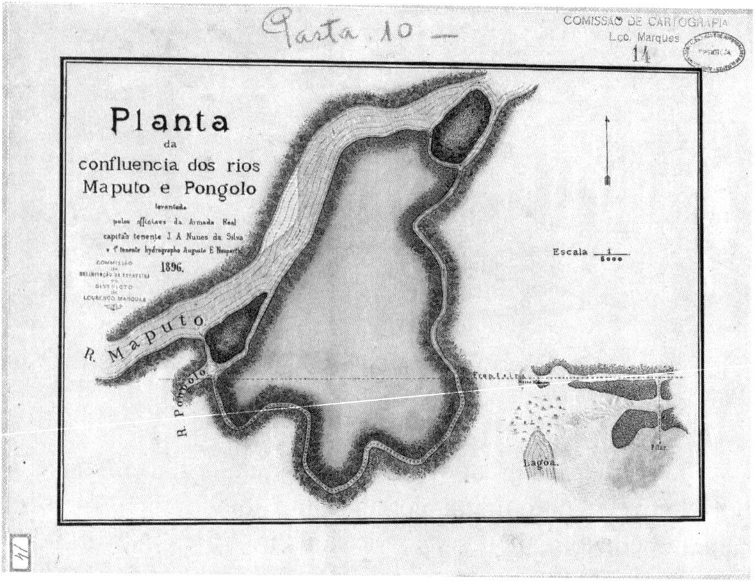

Fig. 2.8. Confluence of the rivers Pongolo and Maputo. Nunes da Silva (1896) *Planta da confluência dos Rios Maputo e Pongolo* IICT — Centro de História, P10CO14.

The Portuguese authorities and Thonga rulers, in contrast, invoked the historical relations between Portugal and the Tembe-Thonga chieftaincy and the treaties they concluded in 1823 and 1870 to preserve the unity of Thonga territory under the Portuguese Crown (Machado 1889a:20).[28] For the Portuguese, preserving this unity was a first step in extending their power much further south than the historical boundaries they had been claiming: this southern limit of the Portuguese territories had been established and internationally recognized at the parallel 26º 30' latitude South.[29] Thonga territory, however, stretched from southern Lourenço Marques Bay to the parallel 72º 30' latitude South, near the Ozimkulo River. For Thonga, the unity of their territory was a guarantee of their survival. Any attempt to carve up the territory would lead to

Fig. 2.9. Beacon, Transvaal border. IICT —AHU Photo Archive of the Portuguese Commission of Cartography, Album 10-3258

Thonga being divided into different colonial systems, depriving them of their original territory and affecting their identity as a community, as well as forcing internal organizational changes. The several petitions that Thonga spokespersons presented during the Luso-British discussion on the border demarcation stressed the geo-climatic differences within their territory; they claimed that these different areas were complementary and supported diverse economic activities and livelihoods. They also pointed out that an arbitrary decision to divide the land would severely affect Thonga socio-economic structure (Roque 2010). Nevertheless, none of the Thonga petitions were considered and all the meetings held by either the British or the Portuguese with Queen Zambili of Maputo proved to be nothing but a means by which to appease Zambili's subjects as Thonga demands were not listened to or considered. Finally, the British succeeded in having a final demarcation accepted at 26º 52' latitude South, along the Maputo River (Fig.7), from the confluence with the Pongolo up to the coast near Ponta do Ouro.

Fig. 2.10. Railway Pretoria-Lourenço Marques: building new rails around Lourenço Marques (late 19th century). IICT — AHU Photo *Archive of the Portuguese Commission of Cartography*, ref.5320.

Even when the works proceeded without too many difficulties, the meetings were often suspended because of different opinions regarding specific aspects of the border, forcing the teams to go back to the field to "enable both commissions to lay on the table their sketches and maps for the better explanation of their arguments."[30] Similarly, the works could be stalled because natural features of the landscape forced the members of the joint commissions to come up with alternatives to the predefined lines. One such occasion was when the joint Anglo-Portuguese commission agreed that the riverbanks at the confluence of the Pongolo and Maputo River (Fig.8), were too unstable to carry the weight of the beacons that were supposed to be constructed there.[31]

Once the borderline design was settled, topographical and geodesic works had to be undertaken, along with the clearing of the places where the beacons (Fig.9) had to be erected. Also, the area around and between these beacons needed to be cleared of bushes and trees, so as to ensure total visibility from one beacon to another. This clearing of the border had a severe impact on both the landscape, and on the land use of local communities; consequences that had not been foreseen by the Europeans in their discussions. Still, the effects of this procedure were quite visible: in a small area such as the Thongaland border, a 27 kilometre-wide strip of woodland was destroyed by the cutting and cleaning of a border that was only 50 kilometres long, making the land useless for the local communities.[32] Even if certain areas witnessed a rapid regeneration of the vegetation,[33] most places were deeply affected by the systematic use of this procedure (Roque 2009). The demarcation of the boundary confronted the local population (that mostly depended on cattle raising, supplemented by hunting and the cultivation of a few crops), with an artificial border that was completely alien to them. More important, however, was that they were being deprived of a substantial part of their resources (such as water, game, grazing, wild fruits, herbs, and fuel). When taking into account Mozambique's almost 3,000 kilometres of inland boundary, one cannot help but fear that the local repercussions of the boundary-making process must have been enormous.

CONCLUDING REMARKS

Obviously, the making of boundaries had profound impacts on the local landscape and its inhabitants. Some of these consequences were intentional, whilst others were not. Almost certain is that the Europeans involved did not lose much sleep in thinking about them. Important, however, is that the very detailed reports by the various commissions on their boundary-making activities provide us with an important source of information on the various issues discussed above, that might help us to understand the particulars of the historical development of this region. Also, these reports are a valuable source on the geography, biology, and ethnography of the colonial landscape before and after the demarcation of the border (Roque 2009). Interesting to note in this regard is that, during the period discussed, photography slowly made its entry into the colonial repertoire and the different survey missions made ample use of this new technology. The PCC was in charge of these photos, and probably for this reason, a first photo laboratory opened in Lourenço Marques in the late 19th century.[34] It is in this photo collection that we often find information that is missing in the written documents. A good example would be the photographs of the construction of the railway between the Transvaal and Lourenço Marques (Fig. 2.10). Since 1874, this railway was high on the agenda of the meetings that were held to negotiate the demarcation of the Transvaal-Mozambique border.

As already mentioned, the analysis in this chapter is the result of only a first, tentative effort to make use of the PCC archives. It does not even come close to an overview of all the information they contain, and can only guess at what the result would be if we were able to cross-reference the various types of documents. However, on the basis of our knowledge of the Commission's maps, and on the basis of the quality of the information that can already be checked, it is apparent that these archives can shed new light on various aspects of the history of this region. Therefore, the various nuclei of the PCC archives will prove not only to be important on the international, political and judicial stage, but could also contribute to a global understanding of the region's past and present.

ACKNOWLEDGEMENTS

This chapter is one of the outcomes of the project *Political Cartography and Colonial Territories* (2003–2006), and of the project *Knowledge and recognition in areas of Portuguese influence: registries, scientific expeditions, traditional knowledge and biodiversity in Subsaharan Africa and Insulindia* (FCT HC0075/2009).

NOTES

[1] Decree of 19 April 1883 of the Ministry of the Navy and Overseas Territories, Barbosa du Bocage.

[2] During the colonial period, the Geographic Survey Mission (MGM) was the institution responsible for geographic missions abroad. Its geographic registries were held in the former Center of Geodesy and are now entrusted to the Center for Geoinformation and Development (GeoDES). They include all the records on the geographic coordinates and descriptions of the boundary marks as well as topographic and geodetic data, photos, reports and instruments used by the MGM.

[3] The IICT's central archive is the Historical Overseas Archive (*Arquivó Historicó Ultramarino*, AHU).

[4] Seventeenth International Congress on the History of Cartography, Lisbon 6–10 July 1997 and map exhibition on "African Borders," Seminar on Cartography and Colonial Political Science, IICT, Lisbon, 12–13 April, 2005 International Colloquium Mapping Africa in the Colonial Times (1876–c.1940), IICT, Lisbon, 7–11 Nov. 2006, Round Table Espólio de Gago Coutinho no IICT, Lisboa, 2 June 2009, Exhibition on Gago Coutinho: exposição bibliográfica e documental, IICT, Lisboa, Jun.–Dec. 2009.

[5] Presently the IICT has two other projects related to the legacy of the PCC, namely "Knowledge and recognition in areas of Portuguese influence: registries, scientific expeditions, traditional knowledge and biodiversity in Subsaharian Africa and Insulindia" (FCT HC0075/2009) and "Half a century of colonial science: crossing views on the archive and the scientific activity of the Comissão de Cartografia (1883-1936)" (FCT HC 0067/2009).

[6] See http://www2.iict.pt/?idc=100&idl=2, accessed June 24 2011.

[7] PALOP (African Countries of Portuguese Speaking Language) are Angola, Cape Verde, Guinea-Bissau, Mozambique and S.Tomé and Príncipe.

[8] The African Union Border Declaration Programme was established during the African Conference of the African Ministers of Border Issues in Addis Ababa, in 2007, in order to implement the Resolution on the Inalienability of Colonial Boundaries assumed in Cairo, in 1964, by the African Union Organization and ratified in Durban, in 2002, during the African Union Assembly of Heads of State and Government.

[9] Mozambique shares its border with South Africa, Swaziland, Zambia, Malawi, Zimbabwe and Tanzania. The maritime border involves, besides Mozambique, South Africa, Madagascar, Comoros and Tanzania.

[10] See the project on "Knowledge and recognition in areas of Portuguese influence..."

[11] At the time of writing, the pictures are inventoried and scanned but remain without context. See http://www2.iict.pt/?idc=100&idl=1 /http://www.tvciencia.pt/tvcicn/pagicn/tvcicn01.asp, accessed June 24 2011. The handwritten materials are summarily inventoried, but hitherto hardly ever used (see IICT 2006).

[12] From the late 18th century onwards, Portuguese travellers started to go deeper in the remote interior and the hinterland between Angola and Mozambique was slowly being absorbed into the Portuguese commercial area of influence. The travel of Lacerda e Almeida to the Cazembe (1788), the first travels down the Zambezi River (before 1803) and to the Alto the Cassai (1803) and the travel of the *Pombeiros* (1802–1811) are some good examples of this.

[13] Accordingly to different periods, the Transvaal can appear under the names of African Dutch Republic (before 1853), Zuid-Afrikaansche Republiek, or South African Republic.

[14] Mussuate or Mussuate chieftaincy.

[15] Maputo, Maputaland or territory of the Amatongas.

[16] MCP 30 5:2 (see list of archival materials).

[17] MCP 33–3 (see list of archival materials). The Portuguese caravan included three wagons pulled by 55 donkeys and one wagon pulled by 14 oxen, four wagon drivers with four assistants and 38 indigenous porters, plus the five members of the Commission, seven horses, all the technical instruments, camping materials and the most possible basic supplies enough to sustain the 51 persons and the 76 animals of the caravan; while

the Boer caravan, other than the five commissioners, included 156 indigenous porters, mostly Swazi, under the rule of seven police agents from Lybenburg district, and 12 horses.

[18] MCP 30 5:1. Mozambique-Thongaland Border Process (see list of archival materials).

[19] MCP 30 5:2. Mozambique-Thongaland Border Process (see list of archival materials).

[20] Art. 23 of the *Treaty of Peace and Friendship, of 29th July 1869,* ratified in 10th July 1871, establishes the parallel 26° 30' latitude South as the southern limit of the District of Lourenço Marques Bay. This agreement was later confirmed by the Art.21st of the Treaty of 11th December 1875, ratified in 7th October 1882 (De Almada 1943).

[21] MCP 33–2. Mozambique-Transvaal Border Process (see list of archival materials).

[22] According to Mr. Von Wielligh, Special Commissioner for both the Transvaal and Swaziland, he had received instructions to consider that the owners of the different concessions had right to demand the borderline demarcation as established in the 1888 Treaty. Minutes of meeting held on the 18th September, on Nomahashe Camp. MCA Env.20. Mozambique-Swaziland Border Process.

[23] Letter of the inhabitants of the Lebombo Portuguese S.E.Africa, to the Special Commissioner da Silva, 18th Sept., 1899, Document in Appendix to the Minute of the meeting held on the 18th September, on Nomahashe Camp. MCA Env.20. Mozambique-Thongaland Border Process.

[24] Inquiry to the Petitioners. Document in Appendix to the Minute of the meeting held on September 18, on Nomahashe Camp. MCA Env.20. Mozambique-Thongaland Border Process.

[25] Namely, the Swaziland Corporation, the Swaziland Mining Commercial and Industrial Chamber and the Swaziland Incomatiport Trading and Land Concession Company.

[26] See, the declarations of Mr. Henri Holtman, Mr. Mitchell Miller and Mr. David Forbes as well as the letter of Mr. Mitchell Miller to the Special Commissioner Mr. Von Wielligh. Documents in Appendix to the Minute of the meeting held on the 18th September, on Nomahashe Camp. MCA Env.20. Mozambique-Swaziland Border Process.

[27] Only by the end of 1925, the borderline will be fixed and confirmed by both governments. Nevertheless the prevailing borderline was the one defined by the Luso-British Treaty of June 11, 1891, signed in London, and

confirmed by the agreement of 1895.

[28] MCP 30 2:12. Mozambique-Thongaland Border Process (see list of archival materials).

[29] Mac Mahon sentence, July 24 1875.

[30] Minute of the meeting held on the 7th August 1894, on the Matingatinga, west of Lebombo Mountains –2.30p.m. MCA Env.19. Mozambique-Swaziland Border Process (see list of archival materials).

[31] Minute of the 2nd session of the Anglo-Portuguese Commission on the delimitation of the Maputo border (Tonga land), Lourenço Marques, 29th Sept.1897. MCA Env.21. Mozambique-Thongaland Border Process (see list of archival materials).

[32] Description of the Anglo-Portuguese border between the English Protectorate of Amatongas and the Portuguese possessions on Eastern Africa according to Art.3 of the Treaty of 11th August 1891 between Great Britain and Portugal. MCA Env.21. Mozambique-Thongaland Border Process.

[33] MCA15,16,18 Mozambique-Thongaland Border Process; MCA 21. Mozambique-Transvaal Border Process (see list of archival materials).

[34] MCA Envs.20 and 21. Mozambique-Transvaal Border Process (see list of archival materials). Until the moment there is no written reference to this laboratory in these archives but the building was photographed in 1889 and 1891, and the photos are lettered and included in the photo albums of this collection.

REFERENCES

Botelho, J. J. T. 1936. História Militar e Política dos Portugueses em Moçambique de 1833 aos nossos dias. Tomo II, Lisboa.

Capello, H. and R. Yvens. 1886. De Angola á contra-costa: descrição de uma viagem através do continente africano. Lisboa: Imprensa Nacional.

De Almada, J. 1943. Tratados aplicáveis ao Ultramar, Tomo V. Lisboa: Agência Geral das Colónias.

Gadal, S. and R. Jeansoulin. 2000. Borders, frontiers and limits: some computational concepts beyond words. Cybergeo: European Journal of Geography (En ligne), Epistémologie, Histoire de la Géographie, Didactique, document 125. Electronic Document, http://cybergeo.revues.or/index4349.html, accessed March 15, 2010.

Gibbs, E. J. 2008 [1889]. England and South Africa. BiblioBazar, LLC.

Instituto de Investigação Científica Tropical (IICT) 2006. Comissão de Cartografia —Catálogos. Lisboa: Instituto de Investigação Científica Tropical.

Instituto do Mar e Fronteiras (IMAF) 2009. Communication by the Director, IICT meeting. Lisbon, January 20.

Landow, G.P. 2001. The Alien Concept of Frontier and Border in Pre-Colonial Times and Places: Political Discourse —Theories of Colonialism and Post colonialism. Electronic document, http://www.postcolonialweb.org/poldiscourse/borders/frontiers.html, accessed Jan. 11, 2010.

Machado, J. J. 1889b. Fornecimento de armas aos Matabeles — Zambézia britãnica e o território dos Swazis. Paper presented to the Portuguese Geographic Society, Nov. 11. Lisboa: Sociedade de Geografia de Lisboa.

——— 1889a. Maputo-Lourenço Marques-Mossamedes. Paper presented to the Portuguese Geographic Society, April 1. Lisboa: Sociedade de Geografia de Lisboa.

Roque, A.C. 2012. Terras de Sofala. Persistências e mudança. Contribuições para a história da costa sul-oriental de África nos séculos XVI-XVIII. Lisboa: Fundação Calouste Gulbenkian / Fundação para a Ciência e Tecnologia

——— 2010. Disputing borders in southern Mozambique: the case of the Mozambique-Thongaland border (19th–20th century). Paper presented to the 8th European Social Science History Conference, Ghent, April 13–16. Electronic document, http://www2.iisg.nl/esshc/ programme.asp?selyear=10&pap=7683, accessed April 8, 2010.

——— 2009. Rethinking Borders in South Mozambique. Paper presented to the ABORNE Conference on How is Africa Transforming Border Studies?, Johannesburg, Sept. 10–14.

Roque, A.C. and L. Ferrão. 2007. Mapping Mozambique Coast in the 19th century. Paper presented to the 22nd International Conference on the History of Cartography, Berne, July 8–13.

——— 2006b. Reconhecimentos Hidrográficos na Cartografia Portuguesa da Costa Centro e Sul de Moçambique no século XIX. Africana Studia, 9:187–204.

——— 2006a. Reconhecimentos Hidrográficos na Cartografia Portuguesa da Costa Norte de Moçambique. *In* O Domínio da Distância. M. Emília Madeira Santos and M. Lobato, eds. Pp. 109–120. Lisboa: Instituto de Investigação Científica Tropical.

Santos, M.E.M. 2006. Political Cartography and Colonial Territories - Final report. Electronic document, http://www.adelinotorres.com/africa.htm, accessed Jan. 11, 2010.

——— 1997. A Comissão de Cartografia e a Delimitação das Fronteiras africanas. *In* As Fronteiras de África — Catálogo da Exposição. Lisboa: Comissão Nacional para as Comemorações dos Descobrimentos Portugueses.

ARCHIVAL MATERIALS

Portuguese Commission of Cartography - Archive of the Frontiers. Tropical Research Institute, GeoDES:

- Mozambique-Transvaal Border - (MCA) Moçambique Cx.Azul., Envs. 15, 16, 18, e 20; (MCP) Moçambique Cx.Preta, 33 vols. 1–3 and 34 vols. 1–2.
- Mozambique-Swaziland Border - (MCA) Moçambique Cx.Azul., Envs. 19 and 20; (MCP) Moçambique Cx.Preta, 31 vols. 1–3, 32 vols. 1–3.
- Mozambique-Thongaland Border - (MCA) Moçambique Cx.Azul., Env. 21; (MCP) Moçambique Cx.Preta, 30 vols. 1–5.

Portuguese Commission of Cartography - Map Collection.Tropical Research Institute. DCH — Archive ex-CEHCA: Moçambique — Pasta 10 refªs 002; 010; 011; 014; 016; 020; 036; 048; 050, 053; 054; 055; 073.

Portuguese Commission of Cartography – Photo Collection. Tropical Research Institute. DCH – Archive ex-CEHCA and AHU

- AHU Moçambique Álbum 1 (Doc.139) - Delimitação de Fronteira em Moçambique com Missão Inglesa (s/d).
- AHU Moçambique Álbum 10 (Doc 148) – Comissão de Delimitação de Fronteira de Lourenço Marques (1890/91).

APPENDIX
ARCHIVE OF THE FRONTIERS: MAPS, MANUSCRIPTS AND PHOTOS CONCERNING SOUTHERN MOZAMBIQUE BORDER IN THE LATE 19TH CENTURY

Area	Year	AF Documents	AF Photos	CC Maps
Transvaal / Lourenço Marques District	1884–91	**1890** Proceedings of 4 meetings (borderline definition of the border line from the Incomati River to the Singuedezi River) **1891** Official Portuguese documents from the Foreign Affairs Office and from the Governor of Mozambique; Documents concerning border demarcation of Lourenço Marques and the Transvaal; Reports of the joint commissions on the border of Lourenço Marques district; Description of the fieldwork and on all the works done during 1891; Sketches of the area along the border line; Reports on the geodesic and topographic works; Description of the marks between the Incomati River to the Singuedezi River; Reports of the Portuguese commissioner on the border of the Lourenço Marques district;	**1890-91** - 85 Photos	**1884-90** - 3 maps (1881, 1887; 1890)
Maputo (Thongaland) / **Lourenço Marques District**	1888–99	**1888–89** Official Portuguese documents from the Governor of Lourenço Marques, the Portuguese Consul in the Cape and the Foreign Affaires Office; Report on the meeting between Portugal and Queen Zambia;	**1896–1898 (?)** - 12 photos	**1896–99** - 9 maps (1896; 1897;1899)

Area	Year	**AF Documents**	**AF Photos**	**CC Maps**
		Account of the occurrences in Maputo and Thongaland;		
		1895 Copy of the Sentence of MacMahon (24th July 1875); Documents regarding the final definition of the southern border of Mozambique accordingly with the Treaty of 11.06.1891; Information on the latitude of the confluence of the Pongolo River with the Maputo River (Usutu River); Opinion of the Portuguese Commission of Cartography (5th Aug.1895;)		
		1896 Proceedings of 4 meetings; Note on the procedures to continue or not the works due to heavy rain during 10 days; Documents concerning the delimitation of Thongaland and the definition of the Maputo border line; Sketch Map of the Maputo River; Official Portuguese documents from the Governor of Lourenço Marques, Portuguese Consul in the Cape and the Ministry of Foreign Affaires; Copy of the British Memoradum; Description of the topographic works;		
		1896–98 Documents concerning Thongaland		
		1897 Proceedings of 2 meetings; Description of the Anglo-Portuguese border between the English Protectorate of Amatongas and the Portuguese possessions on Eastern Africa according to art.3 of the Treaty of 11th August		

Area	Year	**AF Documents**	**AF Photos**	**CC Maps**
		1891 between Great Britan and Portugal (Tongaland - 2nd Oct.); Official correspondence between the Port.gov. and the British gov. confirming the borderline; Report of Captain Nunes da Silva (30.10.97); Reports of Tenent Neuparth (25.10.97);		
Swaziland (Mus-suate) / **Lourenço Marques District**	1888–99	**1888–89** Definition of the luso-swazi border; Proceedings of 2 meetings; **1892** Opinion of the Portuguese Commission of Cartography (14th Jun.1892); Official Portuguese documents from the Foreign Affairs Office **1894** Proceedings of 3 meetings (discussion and definition of the border line from M´Ponduine to the North); **1896–1899** Documents of the joint commissions concerning the disagreement on what concerns the determination of the 1st mark south of the Buchanan mark; Report of the Portuguese commissioner; Opinions of the Portuguese Commission of Cartography (15th Nov.1897 and 26th April 1898); **1897** Proceedings of 3 meetings (discussion and definition of the border line from M'Ponduine to Maputo River's gorge); Registry of the Portuguese objections about the place for the building of the 1st mark South of Buchanan's mark and of the	Not yet identified	**1894-98** - 2 maps (1894;1898)

Area	Year	**AF Documents**	**AF Photos**	**CC Maps**
		arguments of the R.S.A. commission; Report of the Nunes da Silva on the works done in 1897; Official Portuguese documents; Proceeding of the meeting luso-boer; Documents on the approval of the marks between Buchanan and Krogh by the South African Governor; Documents on the demarcation of the rectilinear line Impunduine-Krogh, accordingly with the treaty of 1888; **1899** Proceedings of 5 meetings (discussion and definition of the border line from M'Ponduine to Maputo River's gorge); Petition of the inhabitants in favour of the Portuguese sovereignty; Declaration of Mr. Holtman about the jurisdiction of the king of the Swazis and the Portuguese sovereignty; Registry of the inquiries to several petitioners; Declarations of Mr. Miller and Mr, Forbes in defence of the border line defined in the Treaty of 1888; Letter of Mr. Miller; Registry of the inquiry to Mr. Joissen; Portuguese Appendix to the Proceeding of the 7th Oct. meeting;		

3
MOSSI-FULBE BORDERLANDS: TOWARDS A HISTORY OF INTERCONNECTEDNESS

Mark Breusers

INTRODUCTION

Despite their centuries-long presence, and despite constituting a substantial proportion of the population, Fulbe are not usually considered to be part of the society of the Mossi region in Burkina Faso. They tend to be portrayed as "only passing by," and as "not belonging" to the place where they happen to be, and as bound to leave sooner or later. In the historiography and ethnography of the region they are either conspicuously absent, or regarded as alien entities whose presence, ultimately, has been superfluous to the course of history and to the kind of society, and the structure of the society that resulted.

Considering the Mossi kingdoms' success in accommodating several other likewise trans-local and mobile groups (such as, for instance, Yarse traders and blacksmiths) the institutional non-recognition of Fulbe's encounter with the region's other population groups strikes a disturbing anomaly. Are Fulbe somehow more "other" than others? Are we to interpret their presence in the Mossi kingdoms in terms of distinct social and political practices which allowed them to link up with the various other spaces of Fulbe's pastoral and Islamic diaspora, without significantly affecting the social, political and cultural realities of the kingdoms in whose interstices they penetrated? Or are we to look for an alternative perspective, capable of accounting for the numerous ambiguities and paradoxes that emerge from a close reading of Mossi historiography and ethnography?

My main argument is that it was not "Mossi society" but, rather, a sedentary way of rendering the region's history and society by rulers and ethnographers, that was incapable of and/or unwilling to accommodate Fulbe living there. I show how historiography and ethnography fell victim to a reductive gaze that could not but repeatedly assert Fulbe-Mossi relations and borderlands in terms of discontinuity and disconnection. I argue that a critical reconsideration of modernist concepts of society and culture opens the way for recognizing how Fulbe-Mossi encounters were productive of history and socio-political institutions —two themes systematically discarded in received historiography and ethnography. Such an alternative perspective must acknowledge the impossibility of retrieving Fulbe's "true" role in the region's history; it must avoid trying to simply write Fulbe into Mossi historiography and ethnography, thus adding yet another essentialized category, and of redrawing rather than subverting or transcending the boundaries established in earlier work. Instead, historiography and ethnography are to be reinterpreted in terms of emerging variety and multiplicity, by understanding society and culture not solely in terms of closure and "rooting," but also in terms of openness and "rhizoming" as well. Such an alternative perspective has profound implications. Received historiography and ethnography suggests that Fulbe penetrated the Mossi region without engaging in significant social and political relations with other population groups. Fulbe were portrayed as establishing a separate cultural, social and political space, governed by distinct institutions and value systems, and with evolving alongside —parallel, complementary, in symbiosis or in competition to— but always separate from Mossi society. The alternative perspective allows us to see beyond the usually emphasized pragmatic relations of resource sharing or competition and economic exchange. The translocal practices in which Fulbe in particular tend to be involved in produce variegated relations, not only between different physical spaces, but also, and importantly: between people, between people and their physical environment, and between the this-worldly and the that-worldly.

I start by reviewing received Mossi historiography and by highlighting some ambiguities and puzzling aspects of Fulbe's role in the region's past. Next, I present a rough sketch of ethnographic work carried out in the Mossi region since the early 20th century and show how this work systematically ousted Fulbe from Mossi society. I go on to argue that several factors combined to write Fulbe's encounters with Mossi out of the region's historiography and ethnography. Among these border-making practices are: anthropology's early invention of Fulbe as a distinct people and its restricted concept of society in general; colonial administrators' attempts to sever Mossi-Fulbe political relations; the dominance of dynastic oral historiography; and the unwarranted extrapolation of the region's canonical ethnography on Yatenga to other kingdoms. A last section suggests that Fulbe can take their place in the region's historiography and ethnography if only one abandons the premise of discontinuity between Mossi and Fulbe.

HISTORIOGRAPHY OF THE MOSSI REGION: INCONSEQUENTIAL FULBE

Accounts of the emergence of the Mossi kingdoms after the 15th century accord primary importance to encounters between, on the one hand, *nakombse* ("conquerors" or "people of power," soldiers, warriors) who left the Dagomba-Mamprusi region of present-day northern Ghana, and, on the other hand, *tengbiise* (lit. "children of the earth," the so-called autochthon populations) already present in the basins of the Volta rivers. Ouédraogo, son of a Dagomba-Mamprusi princess and a hunter, left Gambaga to found Tenkodogo in the north. From here the expansion of the Mossi kingdoms took off. Ouédraogo's son, Rawa, traversed a large part of the Volta basin, imposing his fellow kinsmen and warriors as chiefs on local village populations (Izard 1985a:20–21). He epitomized the phase of Mossi conquest, which was not immediately conducive to stable polities. In a second phase, powerful political formations were built, notably by Ouédraogo's grandson Oubri, and by Oubri's grandson Yadega, founders, respectively, of Oubritenga (later to become the Kingdom of Ouagadougou) and the state of Yatenga. Wherever they arrived, the nakombse met with local populations with whom they concluded a pact, following which the tengbiise kept religious authority and custody over land and the nakombse assumed political power. Zahan (1961:15–20) has already argued that one is not to accord historicity to these foundational pacts and, therefore, one cannot distinguish historically between autochthons and conquerors. Rather, these were to be understood as functional categories constitutive of society, not as originally different population groups. Since several other societies in the area were characterized by a similar constitutive model, it was likely that a concept (*naam,* or "power") rather than a people (the nakombse) had travelled north, possibly from Gambaga. Hence, the distinction between naam and *tenga* (earth), or between nakombse and tengbiise, is relational, one not existing prior to, or without, the other (Luning 1997:76–77). Regardless of the factuality of these accounts, however, it was these "pacts" that made the Mossi chieftaincies and kingdoms possible to begin with; the tengbiise providing the nakombse with the religious legitimacy for their power and the territorial fixity they needed for their ancestors not to wander eternally (Bonnet 1988:60).

The histories of the Mossi kingdoms after the foundational encounter between nakombse and tengbiise is usually reduced to a genealogical chart of rulers, compounded by an account of their major accomplishments and of the most striking events in which they were involved (see Izard 1970:143–148,156; Pageard 1965:55; Tiendrébéogo 1963:15; see also Chéron 1924; Kawada 1969; Tauxier 1924). One is left with an image of inwardly turned kingdoms, afflicted by internal warfare or involved in inter-kingdom fratricidal struggle, with the nakombse being the single decisive actors.[1] Izard acknowledged the limitations of dynastic histories, especially those rendered by court dignitaries. He argued for a history based not only on the state or its population, but also on industry and trade as well:

> It will appear that systematic investigations involving the *totality of groups constitutive of Mossi society* and the *totality of local groups* that form each of these larger groups, supply the material that, when processed, allows [...] reconstituting with precision the stages in the formation of the society and the state [...]. [Izard 1970:394; my emphasis and translation]

Crucial, then, is who gets to be included in this "totality of groups constitutive of Mossi society." In Izard's understanding of Yatenga, artisan-traders (Yarse and Marase) and blacksmiths were obviously counted in, indispensable as they were —following the initial pact between the "people of power" and the "people of the land"— to the development of the state of Yatenga: through the artisan-traders, nakombse maintained and extended control of trade, whereas blacksmiths were the kingdom's manufacturers of weaponry and agricultural tools. Blacksmiths were associated, sometimes by force, to the royal court, whereas the integration of Yarse and Marase was institutionalized by having specific royal dignitaries mediate between them and the king (1975:286; 1985a:56–57).

Fulbe, however, were excluded from this effort to add a sociological dimension to Yatenga's history on the grounds that no institutionalized relations existed between them and the royal court. Despite acknowledging their subjection to the Mossi chiefs' tutelage, Izard considered Yatenga's Fulbe to be their own masters and Mossi affairs as incompatible with Fulbe involvement. Izard further accentuated Fulbe's otherness by emphasizing Yatenga's hostile relations with neighbouring Fulbe polities (Maasina, Djelgodji, Liptako, Dokwi, Barani) by which it came to be almost encircled by the beginning of the 19th century. With Fulbe being "the Mossi's principal enemies," (Izard 1982:367–369), Yatenga not only aimed its foreign policy at containing Fulbe to the north, but also regarded Fulbe living within its borders with great suspicion —that is, as untrustworthy, requiring special surveillance and to be kept at a distance from Mossi institutions. However, the Mossi rulers' greatest fear —a jihad involving the various Fulbe polities and Fulbe living within Yatenga's borders—never materialized.[2] Rather, Yatenga engaged in shifting alliances and sometimes even in friendly relations with these Fulbe polities, each of which proved to cherish their relative independence (Diallo 1997:189; Izard 1982:379).

By thus sidelining Yatenga's Fulbe, Izard followed earlier historians of the Mossi kingdoms, who, though usually mentioning the arrival and origin of various Fulbe groups and acknowledging the latter's cordial relations with Mossi chiefs, nevertheless portrayed Mossi-Fulbe interactions as depoliticized and depersonalized.[3] Though interacting with Mossi through practices such as cattle entrustment and grain-milk exchanges, and joining Mossi nakombse in wars and pillages for which they supplied horsemen and footmen, Fulbe were not considered to be a group necessary for the kingdoms' development in the way blacksmiths, Yarse or Marase were (Izard 1982:367–372; 1985a:102–103). In the historiography of the Mossi kingdoms, then, Fulbe's presence and involvement in events is either implicitly or explicitly understood to have been ephemeral and circumstantial: Fulbe were either free to come and go as they pleased or regarded with suspicion, but were always —or so it seems— inconsequential.

HISTORIOGRAPHY OF THE MOSSI REGION: PUZZLING FULBE

Nevertheless, Fulbe feature at important moments in these same historical accounts of the Mossi kingdoms. The King of Ouagadougou sent Fulbe —"apparently people of primary importance"— on a diplomatic mission (the only one of its kind in the kingdoms' history) to the Royal Court of Yatenga (Izard 1985a:66). Fulbe safeguarded the creation of Oubritenga, the later Kingdom of Ouagadougou, from which all the other kingdoms —Tenkodogo excepted— were to originate (Kabore 1966:23); an important Fulbe military force assisted the rebel prince Bagare to become the first King of Yatenga under French rule (Izard 1985a:127–144). In the history of smaller kingdoms, Fulbe likewise sporadically figure as accomplices of nakombse kings or chiefs in settling internal or external conflicts (Chéron 1924:686–688).

Most enigmatic is *naaba* (chief) Motiba, who reigned over Ouagadougou from 1729 to 1737, and who, according to some accounts, was a Fulbe.

> The Fulbe does not have a village of his own where he can say: "this is a Fulbe village," except for Barkoundouba. The chief of Barkoundouba is nominated by the Moogo naaba. The Diallobe of Barkoundouba belong to the

> family of the Moogo naaba. [...] The seventh [sic] Moogo naaba, Modibo, was a Fulbe. He followed the Moogo naaba [Oubi], deceived him and, then, following the king's death, was nominated his successor. However, when the former king's own child had grown up [...] Modibo was deposed and killed. The new Moogo naaba nominated Modibo's sons as Fulbe chiefs, to compensate for the supreme power they were supposed to inherit. That is why Barkoundouba is a village belonging to the family of the Moogo naaba. [Interview with Luc Ouédraogo, royal lineage of Piugtenga kombere, Boussouma Kingdom, July 2002; see also Izard 1970:92]

Of interest is that this episode provides a possible explanation for the fact that certain Fulbe chiefs were inaugurated and received naam from the King of Ouagadougou. These factors suggest that Fulbe chiefs were integrated in the political organization of the kingdom (also see, for instance Pageard 1965:26–29).

Furthermore, Motiba (also called Modibo), is suggestive of the Fulfulde word *moodibbo* ("man of God"). It can be speculated that Motiba was not an arbitrary confidant but associated to naaba Oubi's court because of his religiousness, and, following Oubi's death, was not only a regent but also responsible for the religious education of the future naaba Warga, one of the greater kings of Ouagadougou. This possibility is supported by Pageard's (1965:37) observation that Warga was considered a *wali*, a "great Muslim" or "Muslim saint." This possible involvement of Fulbe as Muslim confidants in court life rarely gets a mention in received Mossi historiography. In general, Muslim scholars, advisors and proselytisers are held to have been Yarse (Duperray 1985; Ilboudo

1990; Kouanda 1988, 1995). They are esteemed in Mossi historiography on account of their religion, whereas Fulbe are portrayed as dangerous for the very same reason. Here is a paradox, then, between the fear of Fulbe calls for a jihad, and their complete absence from the historiography of the spread of Islam in the Mossi kingdoms.

These puzzling appearances, ambiguities, and paradoxes raise questions about what the relations were between Fulbe and other groups in these kingdoms. Who were these Fulbe who appear sporadically in the historiography of the Mossi region as often disloyal, capricious, and dissembling people, as dubious mercenaries or allies, as not having affected significantly the course of Mossi history and state formation, but nevertheless as having succeeded, as a Muslim people, to have penetrated into the interstices of a group of polities that, generally, is characterized by the cohesion of its institutions and portrayed as extraordinarily stable and particularly resistant to Muslim influences?

Little progress seems to have been made since Lieutenant Marc (1909:143–144) noted the mysteriousness of Fulbe's presence in Mossi country, and the difficulty of understanding "the exact situation of Fulbe with regard to the Mossi" and the reasons for "those nomads who were so different from the Mossi, to settle in large numbers in [this] country." One hundred years later, the mystery surrounding Fulbe's role in Mossi history remains.

ETHNOGRAPHY OF THE MOSSI REGION: FULBE'S OUSTING FROM MOSSI SOCIETY

At the advent of French colonial rule, at the end of the 19th century, 19 Mossi kingdoms existed. They had been founded by descendants of the mythical ancestor, naaba Ouédraogo (Izard 1970:85–86). Systematic ethnographic studies were first carried out when, in 1904, the administrators of the *Afrique*

Occidental Française (French West-Africa) were ordered to gather information on a wide variety of issues regarding the regions and populations they were to administer (Wooten 1993:430–434). This resulted in a number of *Monographies de Cercle*, which became the initial basis of the canonical texts in Mossi historiography and ethnography.[4]

Noiré, administrator of Yatenga in 1903/1904, distinguished five "races" in his *cercle* (his administrative unit). These he divided into two categories. On the one hand, there were those who till the land (the "autochthonous" groups: Mossi, Samo, and Dioula/Yarse). On the other, there were those (Fulbe) who engage only in herding, and who have their fields worked upon by men from the other groups.[5] Tauxier also considered "autochthons," Yarse and Fulbe, as "races" distinct from Mossi. But whereas he took "autochthons" and the Yarse to be an integral part of Mossi society — disregarding them would "disfigure" Mossi society since they were Mossi's farmers and traders— Fulbe were but "an adventive element that succeeded entering up to a certain point [...] under Mossi domination, but was never part of [Mossi society]" (Tauxier 1917:332–337). They could therefore be "suppressed" without modifying Mossi society whatsoever.

To authors such as Tauxier, Fulfulde-speaking pastoralists belonged to a widely dispersed population group rather than to, for instance, Mossi society. He (1937:7) opened his study *Moeurs et histoire des Peuls,* which includes an appendix on Yatenga's Fulbe, with the question "What [sic] are the Fulbe?" to conclude a few pages later that they are "multiform," explaining this heterogeneity in terms of a distinct evolutionary scale along which Fulbe moved from a "natural state" of nomadic cattle herdsmen, paying tribute to "negro chiefs," to a stage in which they came to rule these very same farmer populations (Tauxier 1937:8–10). He reduced the populations among which they happened to live to an amorphous environment in which Fulbe —all assumed to have a common origin— evolved "naturally" from subordinate, pagan nomads to ruling Muslim aristocrats. A clustering of characteristics was thus effectuated, with ascendancy and Islamic faith associated with sedentary life and long-term presence, and subordination and paganism with mobility and recent arrival. The Mossi kingdoms' Fulbe were situated on this Fulbe-related evolutionary scale as well and ascribed all Fulbe stereotypes (wealthy and individualized, but also lazy, cunning and dishonest people —more intelligent though and nearer to the white colonizers than their neighbours). To further understanding of the Fulbe, they were to be studied comparatively with other regions' Fulbe (Tauxier 1937:155).[6]

Tauxier's work set the scene. Later authors never questioned that Fulbe, although often recognized to be "subordinated" and "paying tribute" to Mossi leaders, constituted a politically autonomous group and a separate society. Izard (1970:20), for instance, distinguished between "inhabitants of the Mossi kingdoms" and "Mossi society," emphasizing Fulbe's otherness:

> Mossi society obviously […] does not include all inhabitants of the "Mossi kingdom." On the Mossi sice, the king has authority over those groups of foreign origin who settled in Mossi country after the Nakombse conquest: Yarse [...], Maranse [...] et Kambwese [...]. These groups are in a relation of direct subjugation to the king, even if royal authority is delegated to a mocal chief. The position of Peul is different: they do not participate in any institutionalized way in the fonctionning of Mossi society […]. [Izard 1970:20, my translation]

The Mossi system implied that the four groups that constituted the Mossi kingdom (the tengbiise, Yarse, the nakombse and the *bagrse*, royal captives of Fulbe origin) were represented in court organization by four high-ranking dignitaries (respectively the *togo naaba*, the *balum naaba*, the *weranga naaba* and the *rasam naaba*) who were charged with their administration. Fulbe were not represented in court. This led Izard (1982:370; 1985b:466–467) to conclude that Fulbe did not entertain hierarchical power relations with the king, and therefore did not belong to Mossi society.[7]

Other reasons to exclude Fulbe from Mossi society were: language (Moore versus Fulfulde, see Luning 1997:80; Izard 1985b:68); marriage (because of their religion and their pastoral lifestyle, Fulbe were exluded from the Mossi system of marriage exchanges, see Izard 1982:368; Kabore 1966:27); and their livelihood. Izard's opus magnum (*Gens du pouvoir, gens de la terre*, Izard 1985b:5–6) opens with the statement that Yatenga's inhabitants can be "phenotypically" divided into two groups: sedentary farmers ("autochthons," nakombse, Yarse, Marase and bagrse captives) and Fulbe herdsmen with their *riimaybe* (servants).[8] According to Izard, each group constituted a separate society, and was linguistically and socio-culturally homogeneous.

Izard's analysis included a total of 476 Mossi villages, but Yatenga's 146 Fulbe settlements were explicitly left out. By thus establishing the kingdom as a society without Fulbe, Fulbe's relations with Mossi did not have to be explained. Rather, Fulbe relations with other groups could not but become conceived of as intrinsically different from the relations between so-called integrated groups. In contrast to intra-society relations, these inter-society relations were depoliticized and phrased in terms of "common interest" and "contract" (Izard 1983:256). Moreover, Izard saw Mossi-Fulbe relations as purely practical, though he minimized their economic importance, stressing that cattle tended to be owned, besides by Fulbe, only by Mossi chiefs. The principal if not single large cattle owner in Yatenga was the king, and his animals were kept, not by free Fulbe, but by bagrse (Izard 1982:368; 1970:384).

Izard's findings and propositions regarding Yatenga were sometimes too easily transposed to other Mossi kingdoms. For instance, Savonnet-Guyot (1986:87, 90–91) represented Mossi as a people with a single myth of origin, a founding ancestor, and a principle of naam, who speak a single language: "[The] Mossi dynasties engender kingdoms all identical among each other, that produce new dynasties, which all claim [descent] from Wedraogo" (Savonnet-Guyot 1986:88).[9] The prosperity of the state depended on the presence and activities of tengbiise farmers, blacksmiths, and artisan-traders, and conversely, which groups came to belong to Mossi society and how they were categorized was dictated by the logic of state development (Savonnet-Guyot 1986:106). If Izard mentioned Fulbe as a category of people living within the boundaries of Yatenga —albeit not belonging to Mossi society— Savonnet-Guyot's reinterpretation of Izard's work mentioned them not even once.[10]

REVISITING HISTORIOGRAPHY AND ETHNOGRAPHY: DISENTANGLING ESSENTIALIZED CATEGORIES

Judging from the historiographies and ethnographies reviewed above, Mossi society appears as heterogeneous and capable of accommodating difference. "Autochthons," "conquerors," Yarse, blacksmiths, Marase: all are acknowledged to have different origins, occupations, and religions. These differences did not preclude them from the Mossi kingdoms. On the contrary: they were the basis for their inclusion. Fulbe, however, emerge as too different to be accommodated.

Still, we know that, first, some of the royal courts had a specific dignitary responsible for "Fulbe affairs," implying an institutionalization of Fulbe presence. Second, marriage between Fulbe and nakombse was not always that exceptional (Chéron 1924; Kabore 1966).[11] Third, two other often cited criteria for belonging to Mossi society, such as religion and language, did not preclude the inclusion of groups such as Yarse (Muslims and polyglot) and bagrse (Muslims and often having Fulfulde as their mother tongue). Furthermore, in the kingdoms' myths of origin Fulbe feature side-by-side with nakombse, tengbiise, Yarse and/or blacksmiths. Such myths legitimize a particular labour division; also, they justify a group's position in society, in particular vis-à-vis the ruling nakombse.[12] Finally, one would expect Fulbe to have a prominent place in Mossi society because of their central economic role, as they had a quasi-monopoly on cattle herding in a region known for its cattle production and export (Izard 1970:385–387). In other words, so-called objective reasons for *a priori* excluding Fulbe from Mossi society can be easily refuted.

There are different elements that need to be cited in answering the question of why Fulbe were considered "too different" to be included in the Mossi kingdoms. First, Izard's work had defined "the quintessential and dominant questions" (Appadurai 1986:357) and the theoretical, hence empirical, scope of anthropological interest on the region. Subsequent researchers tended to address Izard and often assumed his contentions as premises for their own work (e.g. Bonnet 1988; Luning 1997; Savonnet-Guyot 1986). Izard's predominance in the study of the Mossi kingdoms, and the extrapolation of his findings on Yatenga to other kingdoms, may help explain Fulbe's marginalization in social research on the region. But why did Izard leave out Fulbe? After all, he was not the first to write on the Mossi kingdoms.

To an important extent, Izard's work was based on investigations and reports by early colonial administrators-ethnographers, of which Tauxier was the most important. In general, these administrators-ethnographers were convinced that Fulbe were "whiter" and consequently higher up on the "evolutionary ladder" than the populations among which they lived. This scientific racism was the dominant paradigm in early 20th century France, where it had gained the upper hand over the social evolutionary school: races were biologically determined and could be ranked into an innate hierarchy of races. This hierarchy was based on physical characteristics (such as skin colour), but it also implied a hierarchy of moral virtue and intellectual capacity. Moreover, the fact that Fulbe were widely dispersed but spoke a language of their own triggered a fascination in many a traveller (Botte et al. 1999:19). Also, finally, colonialism over-determined the opposition between sedentary people and nomads (Boëtch and Ferrié 1999:73–76; see also Babiker 2006).[13]

Therefore, early 20th century administrator-ethnographers understood Fulbe living within the Mossi kingdoms as belonging firstly to the larger, widely dispersed Fulbe entity. Also, they perceived these "white" or "whiter" groups as predestined founders of states (Botte et al. 1999:20–21). Hence, to find the "very intelligent" Fulbe —"civilising elements" among the colonized subjects— to be subordinated to the "lazy," "quarrelsome," "improvident" Mossi was to them an anomaly to be corrected wherever possible.[14]

In 1901, for instance, captain Ruef, the then administrator of the *Cercle de Ouagadougou* deprived the king of Ouagadougou of his authority over three Fulbe groups. A few years later, his successor, Dubreuil, acclaimed this measure as "one of the most fruitful reforms" realized in the Mossi kingdoms up to that date, having ended Fulbe's alleged "shameful exploitation." Dubreuil called for a continuation of this policy, especially in the Kingdoms of Boussouma and Boulsa, where Fulbe population density was particularly high, but also pointed out that reforms had become less urgent because, following Ruef's first measures, Mossi chiefs had decided to no longer subject Fulbe to "the humiliations that they were used to inflict on them."[15] "Liberating" Fulbe from the Mossi courts became even less of a preoccupation once the French administration of West Africa shifted from direct rule to a pragmatic form of indirect rule.[16]

Hence, it was especially during the first decade of the 20th century that the French administration attempted to make the existing political hierarchy more in line with prevailing colonial perceptions and expectations (see Nana 1994:16–17). This attempt by colonial administrators to "invent" a tradition, according to which there was no institutionalized relation of subordination of Fulbe to royal courts, contributed to the representation of Fulbe as a distinct, separate group that existed outside of Mossi society and, instead, was part of a widely dispersed population, the essence of which was their cultural identity as nomadic herds people. Since, however, in the pragmatics of colonial administration, the ideal of freeing Fulbe from the Mossi yoke was soon abandoned, royal and *kombere* (regional chief) court organization, in at least some of the kingdoms (among them, Boussouma) continued to include institutionalized arrangements for the management of relations with Fulbe.

Still, in their indignation about the subordination of the —in their eyes— superior Fulbe, early administrators seem to have grossly exaggerated the inflicted extortions. Indeed, the presumably heavily-exploited Fulbe proved to be also the region's wealthiest inhabitants —a paradox that could be resolved only by resorting to racist prejudices. Thus, Dubreuil argued that, despite being persecuted, Fulbe succeeded "to acquire an affluence very superior to that of the Mossi" and controlled "an important part of the country's wealth," thanks to "their economic spirit, their subtlety, [...] their duplicity, in their transactions with the Mossi."[17] As I will demonstrate, the paradox of Fulbe being "subordinated" yet relatively wealthy, is more convincingly resolved when taking into account the fact that Fulbe subjects and Mossi chiefs engaged in various kinds of social and political relations that had at least a minimal legitimacy in the eyes of both Mossi and Fulbe.

Colonial categories were, however, not created *ex nihilio*. The administrators-ethnographers' sources were closely affiliated to the courts of the major kingdoms (Ouagadougou, Yatenga, Boussouma). Rulers and leading court dignitaries rendered the kingdoms' past as a dynastic succession of kings, chiefs and nakombse, reducing others to the status of passive playthings of these actors' ambitions and frustrations. They monopolized historical agency, and claimed selected actual or asserted historical events as their exclusive cultural property (Wilmsen 2002:841). Later anthropologists, in their turn, focused disproportionately on recognizable and generalizable features that were often literally articulated by their informants. Their models and theories were at least partly a response to the representations and ideologies of local elites (Tonkin 1990:141–142).

As cultural specificity gradually replaced race, Fulbe studies survived as a separate field of research. This field focussed on the comparative study (in linguistics, sociology and technical-economic fields) of dispersed Fulbe groups, often cutting them loose from the groups among whom they lived (Boesen 1999:84–85; Botte et al. 1999:19–22). As a consequence, they reproduced the rather stereotypical images of Fulbe herdsmen, which in turn influenced how Fulbe were represented in studies of regions where they constituted a minority. The persistent decontextualization and reification of Fulbe resulted in one study after the other assuming that Fulbe living in the Mossi region were "more different" than other population groups.

The representation of a society as consisting of a distinct people, speaking the same language, having a particular culture and living in accordance with specific institutions, dominated anthropology for the most part of the 20th century (but see Herskovits 1926; Fortes 1945). This concept of society as a bounded and self-contained entity implied clear-cut boundaries, finitude, break, rupture, and disjunction (Gupta and Ferguson 1992:6). Following the idea that individuals should be understood as members of well-bounded groups, the Mossi region's population was classified into unitary categories. This meant that researchers were to imagine a boundary between Fulbe and Mossi that was impermeable to sustained socio-political intercourse, even if this implied such a boundary would extend *ad infinitum* into the interstices of the kingdoms (see Alvarez 1995:454; Kearney 2004:228). From this perspective, including Fulbe —distinct but de-territorialized— in the region's society would jeopardize its finitude.

Paradoxically, Izard (1985b:68) claimed that "being a Mossi is being nothing." Usually the "other" is designated as Mossi, whereas the "self" is identified with a title or status group label (such as nakombse, tengbiise, blacksmiths, or Yarse). Only those contemptuously designated as commoners (*talse*) may identify themselves as Mossi. "Mossi" thus designates a negative, residual category (see also Izard 1976:69; 1983:255). Furthermore, Izard (1976) stressed the relativity of socio-ethnic statuses and the frequency of identity changes. He, however, interpreted this unfixity in terms of the successful efforts by Mossi rulers to transform ethnic groups with a history into an ahistorical matrix of functional groups from which Fulbe were excluded. As a result, "the Mossi" emerged as an essentialized ethnic label, even if "naked" ethnicity — that is, the "Mossi category"— was little valued in this heterogeneous society. Despite Izard's efforts not to relinquish the dynamics of boundary-making and change, he endowed Mossi society with structural coherence and functional purpose — especially *vis-à-vis* Fulbe.

REINSCRIBING FULBE: TOWARDS A HISTORY OF INTERCONNECTEDNESS

The invention of tradition, then, is not a colonial prerogative. At every instance, Mossi society, its past and its categories, were imagined from the point of view of a particular present, and with social, moral, and political considerations in mind. All actors involved —whether pre-colonial praise singers, Arabic *tarikh* authors, royal court dignitaries, or administrator-ethnographers— can be shown to have been selective in their treatment of the past. Closures —mute and multiple, unintelligible and undecipherable— can be assumed to have been everpresent in a dialectic of intertextuality that, for instance, connected western models of historical discourse to indigenous traditions of narrative (Chapman et al. 1989:5-7; Spear 2003:8). As Spear (2003:23) argues, colonialism and its representations were embedded in an endless process of becoming: they were born out of earlier eras and representations and brought forth later ones. With regard to Fulbe in the Mossi region, this resulted in their "not belonging" to mainstream Mossi society.[18]

These interactive processes of inventing the past tend to muffle subalternate voices. These voices, however, can be heard if only one cares to listen. My own fieldwork in the Kingdom of Boussouma suggests that subalternate histories, contesting Mossi rulers' exclusive cultural property of historical events, continue to flourish.

> When [Nabigeswende, founder of Boussouma] left Ouagadougou for Boussouma, he was accompanied by a Fulbe, who [upon arrival] was nominated jooro [chief, in Fulfulde, pl. *joorobe*] of Baskouda. Nabigeswende came to Boussouma together with the earth priest of Tangpoore, [...] the Yar-naaba [Yarse chief], his tasoba [war chief] and the Bagre naaba as

> well. […] Since he followed the naaba from Ouagadougou to Boussouma, he is considered the most important of the Boussouma joorobe […]. This is what we learned and this is also what [is confirmed in what] we see, since when we go to visit the Boussouma naaba, the jooro of Baskouda is the first to greet him. Only thereafter the other joorobe can greet the king. [Interview with the Balbou jooro, August 2002]

> Boussouma's force was the force of [its] Fulbe. Boussouma relied on its Fulbe. […] Whenever the nakombse went to battle, the Fulbe were there as well. They were even first. It was they who had the good horses, who had the good armour, it was they who were reckless and had a strong heart. […] Thanks to the Fulbe, no pillagers dared entering Boussouma. The Fulbe were Boussouma's fortress. [Interview with Amado Bande, Louda jooro, July 2002]

> There were no bagrse before the Fulbe's arrival. It was only after Fulbe came [to Boussouma] that the king designated one of his captives as chief of his cattle enclosure, simply because it was only then that he started to receive cattle and captives. By giving the king cattle, Fulbe were at the origin of Bagre. [Interview with Amado Bande, Louda jooro, March 2002]

These fragments suggest that Fulbe credit themselves with more agency than they are granted in received historiography, which neglected to ask certain questions regarding Fulbe and their relations with other groups in the Mossi region. Also, it is likely that historiography ignored or dismissed as invalid certain types of evidence, thus giving rise to the kind of paradoxes and contradictions mentioned earlier on in this paper. Similarly, received ethnography also contains fragments demonstrating that the trans-local encounter between Mossi and Fulbe did result in institutionalized socio-political arrangements. Kabore (1966:57), for instance, maintains that at the Ouagadougou Court a "secondary" dignitary, the "Fulbe chief" (*Silmi naaba*), mediated between the king and Fulbe. He also suggests that Fulbe, like the other groups, were subjected to the Mossi chiefs. At the Boussouma Court, a "chief of the captives" (*Bagre naaba*) mediated between the king and Fulbe; in case of war, the kingdom's Fulbe marched under his command (Chéron 1925:309–310). Without great difficulty, such instances can be confirmed by findings from my fieldwork in Boussouma, where the "chief of the captives" still is the intermediary between Fulbe and the king. Furthermore, Boussouma numbers twelve *joorobe* (Fulbe chiefs) who are inaugurated and receive their naam directly from the king. This suggests that the authority of the *jooro* (Fulbe chief) does exist not parallel to or outside the Mossi political organization, but is rather integrated within it (see Breusers 2002):

> There is no difference with regard to [the] power [of Mossi and Fulbe chiefs]. What differs is the way in which subjects follow their chief. A chief must settle problems between people. If he does not succeed, he submits the problem to the […] naaba, whether he is a Fulbe or a Mossi chief. [Interview with Jobo Sonde, son of the Bandega jooro, July 2002]

Hence, it seems possible to write Fulbe into the region's historiography and ethnography. But how can this be done? Even if, to an important extent, the independent history of groups such as the Fulbe is lacking, the fact that alternative Fulbe versions of the past are signalled by paradoxes, ambiguities and contradictions does not mean that "Fulbe history" is "really there"; the fact that fragments of their past can be retrieved, does not imply that this past is waiting to be rediscovered and expressed (see Chapman et al. 1989:8). Any attempt, then, to write "Fulbe history" risks producing yet another invented, truncated history; it risks reproducing Fulbe as yet another essentialized sub-category befitting of the inexorably unfolding logic of the development of the Mossi state. In that case, such an attempt would not be able to account for the heterogeneity (noblemen, *riimaybe*, cattle herdsmen, agropastoralists, bagrse, etc.) beneath the "Fulbe" label, nor would it account for Fulbe's variegated relations with the kingdoms' other groups. Such an attempt is, finally, also at risk of creating a new boundary between Fulbe from the Mossi region and from neighbouring societies. As a result, it would not address the more fundamental issues but only displace them. What is needed, then, is not to shift an external boundary or reshuffle the internal ones by adding new subcategories. What is needed is to question the modernist concept of society itself.

If one is to resign oneself to the impossibility of retrieving the "true" history of Fulbe in the Mossi region —and, hence, to the insurmountability of uncovering the multiple paths that characterize relationships between Fulbe and other groups— and if one is to avoid adding yet another bounded subcategory to Mossi society, then how should we study this region's society and culture while doing justice to Fulbe presence? How can we account for Fulbe's part in both past and present day processes of change? How are we to render the paradox that Fulbe represent themselves as travelers and strangers who are only passing by, while they have been involved in local social, political, and religious relations for centuries?

One way out is suggested by Gupta and Ferguson (1992:16). They argue that the starting point must be altered, and instead of a pre-given world of separate peoples and cultures, they propose a difference-producing set of *relations* as a point of departure. Instead of starting from the premise of discontinuity and autonomy to theorize contact, conflict and contradiction they propose to start from existing, interconnected spaces. This implies privileging interconnectedness instead of assuming disconnectedness, and understanding cultural difference as "a product of a *shared* historical process that differentiates the world as it connects it" (Gupta and Ferguson 1992:7–8, 16; emphasis added). Indeed, these authors argue that "the separateness of separate places is not a natural given but an anthropological problem" (Gupta and Ferguson 1992:17); so is the separateness of separate identitary categories. How was separateness constructed and how is it maintained? But also, how is connectedness realized? How do people confound established spatial and conceptual orders, either through physical movement or through their own conceptual and political acts of re-imagination? Claims to authenticity or purity and other forms of essentialism are to be related to acts of power or "rooting," against which, or in simultaneity with which, subalternate acts of confounding, subverting or "rhizoming" continuously take place. The former were disproportionately emphasized in modernist epistemology, of which Mossi historiography and ethnography are manifestations. Needed now are concepts and approaches that redirect attention to change, interconnectedness, heterogeneous becoming, and transformation: qualities of reality that have been substantially marginalized by a focus on permanence, discreteness, linear progress, and equilibrium (Styhre 2001).[19]

As Wilmsen (2002:841) argues, a successful approach dissolves the surface appearance of disconnectedness and fragmentation and re-establishes historical connections. A first step —probing for contradictions amongst the discourses that generated these surface appearances— was tackled above. Next, an ethnographic focus is required on spatial and conceptual boundaries, borderlands and borderlines, on how they are defined and established, but also transcended and denied, on how categories are mixed up, destabilising the fixity of what is "ourselves" and "others" (Gupta and Ferguson 1992:19), of what is "inside" and "outside." In this regard, Bhabha (1989:72, quoted in Gupta and Ferguson 1992:19) calls for focusing on the borderline of "ourselves-as-others, others-as-ourselves." Such ethnography would challenge modernist ethnography and historiography without resorting itself to yet another (re)construction and essentialization of identities; it would avoid resorting to a binary logic of either/or categories, and, instead, allow for a logic of "both-and-and-..." (Kearney 2004:228–229).

What then are these borderlands and borderlines in the Mossi region? Where can we expect the notions of ourselves-as-others and others-as-ourselves to be expressed? Obviously, some issues and processes are more likely to reveal interconnectedness and heterogeneous becoming. For instance, marriage and kinship tend to be structured and rule-governed. Instead, one could focus, on friendship (*zoodo*), which is particular among Mossi, in the sense that, initially, a friend should be a stranger, that is, someone one did not grow up with, someone who is not one's kinsman. Friendship is, however, engaged in with the expectation of establishing in-law relations. Hence, besides being an expression of individual freedom, Mossi friendship plays a significant role in the never-ending process of creating alliances between kin groups; it constitutes an intermediary phase that transforms "strangerhood" into kinship (see Breusers forthcoming). It is a relationship that resolves the spaces of uncertainty that arise in encounters characterized by "radical otherness" (Martinelli 1999:357). As such, friendship defies established boundaries and expresses social contingency; it operates by variation, expansion, and conquest (see Deleuze and Guattari 1988:7–17). This is even more true for friendship between Mossi and Fulbe, which, in contrast to friendship between Mossi, is unlikely to be realized in kinship organization (see also Martinelli 1999:382–383).

Another borderline, crucial to explanations of, and coping with, illness, infecundity and misfortune is the realm between the world of the living, on the one hand, and the world of the dead and the unborn, on the other. During sexual intercourse, one of a twin-pair of *kinkirse* (spirits) is said to enter the woman's womb. Then, the world of the living opens up to the other world; it becomes vulnerable to a transgression that, if it occurs, must be accommodated for. When, for instance, a Mossi womb is entered by a Fulbe kinkirga, the child must be recognized as a Fulbe to prevent it from returning to the other world. Fulbe should be involved in the name-giving ceremony, after which the child grows up in a —symbolical— Fulbe environment. Afterwards as well, the child's destiny remains linked to Fulbe, with whom it should establish connections to safeguard health, fecundity, and good fortune (e.g. through spiritual parenthood; see Breusers forthcoming). Such cases of Fulbe ascendancy among Mossi exemplify the possibility of "ourselves-as-others, others-as-ourselves."

In between, as well, are the bagrse. The analysis above suggested that it is possible to write a historiography and ethnography of the Mossi region representing Fulbe as incorporated or, in other words, "rooted" in Mossi socio-political institutions, for instance through royal court organization and the incorporation of Fulbe chiefs into the realm of power or naam. Fulbe were also "rooted" as royal captives. In contrast to other categories of royal captives, who were completely robbed of whatever historical and social identity they might have possessed as free men (Izard 1975:285), Fulbe captives were classified into a separate category, bagrse. Whereas other captives' identity makes sense only within the realm of Mossi power, bagrse either claim or are ascribed a Fulbe identity, which they express by speaking Fulfulde, maintaining or adopting a Fulbe patronymic, and/or a preference for cattle herding (see Luning 1997:81–82). Hence, though incorporated into Mossi institutions, bagrse imagine a history prior to captivity as well as connections with a world outside Mossi power (see, for instance, Tiendrébéogo 1963:20–22).

The last example of a borderline is probably the most obvious one, namely the physical borderlines such as no-man's lands between different polities and "unsocialized" spaces in between the domesticated places of villages and fields, where Fulbe tend to be prominently present. Fulbe often claim to have initiated the humanization of space. In their search for pastures, they tore open the bush and confronted and chased wild animals, thus facilitating the subsequent arrival of Mossi farmers: "All Mossi fear the frontier [...]. The Fulbe tore the bush apart, killed the wild animals and chased others away. Only thereafter the Mossi come and claim the land is theirs" (Interview with Amado Bande, Louda *jooro*, July 2002).

Luning (1997:226) describes how, in a final phase of the inauguration of the king of Maane, Fulbe build a Fulbe hut in the royal court. For a few weeks, this hut will be the new king's residence, until he is allowed to occupy a "normal" house. Luning's interpretation comes close to Fulbe's exegesis of their role as "openers of the bush": when a new settlement is established, one must first find out if place and new occupants match; therefore, the foundation of a house must be preceded by building a temporary hut.

Fulbe, then, are present in between and in the interstices of kingdoms, chieftaincies and villages, and to a certain extent they can be portrayed as the vanguards of Mossi society. In this regard, it can be noted that in Mossi oral traditions Fulbe's capacity to go unnoticed is a recurrent theme. When, for instance, naaba Karfo, King of Ouagadougou from 1834 to

1842, sent a Fulbe to kill a political opponent, the assassin was actively sought for but not found since “nobody bothered disturbing the poorly dressed Fulbe who was resting, stretched out on the ground near the village” (Tiendrébéogo 1963:32). When, later in the 19th century, Boussouma was in conflict with Ouagadougou, the king of Boussouma armed some hundred horsemen to arrive before the gates of Ouagadougou:

> This progress was made possible by the fact that the inhabitants of the Boussouma region were dressed like Peul [this detail was omitted by Izard 1970:178, 250]. Their approach was not noticed in Ouagadougou and the noblemen in the capital were caught unarmed. [Tiendrébéogo 1963:36, my translation]

Their capacity to navigate these no man’s lands and to go unnoticed, meant that Fulbe became excellent scouts and precious intelligence officers (also see Izard 1982:367–368):

> The Fulbe chiefs receive more information than the Mossi. We settle them somewhere so that they listen and come and tell us. A Mossi speaks as he speaks, but a Fulbe acts as if he comes to talk, to ask a question. He hears what is said, leaves and goes and tells the kombere: “Watch out, in that or that village they talk about this or that.” […] [The Fulbe] settle on the frontiers to listen to what people say. […] If there is going to be a war, he goes to inform the chief: “Watch out, that day there will be a war. [Interview with Luc Ouédraogo, royal lineage of Piugtenga *kombere*, Boussouma kingdom, July 2002]
>
> When two Mossi speak with each other and

> there is a Fulbe at their side, the Mossi consider there is nobody present, and so the Fulbe can listen and inform us. [Interview with the king of Boussouma, July 2002]

Whether as friends who are not easily turned into kinsmen or as capricious kinkirse spirits, whether as captives claiming a Fulbe identity or as vanguards and the eyes and ears of the kingdom, Fulbe operate at the fringes of Mossi socialities and polities. They make new paths, and forge new relationships between political factions, or between the human and the spirit world.

CONCLUSION

In order to grasp Fulbe's presence in the Mossi region one is not to reject *en bloc* "modernist" understandings in terms of rules, traditions, or unified identities (Styhre 2001). Like other groups in the region, Fulbe are incorporated into and subordinated within Mossi polity. I demonstrated that this trans-local Mossi-Fulbe encounter was institutionally productive. This is relevant especially in the light of previous work that emphasized the pragmatic and contractual aspects of relations between Mossi and Fulbe, thus suggesting that the basis for their collaboration is not inscribed in previously institutionalized social relations.

Yet, this sedentary perspective does not tell the whole story. In fact, such a perspective can *never* do that: wherever one finds the naming, codification, or the fixing of boundaries, one also finds strategies to avoid categorization (or alternative categories), decodification, and attempts to slip out from structures and boundaries (see Rice 1990:156). Therefore, I argued in favour of an explicit focus on interconnectedness and on multiple differences, on continuous becoming instead of preestablished discontinuity. Consequently, Fulbe are to be understood as not in *or* out of Mossi society, but rather, as in *and* out.[20] Analysis of social and political life in this region is to start, not from the assumption that Fulbe and Mossi constitute separate societies, nor from the idea that Fulbe are a category integrated into a bounded, Mossi-dominated, society.

It is not my intention to oppose Fulbe as a meandering, rhizoming force to the "rooted" categories of, for instance, nakombse or "autochthons." As much as any other group "constitutive" of society, Fulbe are involved and captured in processes of both "rhizoming" and "rooting." Yet, their pastoralism, their settlement in the interstices of Mossi polities, or the fact that they embody "otherness within self" for other groups, makes them into privileged agents of transgression and creative interconnections. As such, they constitute a particularly interesting point of entry for grasping this society's openness and for studying change in terms of multiplicity and becoming —for an ethnography that does not resort to essentialized categories.

Such a perspective may help to resolve the mystery of Fulbe presence in the Mossi region. Fulbe are involved in trans-local encounters with other groups. Sometimes, these encounters give rise to institutionalized socio-political relations; at other times, though, they allow Fulbe and others to slip out from under established institutional arrangements. This partly explains why Fulbe are "passing by," without origin or destiny, yet are always present and to be accounted for if one is to understand this society and its dynamics of change. As one of my interviewees phrased it:

> We don't know where the Fulbe came from. [...] They came just like that, and we see them since a long time. We are together. [...] The Fulbe has no point of departure, he has no other basis than where he happens to be at the moment. Wherever he is, he is at home. [...]

But, sooner or later he will leave […]. [Interview with the Nessemtenga *tengsoba*, February 2002]

NOTES

[1] Only in the historiography of Yatenga, substantial interest is taken in the kingdom's relations with non-Mossi polities (Ségou, Maasina and Djelgodji; see Izard 1982; Tauxier 1924).

[2] An immediate consequence for Yatenga of such a *jihad* would have been the cutting off of salt routes and the running dry of the supply of captives (Izard 1985a:71).

[3] For instance, Tauxier (1917:621–629; 1937:385) traced how various Fulbe groups arrived in Yatenga from the mid-17th century onwards, after several wanderings had brought them from the Futa-Toro or Futa-Djallon to places such as Douentza, Bandiagara, Liptako or Sokoto. Tauxier's most important source was the *Monographie du cercle de Ouahigouya* of 1904. Izard (1985a:68–70) reproduced Tauxier's account of Fulbe settlement history without adding new information. See also Chéron (1924:647,668), Marc (1909), Pageard (1965:26–29).

[4] Not only did Delafosse (1912) draw upon them in his *Haut-Sénégal Niger* and were they extensively quoted by Tauxier (1912; 1917), but they continued to be referred to by historians throughout the 20th century, especially because of the records of oral accounts of dynastic histories they comprised (Izard 1970:21–27).

[5] Archives Nationales Section Outre-mer (ANSOM) 14MIOM/690 (1G326). Etude sur le Yatenga, établie suivant les instructions de M. le Gouverneur Général de l'AOF, Commandant du Cercle Capitaine Noiré de l'Infanterie Coloniale, 1903–1904.

[6] Hence, Fulbe in southern kingdoms (e.g. Ouagadougou) were relatively mobile, living in isolated households and subordinated, whereas the Yatenga Fulbe had evolved somewhat towards supremacy, being more sedentary and having their own chiefs, albeit still subordinated to Mossi rulers (Tauxier 1937:154–155).

[7] In practice, relations between Fulbe and Yatenga's central authority were mediated by the *weranga naaba* and the *rasam naaba*, high dignitaries responsible for relations with nakombse and captives, as well as for the

kingdom's northern and eastern territorial sectors. According to Izard (1985b:466–467) this was because of pragmatic considerations, since most of Yatenga's Fulbe happened to live in these two sectors.

8 Note how this distinction is reminiscent of the one made by Noiré some 80 years earlier.

9 Savonnet-Guyot (1986:112–113) nevertheless acknowledged that the initial model tended to be adapted somewhat in each kingdom (e.g. Yatenga's centralized organization *versus* Ouagadougou's looser structure).

10 Izard (2003:12) recognized the danger of his vision becoming all too easily accepted as orthodoxy.

11 Izard (1970:401) relegated the observation that the "solidarity between Fulbe and Mossi is particularly strong in [the kingdom of] Ratenga where matrimonial exchanges exist between the families of Fulbe chiefs and the royal family" to a footnote.

12 In this manner, Duperray (1985:189), interprets a lengthy myth reproduced in Dim Delobsom (1932:118–132) as justifying the privileged place of the Yarse among the nakombse's subjects. This myth, in which God instructs the ancestors of blacksmiths, Fulbe, Yarse and nakombse to go and build their house in the world —by which is meant the Moogo or the 'Mossi world'— can be taken to legitimize both Yarse's and Fulbe's belonging to Mossi society.

13 Note that in Izard (1985b:5), too, the sedentary-nomadic contrast was advanced to underscore the irreducible, "phenotypical" difference between Mossi and Fulbe societies.

14 ANSOM 14MIOM/689 (1G316). Notice sur le Mossi rédigée par le Capitaine Pinchon, Résident de France au Mossi, 1903; Monographie du Cercle du Mossi, Gouvernement Général de l'AOF, Colonie de la Haute Volta, 1920. ANCI Monographies de Cercle.

15 ANSOM 14MIOM/690 (1G326). Rapport du Capitaine Dubreuil, Commandant le Cercle de Ouagadougou sur la nécessité de diviser le Cercle actuel de Ouagadougou en deux cercles, sur les conditions dans lesquelles pourra s'effectuer cette division, et Note sur l'Administration du Mossi, AOF, Haut Sénégal Niger, Cercle de Ouagadougou, février 1905. ANCI Monographies de Cercle.

16 After World War I, administrators were to maintain indigenous office holders in their authority, prestige and power, albeit within the limits of

French sovereignty (Dimier 2003:87).

[17] ANSOM 14MIOM/690 (1G326). Rapport du Capitaine Dubreuil, 1905 (see above). Fulbe's relative wealth was reflected in taxation levels, which took into account the material situation of each "race"; for instance, for the year 1906 the head tax was set at 0.25 francs for Mossi, 0.75 francs for Yarse and 1.00 francs for Fulbe.

[18] Today, development efforts based upon stereotypic understandings of "pastoralists" and "farmers" continue to further the separation of Mossi and Fulbe (Breusers et al. 1998). See also Babiker (2006:180) who observes that "[the] 'herder/farmer' dichotomy is an example of oppositions that reflect the general tendency to convert differences of degree into differences of kind."

[19] Amselle (1998) argued that West African corporate groups' identities were characterized by fluidity until 19th century colonial administrator-ethnographers invented more rigid ethnic identities for administrative convenience. Nevertheless it can be hypothetized that, even if group identities were more fluid and malleable in pre-colonial times, that naming and categorising also occurred then and boundaries —however permeable— were drawn. Conversely, the extent to which colonial administrator-ethnographers were successful in inventing rigid ethnic identities is likely to have been limited as well.

[20] "The Fulbe always speaks two languages. He speaks Fulfulde, but he speaks Moore just as well as we do. The Fulbe are nomads, but, even if they go as far as Ghana where they can stay for years they continue to claim to be of Boussouma" (interview with the king of Boussouma, July 2002).

REFERENCES

Alvarez, R. R. 1995. The Mexican-US border: the making of an anthropology of borderlands. Annual Review of Anthropology 24:447-470.

Amselle, J.-L. 1998. Mestizo logics: anthropology of identity in Africa and elsewhere. Stanford University Press.

Babiker, M. 2006. African pastoralism through anthropological eyes. Whose crisis? *In* African anthropologies : history, critique and practice. M. Ntarangwi, D. Mills and M. Babiker, eds. Pp. 170–187. Dakar: CODESRIA.

Boesen, E. 1999. *Pulaaku*. Sur la foulanité. *In* Figures peules. R. Botte. J.

Boutrais and J. Schmitz, eds. Pp. :83–97. Paris: Karthala
Boëtsch, G. and J.-N. Ferrié. 1999. La naissance du Peul. Invention d'une race frontière au sud du Sahara. *In* Figures peules. R. Botte. J. Boutrais and J. Schmitz, eds. Pp. 73–82. Paris: Karthala.
Bonnet, D. 1988. Corps biologique, corps social: procréation et maladies de l'enfant en pays mossi, Burkina Faso. Paris: ORSTOM.
Botte, R., J. Boutrais and J. Schmitz. 1999. Préface. *In* Figures peules. R. Botte. J. Boutrais and J. Schmitz, eds. Pp. 7–50. Paris: Karthala.
Breusers, M. Forthcoming. Friendship and spiritual parenthood among Mossi and Fulbe in Burkina Faso. *In* Friendship, descent, and alliance in Africa. Y. Diallo, T. Grätz and M. Guichard, eds. Oxford: Berghahn.
——— 2002. 'The teeth and the tongue are always together, but it happens that the teeth bite the tongue': Fulbe's social and political integration in Moaga society and their access to natural resources. A case study from Burkina Faso. Paper presented at the workshop '*The landed and the landless? Strategies of territorial integration and dissociation in Africa*,' Max Planck Institute for Social Anthropology, Halle/Saale, May 27–29.
Breusers, M., S. Nederlof and T. van Rheenen. 1998. Conflict or symbiosis? Disentangling farmer-herdsman relations: the Mossi and Fulbe of the Central Plateau, Burkina Faso. The Journal of Modern African Studies 36(3):357–380.
Chapman, M., M. McDonald and E. Tonkin. 1989. Introduction. *In* History and ethnicity. E. Tonkin, M. McDonald and M. Chapman, eds. Pp. 1–21. London: Routledge.
Chéron, G. 1925. La cour du Boussouma naba. Bulletin du Comité d'Etudes Historiques et Scientifiques de l'AOF 8(2):304–312.
——— 1924. Traditions relatives au cercle de Kaya. Bulletin du Comité d'Etudes Historiques et Scientifiques de l'AOF 7(4) :639–691.
Delafosse, M. 1912. Haut-Sénégal-Niger (Soudan Français). Paris.
Deleuze, G. and F. Guattari. 1988. A thousand plateaus : capitalism and schizophrenia. London: Continuum.
Diallo, Y. 1997. Les Fulbe du Boobola. Genèse et évolution de l'Etat de Barani (Burkina Faso). Köln: Rüdiger Köppe Verlag.
Dim Delobsom, A.A. 1932. L'empire du Mogho-Naba. Coutumes des Mossi de la Haute-Volta. Paris: Domat-Montchrestien.
Duperray, A.-M. 1985. Les Yarse du royaume de Ouagadougou: l'écrit et l'oral. Cahiers d'Etudes Africaines 98(2):179–212.
Echenberg, M.J. 1971. Late nineteenth-century military technology in Upper Volta. The Journal of African History 12(2):241–254.
Gupta, A. and J. Ferguson 1992. Beyond "culture": space, identity and the politics of difference. Cultural Anthropology 7(1):6-23.
Ilboudo, P. 1990. Croyances et pratiques religieuses traditionnelles des

Mossi. Stuttgart: Franz Steiner Verlag.
Izard, M. 2003. Moogo: l'émergence d'un espace étatique ouest-africain au XVIe siècle. Paris: Karthala.
——— 1985b. Gens du pouvoir, gens de la terre. Cambridge : Cambridge University Press.
——— 1985a. Le Yatenga précolonial. Un ancien royaume du Burkina. Paris: Karthala.
——— 1983. Le royaume du Yatênga et ses forgerons: une recherche d'histoire du peuplement. Métallurgies Africaines. Nouvelles contributions. Mémoires de la Société des Africanistes 9:253–279.
——— 1982. La politique extérieure d'un royaume africain: le Yatenga au XIXe siècle. Cahiers d'études africaines 23 (3–4):363–385.
——— 1976. Changements d'identité lignagère dans le Yatenga. Journal des Africanistes 46(1–2):69–81.
——— 1975. Les captifs royaux dans l'ancien Yatenga. *In* L'esclavage en Afrique précoloniale. C. Meillassoux, ed. Pp. 281–296. Paris: Maspero.
——— 1970. Introduction à l'histoire des royaumes mossi. Tomes 1 et 2, Recherches Voltaïques 12–13. Paris-Ouagadougou: CNRS-CVRS.
Kabore, G.V. 1966. Organisation politique traditionnelle et evolution politique des Mossi de Ouagadougou. Recherches Voltaïques 5, Paris : CNRS.
Kawada, J. 1969. Chronologie des Busuma naaba. Notes et Documents Voltaïques 2(2):42–53.
Kearney, M. 2004. Changing fields of anthropology: from local to global. Lanham: Rowman and Littlefield Publishers.
Kouanda, A. 1995. La progression de l'islam au Burkina pendant la période coloniale. In La Haute-Volta coloniale. Témoignages, recherches, regards. G. Massa Y.G. Madiega. Pp. 233–248. Paris: Karthala.
——— 1988. L'état de la recherche sur l'islam au Burkina. In: *Islam et sociétés au sud du Sahara*. Paris: Editions de la Maison des Sciences de l'Homme:94–105.
Luning, S. 1997. Het binnenhalen van de oogst. Ritueel en samenleving in Maane, Burkina Faso. Leiden: CNWS.
Marc, L. 1909. Le pays mossi. Paris: Larose.
Martinelli, B. 1999. Logiques masculines et féminines de l'amitié chez les Moose du Burkina Faso. *In* Amitiés. Anthropologie et histoire. G. Ravis-Giordani, ed. Pp. 355–385. Aix en Provence: Publications de l'Université de Provence.
Nana, M. 1994. Modalités et outils de 'pacification' en pays moaaga (1897–1919). Revue Française d'Histoire d'Outre-Mer LXXXI (302):5–25.
Pageard, R. 1965. Une enquête historique en pays mossi (Ziniaré, Gaongo, Koubri, Kombissiri, Sapone, Tanghin-Dassouri, Niou et Yaco) avec appendice sur 'L'histoire des peuples mossis' de Leo Frobenius. Jour-

nal de la Société des Africanistes 35(1):11–66.
Rice, L. 1990. 'Nomad thought': Isabelle Eberhardt and the colonial project. Cultural Critique 17:151–176.
Savonnet-Guyot, C. 1986. Etat et sociétés au Burkina. Essai sur le politique africain. Paris: Karthala.
Spear, T. (2003). Neo-traditionalism and the limits of invention in British colonial Africa. Journal of African History 44(1):3–27.
Styhre, A. 2001. The nomadic organization: the postmodern organization of becoming. Tamara: Journal of Critical Postmodern Organization Science 1(4):1–12.
Tauxier, L. 1937. Moeurs et histoire des Peuls. Paris: Payot.
——— 1924. Nouvelles notes sur le Mossi et le Gourounsi. Paris: Larose.
——— 1917. Le Noir du Yatenga. Mossis – Nioniossés – Samos –Yarsés – Silmi-Mossis – Peuls. Paris: Larose.
——— 1912. Le Noir du Soudan. Paris.
Tiendrébéogo, Y. 1963 Histoire traditionnelle des Mossi de Ouagadougou. Journal de la Société des Africanistes 33:7–46.
Tonkin, E. 1990. West African ethnographic traditions. *In* Localizing strategies: regional traditions of ethnographic writing. R. Fardon, ed. Pp. 137–151. Edinburgh: Scottish Academic Press.
Wilmsen, E. N. 2002. Mutable identities: moving beyond ethincity in Botswana. Journal of Southern African Studies 28(4):825–841.
Wooten, S. R. 1993. Colonial administration and the ethnography of the family in the French Soudan. Cahiers d'Etudes Africaines 33(3):419–446.
Zahan, D. 1961. Pour une histoire des Mossi du Yatenga. L'Homme 1(2):5–22.

4
SHAPING NEW TERRITORIES: THE DISCURSIVE CONSTRUCTION OF BOUNDARIES IN SUBURBAN DAKAR

Eline Versluys

INTRODUCTION

This chapter examines how young inhabitants from a suburban neighbourhood in Dakar construct multiple identities in relation to their language use and linguistic attitudes. The research is based on several periods of ethnographic fieldwork conducted in the neighborhood of Yoff from 2004 to 2009. Twenty-two young inhabitants between the ages of 18 and 30 participated in individual interviews and group discussions on their lives in the neighbourhood and their linguistic practices. The analysis combines an ethnographic approach with discourse analysis in an attempt to understand the social mechanisms behind the different identities these youngsters construct, and focuses on these processes of boundary-making. Important to note, however, is that these boundaries are always plural and intersecting: on a first level, boundary-making takes place with regard to ethnic, spatial, and cultural identities. On a second level, moreover, each of these domains implies various and ambiguous identity positions.

The analysis will first briefly introduce the theoretical foundations of this study. Next, it sketches the urban context of Dakar, in particular the specific situation of Yoff and the sociolinguistic landscape that it finds itself in. A third section presents the research context, discussing the main research findings.

SOCIAL IDENTITY AND DISCOURSE ANALYSIS

This study considers the notion of boundaries from a narrative perspective: how do youngsters delineate *us* from *them* in discourse? Such boundaries have been extensively studied in social identity theory. Although the notion of identity that emerges from this academic research is rather broad and complex, it can be brought down to what Paulin Djité (2006:6) describes as "the everyday word for people's sense of who they are." Social identity then is the collective side of this sense, or, as in Tajfel's definition, "that part of an individual's self-concept which derives from his knowledge of his membership of a social group" (Tajfel 1981:255). Rephrasing Djité's basic definition, I understand social identity as people's sense of where they belong and to what or to whom they belong. This sense, however, should be interpreted in an active or agentive way: for a long time, social science has acknowledged the fact that people actively construct and negotiate their social identities. In this process of identity making, authors such as Billig (1976), Fairclough (1992), Bauman and Briggs (1990), Davies and Harré (1990) attribute a central role to language. This linguistic turn, then, reconsiders social identity as "the linguistic construction of membership in one or more social groups or categories" (Kroskrity 1999:111). Within these confines, discourse analysis proves to be a very useful research tool with which to lay bare the fine-grained mechanisms and techniques of the process of boundary-making. What is often lacking in studies on social identity, though, is a detailed account of the minute particulars of this process. Documenting these particulars, then, constitutes the first and main goal of this contribution.

Boundary-making takes place in four stages. Firstly, a person identifies a particular social category. This can be, for example, "the family," "the poor" or "the Catalan people." Sacks (1972) has called these labels "membership categorization devices." Through these devices one can delineate a specific social group. Secondly, a person associates himself with this category through the use of pronouns and determinants such as "we" and "our." A third stage is the ascription of meaning to this category. This is often done through the use of essentialist remarks. In presenting particular characteristics as "typical" or "inherent" of a certain group, a social identity is being constructed (cf. Fuss 1990, Hirschfeld 1996, Stoler 1997). Finally, actors generate a notion of otherness, also called othering (Spivak 1988). A social identity can only be shaped through the construction of an other, or as Tajfel and Forgas put it: "We are what we are because they are not what we are" (1981:124). Hall calls this the "production of frontier-effects" (1996:3): creating boundaries by drawing lines between an imagined "us" group and a "them" group.

Alongside its focus on the process of identity construction, the analysis concentrates on the polyvalence and multiplicity of social identity. This phenomenon, too, has been studied extensively in social theory. Here, I consider two types of multiplicity: diversity and gradation. The first notion, diversity, refers to an individual's capability of combining several identities. As Davies and Harré (1990:49) put it, "the positions created for oneself and the other are not part of a linear non-contradictory autobiography." Even at the micro-level of conversation, identities can vary in the course of one conversation according to the different storylines that are adopted (Davies and Harré 1990). In this paper, diversity refers to three domains within which boundary-making takes place: ethnicity, space, and culture. The second notion, gradation, refers to the fact that most social scientists agree that identity cannot be seen as a monolithic entity to which individuals do or do not correspond (Davies and Harré 1990, Duszak 2002, Geschiere and Meyer 1998, Pavlenko and Blackledge 2004). As Duszak (2002) expresses it, identity rather constitutes a continuum of "ingroupness" to "outgroupness" in which every person can take on different positions. This also implies there are different, and shifting, hues or gradations of "in" and "out." One can, for example, position oneself strongly as "Flemish" during a political meeting, but adhere less to this identity when traveling abroad, by stating oneself to be "Belgian."

DAKAR: THE BOUNDLESS CITY

Dakar is literally unbounded because it keeps on growing and occupying new land. The Senegalese Demographic Agency (*Agence Nationale de la Statistique et de la Démographie*) estimated Dakar's population at 2,168,314 inhabitants in 2002 (22 per cent of the national population), at 2,428,155 in 2007, and it foresees a population of 2,703,203 inhabitants in 2012 (ANSD 2008). Over the past few decades, in other words, the city has seen an extremely rapid urbanization. These consecutive waves of population growth have caused a second type of boundlessness, namely the panoply of social and cultural spheres: alongside the indigenous Wolof culture, one finds the various cultures of migrants from inside and outside Senegal. Dakar also testifies to the influence exerted by the former (French) colonizers, the Muslim world, and to presence of the English-speaking world in the city. These different spheres do not exist in isolation: they interact with each other, and with the variety of spaces the city has to offer.

One of these spaces is the suburban neighborhood of Yoff. Situated at the northern end of the Cap-Vert peninsula (on which Dakar is located), this fishermen's village evolved into one of Dakar's suburbs because of the city's rapid expansion. Yoff was, and still is, home to the Lebou ethnic group, who settled in the western coastal areas of Senegal after a long period of migration.[1] Today, Lebou consider themselves to be the original inhabitants of the Cap-Vert peninsula, spread over different coastal localities such as Ouakam, N'Gor and Yoff. In Yoff, they still make up the majority of the population, even though many migrants from diverse backgrounds have settled there. Walking through Yoff, one cannot fail to observe that the suburb constitutes a fascinating in-between space. Although it has incorporated many urban elements (such as public transport, cybercafés, and a motorway), at the same time it manages to preserve its village atmosphere and community organization (exemplified, for instance, by the village chief, or the board of elders). This makes Yoff a unique melting pot of different worlds and opposing tendencies.

As in many other African countries, the sociolinguistic complexion of Dakar and Senegal is marked by a high degree of multilingualism. In Yoff this multilingualism has evolved along three lines: French, Urban Wolof and the ethnic Lebou dialect. The ex-colonial, official French language finds itself in the same situation as many official languages in Africa, as it is characterized by a highly institutionalized status but spoken on relatively few occasions: French is used in administration, education and formal employment. This makes French a symbol of socioeconomic progress (Ndao 1996, Cissé 2005, Mbaya 2005), although this status is increasingly threatened by the rise of Urban Wolof, a variety of the language spoken by the largest ethnic group in Senegal, which consists of a type of code-switching and a mixing between French and Wolof. Many scholars regard the rise of Urban Wolof as threatening the privileged position of French (Thiam 1992, Calvet 1994,

Swigart 2001). As we will see, a lot of identity discussions evolve around the choice of whether to speak Urban Wolof or French. The Lebou dialect, finally, is part of the Wolof language family. As with many other ethnic languages in Dakar, it has tended to become used less and less, and young people claim to speak it only in particular situations, such as in conversations with elderly people and when telling jokes. Still, it seems to remain an important element in ethnic identity construction. In the analysis of the data we will see how these languages play a role in the narrative construction of social identities.

THE CONSTRUCTION OF IDENTITY FRONTIERS IN DAKAR

The making of ethnic boundaries

The majority of my interviewees claim to belong to the Lebou ethnic group. In our conversations, the theme of ethnicity was brought forward several times. Most interesting, however, is that ethnic identity is not constructed in a univocal way. My informants engage in a very ambiguous creation of ethnic group belonging, as they constantly shift between different positions. It follows that ethnic boundaries are not stable; they are fragile and unfixed.

First of all, my informants adopt an identity position that can be characterized as "convinced, proud, and monolithic." They construct ethnicity by using the term *les Lebou* (the Lebou), thus defining it as a specific category. Secondly, they identify with this category by using certain pronouns and other lexical items, such as *nous* (we) and *notre culture* (our culture), and most informants proudly confirm their belonging to Lebou culture. In the words of Bara,[2] a 28 year-old single man engaged in community development projects, this association is quite explicit: *Je m'identifie à ce groupe-là j'appartiens à ce groupe-là.*[3] Also, thirdly, these interviewees engage in a series of essentialist claims, linking "Lebou" to various so-called typical characteristics. First among these is the language: in all the conversations we had, participants establish a "natural" and evident link between their ethnic affiliation and language, as can be observed in the following quotes:

> *–c'est mon identité ... je suis Lebou sur le plan ethnique ... si je parle pas cette langue c'est un peu si je renie une part de moi;*[4]
> *–nous sommes des Lebou on parle le langage lebou;*[5]
> *–je parle lebou donc ... parce que je suis né Lebou.*[6]

This form of "ethnolinguistic linking" (McIntosh 2005:1926) is paralleled by other instances of essentialism, for example when informants make an evident association between the social group that they belong to and its supposed traditional way of life. In most of the conversations the words "lebou" and "tradition" were interchangeable, and very often pronounced in the same breath —with tradition referring to Lebou's founding history, their political organization, and the religious cult of spirits (cf. Versluys 2010). Lebou identity is also associated with the Dakar region, with fishing and with proximity to the sea, and with being very solidary but also hot-tempered. Fourthly, and finally, this group identity is solidified by an action of othering. Many informants explicitly use the term *les autres* (the others), either referring to the non-Lebou inhabitants of Yoff or to the totality of other Senegalese citizens. This first boundary-making movement creates the idea of a strong and clear ethnic identity that is highly identifiable in terms of language, space, and occupation: a "real" Lebou speaks Lebou, is an original inhabitant of Dakar, is a fisherman, observes Lebou tradition, and is community-minded and exuberant. Such stereotypical images, however, are blurred and challenged by another and far less univocal dimension of ethnic boundary-making, and interviews testify to much more ambiguous utterances on being Lebou.

First of all, there is confusion as to the category of Lebou. Talking about his personal situation, Malick —another informant— points out this ambiguity:

> *–demande-moi de dire que je suis Lebou quand je suis là je dis "JE suis Lebou" ... mais quand on me demande "dis-moi la vérité" là je te dis ... "je suis métissé entre ... Lebou et Toucouleur."*[7]

Secondly, from a collective point of view, ethnic boundaries remain far from clear. Given the perceived proximity between Wolof and Lebou, these groups are often confused in the interviews:

> *–bon ... les Lebou ... ce sont des WOLOF ... des véritables Wolof.*[8]

Sonar goes even so far as to question the very existence of the ethnic group:

> *–Lebou il contient des Sereer ... Lebou il contient des Se –c'est un peu Sereer trop même ... il contient des Peul ... il contient des Toucouleur ... Lebou n'est pas une ethnie.*[9]

What is striking here is not so much the blurred boundaries between Senegal's ethnic groups, but the fact that these findings contradict the first identity position outlined above —when informants claimed to belong to a clearly definable social group. Related to this ambivalence is the observed malleability or manipulability of ethnic belonging. For example, in one group discussion the participants tell how some Pulaar inhabitants of Yoff claim to be Lebou, purely by virtue of the area they are living in. In another conversation Sonar — as mentioned earlier, not of Lebou descent— calls himself and his friends *nous les petits-fils lebou* (we the Lebou grandchildren). Thus we see that ethnic belonging is far less clear-cut than the informants' explicit claims suggest. Also with regard to language, boundaries are rather fuzzy. Lebou is often identified with Wolof, and one informant even questions its very existence:

> *–la langue lebou en général même si on dit – il faudrait même voir exactement si cette langue-là existe ... parce que nous parlons wolof ... nous parlons wolof mais un patois quoi en fait.*[10]

In general, informants engage in a bizarre play of claiming Lebou identity and then distancing themselves from it. In this respect, the most visible means of establishing such a distance (and a specific type of "othering"), are the internal distinctions informants make. Among Lebou, they distinguish between more and less "real Lebou." Informants claim that older people, or people living in other Lebou neighbourhoods, are somewhat more "Lebou" than they are: they pay more respect to traditions, speak a "truer" Lebou language, and correspond more intensively to the "typical" Lebou characteristics. What this boils down to is that the youngsters interviewed here construct a multi-faced ethnic identity. On the one hand, they present themselves as marked by a strong ethnic belonging, listing all the characteristics they claim go with it. On the other hand, however, they minimize this identity and distance themselves from it. These young men and women continously cross the boundaries that they themselves construct.

Fig. 4.1. The board at the entrance of Yoff. Photo by E. Versluys, February 3, 2009).

Social identity and space: villagers or urbanites?

A second type of identity constructed in the conversations examined is a spatial one. As shown by authors such as Lefebvre (1991), Keith and Pile (1993), Appadurai (1995), Gupta and Ferguson (1992) and van Binsbergen (1998), space itself is a socially constructed entity. This is also true for the inhabitants of Yoff, as for many interviewees the Yoff neighbourhood constitutes a central element they identify with. Yoff evokes a sense of belonging, crystallized in a specific label for its inhabitants —*les Yoffois* (the Yoff inhabitants)— with which informants identify by using the words "we" and "our": *on le règle entre nous on est tous parents*, *NOUS qui habitent à Yoff, notre quartier.*[11] The most important means of constructing a Yoff spatial identity, however, is by means of a form of othering, namely, in contrasting it to other localities. This reminds us of Appadurai's statement that every production of locality implies the generation of context (Appadurai 1995). My informants produce context by constantly opposing "here" to "there," an opposition which is paralleled by an "us" versus "them" contrast. In general, Yoff is compared to two images of extremes, the city and the village, with Yoff being positioned somewhere in between. In two essentialising movements, Yoff is characterized both as a village-like space in opposition to the city centre, and as an urban place in contrast to the rural village. Informants constantly shift between the categorizations of villager and urbanite, making and crossing boundaries throughout their discourse. Some of them try to mould these oppositions into a definition of Yoff as an ideal place that combines the best of two worlds:

> *–ce n'est pas donné à n'importe qui d'habiter DANS un village qui se trouve .. DANS une ville et que cette ville soit la capitale (du pays) [...] on connaît toutes les tendances quoi.*[12]

A first, major, image that Yoff is contrasted to is that of the city centre of Dakar (usually simply called Dakar or "the city"). Yoff is then referred to as "the village":

> *–Dakar c'est une VILLE, là-bas c'est le centre ville ici c'est un village!*[13]

My respondents further elaborate this essentialising opposition by listing differences deemed crucial between the two places: characteristics related to architecture, fashion, infrastructure, and atmosphere. But the difference they emphasize most is the general way of life of Yoff's inhabitants. Yoff's way of life is explicitly presented as that of the village, where aspects of community building and social relatedness are central. Also, they associate this essentialized image of the village with traditionalism. As one informant remarks:

> *–[Yoff est] un village lebou qui a su ... merveilleusement préserver sa tradition ... sa culture.*[14]

The city centre, by contrast, is presented as a space where modernity has left its marks. Fatou, for instance, identifies its inhabitants as *modernes* (modern).

Finally, these social meanings are intertwined with a difference in language use between the people living in the city centre and the *Yoffois*. The latter pretend to be much less inclined to use French than their urban counterparts, a difference that is evaluated in terms of "authenticity," because of their linguistic habits, inhabitants of the city centre are labeled as *assimilés* (assimilated) or *déracinés* (uprooted), referring to their assimilation of European culture. The fact that the *Yoffois* speak less French is interpreted as a sign of respecting the traditions:

> *–par rapport aux traditions ... ceux qui habitent ... Yoff ... sont beaucoup plus fiers.*[15]

Again, this general attitude is starkly contrasted to the habits in the more urban neighbourhoods:

> *–par example ici c'est c'est ... ça n'a –le français n'a pas une ... telle importance parce qu'on vit en communauté ... on est en ... en Lebou ... on ... on n'est pas très individualisé ... on n'habite pa :s des... des chics comme les Almadies ... comme Fann*[16] *etcetera @ ... on vit en communauté on parle lebou tout le temps on part partout on est solidaire.*[17]

Here, a series of dichotomies combine place, language, and social categories: "here" versus "Les Almadies/Fann," "Lebou" versus "French," "community" versus "individual," or "solidarity" versus "chic."[18] My informants thus construct their place of residence as clearly village-like, in contrast with the centre of Dakar —the "city." Therefore we see how categorization, essentialism and othering are combined in order to construct a solid spatial identity.

At the same time, though, informants also move in an opposite direction, emphasizing the urban dimension of the Yoff neighbourhood. When confronted with questions evoking more characteristic rural settings, they suddenly shift towards the other end of the continuum, characterising Yoff in contrast to the "typical" rural Senegalese village, and identifying themselves with the urban character of their neighborhood.

Informants install a "we–them" distinction between Yoff and the rural villages, now linking the former with modernity and the latter with traditionalism:

> *–d'ailleurs ils se démarquent un peu : <@ de nou :s @> ils disent qu'on peut –qu'on est .. un peu plus moderne qu'eux c'est ce qu'ils disent ;*[19]
> *–comme les villages il y a des cases de :s .. des trucs traditionnels quoi mais ici il y a il y a tout hein ! .. il y a même des centre commercials ! [...] maintenant ça s'est modernisé hein.*[20]

In this example, Binta denies she feels like she is living in a village; as she associates the village with traditionalism, she wants to prove that Yoff does not fit this characterization, trying to describe her neighbourhood by characteristics regarded as urban and modern. Her use of the word *même* (even) suggests that she regards shopping malls as the epitomy of utter urbanity. The rural village and its inhabitants, then, are presented as very different from Yoff and the *Yoffois*:

> *–il y a pas d'abord l'électricité, pas de télé pas de radio, pas de boîtes de nuit,*[21] *c'est très naturel, les gens sont TRÈS simples.*[22]

Likewise, Fatou —the girl who so eloquently praised Yoff's village atmosphere in contrast with the city centre— argues:

> *–la ville quand on habite la ville il y a pas de problème mais <@ QUAND on habite @> euh ... au fin fond c'est difficile parce que moi je me vois mal @ euh ... habiter une ca :se ... faire ... le mil avec un pilon et un mortier aller puiser de l'eau.*[23]

In spite of her previously stated adoration of village life, Fatou's affection towards it seems limited. Her purpose in constructing an idealized village reality appeared to serve the purpose of distancing herself from the city centre life which she firmly condemns. In this we recognize the imaginary and idealistic presentation of the rural world as described by Devisch (1996) and van Binsbergen (1998).

Young people in Yoff thus construct shifting boundaries around their neighbourhoods. The direction in which these boundaries move depends upon the type of othering that is established. When my informants wish to distinguish themselves from the "inauthentic," "assimilated," French-speaking individuals living in the centre of Dakar, they present themselves as true "village people." When, however, they want to establish a clear contrast with the "authentic" and "traditional" people in Senegal's rural settlements, they construct themselves as true "urbanites."

Creating cultural frontiers: Africa versus the West

A last dimension of this process of boundary drawing and

Fig. 4.2. Western influences in Yoff. Photo by E. Versluys, February 10, 2009).

othering among youngsters in Yoff relates to their making and unmaking of "Africanness," and is often triggered by discussions on the use of French. In Senegal, the use of the former colonizing language is shrouded in different and sometimes opposed meanings and interpretations. Some consider it to be a truly appropriated Senegalese language; others denounce its presence as a painful reminder of the colonial period (see Versluys 2005, 2007). When French is explicitly or implicitly associated with France, Europe or the western world, my informants oppose these spheres to a world they consider as closer to themselves, more autochthonous and more familiar. Speaking French is then considered to be a betrayal of some sort of own identity, and those who speak it become the object of othering. Malick, for example, explains the conduct of someone speaking French as follows:

> *–il a le complexe d'afficher sa véritable nature.*[24]

Bouna expresses himself in a comparable way:

> *–j'estime que .. ça c'est c'est un peu indigne quoi ... bon parce que quoi qu'il en soit ... l'homme doit être .. DIGNE de ce qu'il est.*[25]

What this dignity consists of, Bouna clarifies as follows:

> *–moi je ne suis pas ... assimilé quoi man*[26] *je suis pas assimilé ... je suis TRÈS digne de ce que je suis .. je suis TRÈS TRÈS fier d'être UN Africain .. d'être UN Sénégalais ... d'être un noir quoi.*[27]

This contrast between a "foreign" and an "African" world is negotiated by means of an ongoing discussion about language use. "Africanness" is built up as a group identity, as demonstrated again in the use of categorization devices. Informants use the common denominator *les Africains* (the Africans) to define a certain group with which they, in a second step, identify by using the pronoun "we":

> *–nous ... jeunesse africaine;*
> *–de loin on est beaucoup plus traditionaliste que les Européens;*
> *–nous sommes un peuple très musical ;*
> *–nous tous;*
> *–notre sang.*[28]

Thirdly, the group of "Africans" is characterized by a series of essentialist associations. One of the first characteristics mentioned is African community life. Fatou constructs it as a natural characteristic of African society:

> *–j'aime BIEN la vie communautaire parce que ... l'Afrique .. je crois que c'est ça son atout.*[29]

She even presents community life as innate to every African citizen:

> *–ça doit être quelque chose de naturel pour les Africains .. parce que c'est inné en nous.*[30]

Other essentialising characteristics mentioned in this regard are solidarity and the extended kinship system (Fatou, Bara), traditionalism (Djibril) and musical talent (Malick):

> *–et si on parlait des relations humaines ou des relations sociales ? [...] mais toute cette chaleur-là on peut pas .. on peut pas la quantifier!*[31]
> *–de loin on est beaucoup plus traditionaliste que les Européens;*[32]
> *–nous sommes un peuple très musical.*[33]

These perceived or imagined characteristics are then starkly contrasted to those of the other: Bara, for example, strongly opposes *les gens* (the people) to *nous* (us) to express the following concern:

> *–sur quels critères les gens nous évaluent ? .. sur un critère purement économique.*[34]

Limane, in his turn, constructs a group identity which is based on the common experience of colonization and economic oppression:

> *–nous dépendons des ... des autres quoi ... on n'est pas libre - on n'est pas encore libre nous .. nous les Africains.*[35]

When I ask him to explain who these others are, he answers:

> *–les étrangers le :s .. des des F - les Européens les Américains.*[36]

In these utterances, "essential" African traits are placed against "essential" western traits. Malick, for instance, establishes an explicit comparison with the western world. He does this by paraphrasing the late president Senghor's words:

> *–le rythme est noir .. la raison est hellène [...] hellène pour dire l'Occident.*[37]

The western world is essentially rational (as opposed to the musical universe of Africans). It is presented as modern (as opposed to traditional), and Senegalese who experience western influence are described as *apprennent à vivre la culture moderne.*[38] In one group discussion Djibril and Fatou establish this association together:

> *D: on s'habille –*
> *F: plus moderne ... c'est plus moderne*
> *D: eux ils disent qu'on s'habille ... à l'Européen quoi.*[39]

Finally, African community life is opposed to western individualism:

> *–là au moins il y a plus de chaleur humain que [...] chez vous*[40]
> *–l'esprit de solidarité qui existe ici il y en a pas là-bas.*[41]

But this last form of otherness is not stable and homogenous. Whereas in some instances the distinction between an "African" and "western" identity is presented as very clear-cut, on other occasions this distinction blurs. Since colonization, for instance, the Senegalese have been struggling with the notion of assimilation, often accusing each other of becoming assimilated, of being too much influenced by the colonizer's culture. In this context of cultural influence, it is obviously difficult to maintain a rigid boundary between the two spheres. For example, in one of the group discussions Limane and Sekou comment on Limane's clothing:

> *L: regarde comme moi .. regarde comme je suis sapé là*
> *S: @ c'est plus Africain quoi.*[42]

In many interviews informants admit to being "assimilated," to being westernized, even if this admission often goes hand-in-hand with feelings of guilt or shame:

> *–oui oui mais <3> j'ai un peu honte quand même de parler français je parle sou –je ... je préfère parler wolof .. parce que ... on me classe .. un peu d'intellectuel ... certains disent que je suis un peu philosophe [...] c'est un terme un peu péjoratif au Sénégal hein quand on dit quelqu'un il est intellectuel ça veut dire que c'est un – c'est .. c'est peut-être quelqu'un ... d'assimilé trop occidental* [43]
> *–on a été colonisé ... n'est-ce pas ... donc euh [...] donc euh .. si on est comme ça ... ce n'est pas de notre faute* [44]
> *–<@ en même temps @> on a un peu honte ... d'assimiler ;*[45]
> *–nous sommes les meilleurs ... élèves de la France.*[46]

The interview fragments testify to a tension between an explicit African identity and a more westernized one. Bara labels this tension as an "identity crisis" and makes a plea for "being oneself":

> *–c'est un défi aussi pour nous .. bon la crise identitaire ok mais tout ça ! .. un défi qu'on soit nous-mêmes.*[47]

CONCLUSION

The presented case study on suburban Dakar demonstrates the strategies youngsters in suburban Dakar deploy in negotiating their identities. This process of the narrative making and unmaking of identity boundaries involves four stages: categorization, identification, essentialism and "othering." Throughout these stages, interviewees use category labels, pronouns, essentialist remarks, and "othering" to create their social identities. The analysis suggests that these social identities are multiple, and that boundaries overlap. This means that an individual's identities are diverse; it also means that identification and distancing come in degrees.

Informants' narratives are indeed witness to the fact that individuals shelter a broad range of ethnic, spatial and cultural identities. Simply put, these youngsters are at the same time Lebou, *Yoffois* and African. But whereas, at first sight, these identities seem to be clearly bounded, in the practical reality of Yoff, they overlap. Moreover, informants never fully adhere to the explicit identities they construct for themselves. Within the ethnic domain, they point at groups of people that can be considered as more "Lebou" than they are. Concerning their place of residence they constantly shift between the labels of villager and urbanite. And on a cultural level they continuously nuance the claims to authenticity that they make themselves. Obviously, these actors feel a need for bordering, to define themselves by establishing boundaries between themselves and others. Equally obvious, however, is that these boundaries are never stable or fixed. Crossing and shifting boundaries is as important as constructing them.

NOTES

[1] This migration presumably began in eastern and northern Africa and lead to West Africa in the 15th and the 16th centuries (Dumez 2000).

[2] The informants' names have been replaced by pseudonyms. The transcription codes used in this paper are inserted in the appendix to this chapter. Unlike in the other contributions, citations are presented here in their original French transcription. English translations are found in footnote.

[3] "I identify with that group I belong to that group."

[4] "It's my identity .. I am Lebou on an ethnic level .. if I don't speak that language it's as if I would deny a part of me."

[5] "We are Lebou we speak the Lebou language."

[6] "I speak Lebou .. because I am born as a Lebou."

[7] "Ask me to say I am Lebou when I'm here I say 'I AM Lebou' .. but when you ask me 'tell me the truth' then I say … 'I am mixed .. between Lebou and Toucouleur.'"

[8] "Well … the Lebou .. they are WOLOF … real Wolof."

[9] "Lebou contains Sereer .. Lebou contains Se – it's even a little too Sereer … it contains Peul .. it contains Toucouleur … Lebou is not an ethnic group."

[10] "The Lebou language in general even when we say – one should even see whether that language exists .. because we speak Wolof … we speak Wolof but a patois actually."

[11] "We arrange it among ourselves we are all kin," "WE who live in Yoff," "our neighborhood."

[12] "It is not given to everyone to live IN a village that is situated .. IN a city and that this city is the capital (of the country) […] we know all the tendencies you know."

[13] "Dakar it's a CITY," "over there it's the city centre here it's a village!"

[14] "A Lebou village that has managed .. marvelously to preserve its tradi-

tion .. its culture."

[15] "With regard to tradition .. the people who live .. in Yoff .. are much prouder."

[16] Les Almadies and Fann are two of the most well-off neighbourhoods in Dakar. They constitute residential areas that are situated more closely to the city centre than the suburban region of Yoff.

[17] "For example here it's it's .. it has – French doesn't have .. that much importance because we live in a community .. we are among .. among Lebou .. we .. we are not very individualized .. we do: n't live in .. in chic neighborhoods such as Les Almadies … or Fann etcetera @ .. we live in a community we speak Lebou all the time we go everywhere we are solidary."

[18] Although the use of dichotomies like these certainly contains an unpleasant resemblance with simplistic structuralist analyses, I do think it is valuable to reveal them for they are so explicitly constructed by the informants themselves.

[19] "Besides they distinguish themselves a little bit <@ from us@> they say that we can – that we are .. a little bit more modern than them that's what they say."

[20] "As in the villages there are huts .. traditional things you know but here you have everything ! .. you even have shopping malls ! […] nowadays it has modernized."

[21] "First there is no electricity," "no television no radio," "no night clubs."

[22] "It's very natural," "people are VERY simple."

[23] "The city when you live in the city there is no problem but <@ when you live @> eh .. in the outback it's difficult because I have difficulties seeing myself eh @ .. living in a hut .. making .. sorghum with a pounder going to draw water from a well."

[24] "He has a complex of showing his real nature."

[25] "I find that .. that a little bit unworthy you know … well because in any way .. a man has to be .. WORTHY of what he is."

[26] "Man" is a Wolof word for "me."

[27] "I am not .. assimilated you know I'm not assimilated .. I am VERY worthy of what I am .. I am VERY VERY proud of being AN African .. of being a Senegalese … of being black you know."

[28] "We .. African youth," "we are much more traditionalist than Europeans are," "we are a very musical people," "we all," "our blood."

[29] "I REALLY like living in a community because … Africa .. I think that's it's advantage."

[30] "It has to be something natural for the Africans .. because it is innate in us."

[31] "And if we would talk of human relations or social relations ? […] but all this warmth you cannot .. you cannot quantify that!"

[32] "We are much more traditionalist than Europeans are."

[33] "We are a very musical people."

[34] "On which criteria do people evaluate us ? .. on a purely economic criterion."

[35] "We depend on .. on the others you know … we are not free – we are not yet free we .. we the Africans."

[36] "The foreigners the : .. the the F – the Europeans the Americans."

[37] "The rhythm is black .. the reason is Hellenic […] Hellenic meaning the West."

[38] "Learn to live the modern culture."

[39] D: "we dress -" F: "more modern … it's more modern" D: "they say we dress .. European style you know."

[40] "Here at least there is more human warmth than […] where you are."

[41] "The spirit of solidarity that exists here doesn't exist over there."

[42] L: "look at me .. look at the way I am dressed" S: "@ that's no longer African."

[43] "Yes yes but <3> I am a little bit ashamed to speak French I often spea – I .. I prefer speaking Wolof .. because … they classify me .. a little bit as an intellectual … some say I am a little bit philosophical […] it's a slightly negative term in Senegal when you say that someone is intellectual it means that he is – he is .. it's maybe someone .. who is assimilated too westernized."

[44] "We have been colonized … isn't it … so eh […] so eh .. if we are like this .. it's not our fault."

[45] "<@ at the same time @> we are a little bit ashamed … of assimilating."

[46] "We are the best … pupils of France."

[47] "It is also a challenge for us .. well the identity crisis ok but all that! .. a challenge to be ourselves."

REFERENCES

Agence Nationale de la Statistique et de la Démographie (ANSD). 2008. Situation économique et sociale du Sénégal: 2007. Dakar. Electronic document, http://www.ansd.sn/publications/annuelles/SES_2007.pdf, accessed Jan. 11, 2012.

Appadurai, A. 1995. The production of locality. *In* Counterworks. Managing the diversity of knowledge. R. Fardon, ed. Pp. 204–225. London: Routledge.

Bauman, R., and C. Briggs. 1990. Poetics and performance as critical perspectives on language and social life. Annual Review of Anthropology 19:59–88.

Billig, M. 1976. Social psychology and intergroup relations. London: Academic Press.

Calvet, L.-J. 1994. Quel modèle sociolinguistique pour le Sénégal? Ou il n'y a pas que la véhicularité. Langage et société 68:89–107.

Cissé, M. 2005. Langues, Etat et société au Sénégal. Sudlangues 5: 99–133.

Davies, B. and R. Harré. 1990. Positioning : The discursive production of selves. Journal for the Theory of Social Behaviour 20(1):43–63.

Devisch, R. 1996. 'Pillaging Jesus': healing churches and the villagisation of Kinshasa. Africa 66(4):555–586.

Djité, P. G. 2006. Shifts in linguistic identities in a global world. Language Problems and Language Planning 30(1):1–20.

Dumez, R. 2000. Yoff, le territoire assiégé. Un village lebou dans la banlieue de Dakar. Dakar: Unesco.

Duszak, A. 2002. Us and others: an introduction. *In* Us and Others. Social identities across languages, discourses and cultures. A. Duszak, ed. Pp. 1–28. Amsterdam: Benjamins.

Fairclough, N. 1992. Discourse and social change. Cambridge: Polity Press.

Fuss, D. 1990. Essentially Speaking: Feminism, Nature and Difference. London: Routledge.

Geschiere, P. and B. Meyer. 1998. Globalization and Identity: dialectics of flow and closure. Introduction. Development and Change 29(4):601–615.

Gupta, A. and J. Ferguson. 1992. Beyond 'Culture': Space, Identity and the Politics of Difference. Cultural Anthropology 7(1):6–23.

Hall, S. 1996. Introduction: who needs identity? *In* Questions of cultural identity. S. Hall and P. De Gay, eds. Pp. 1–17. London: Sage publica-

tions.
Hirschfeld, L. A. 1996. Race in the Making: Cognition, Culture, and the Child's Construction of Human Kinds. Cambridge, MA: MIT Press.
Keith, M. and S. Pile. 1993. Introduction: The politics of place. *In* Place and the politics of identity. M. Keith and S. Pile, eds. Pp. 1–21. London: Routledge.
Kroskrity, P. V. 1999. Identity. Journal of Linguistic Anthropology 9(1–2):111–114.
Lefebvre, H. 1991. The production of space. Oxford: Blackwell.
Mbaya, M. 2005. Pratiques et attitudes linguistiques dans l'Afrique d'aujourd'hui : le cas du Sénégal. München : Lincom.
Ndao, P. A. 1996. Contact de langues au Sénégal. Etude du code-switching wolof-français en milieu urbain. Approches linguistique, sociolinguistique et pragmatique. Ph.D thesis. Dakar: Université Cheikh Anta Diop de Dakar.
Pavlenko, A. and A. Blackledge. 2004. Introduction: New theoretical approaches to the study of negotiation of identities in multilingual contexts. *In* Negotiation of Identities in Multilingual Contexts. A. Pavlenko and A. Blackledge, eds. Pp. 1–33. Clevedon: Multilingual Matters.
Sacks, H. 1972. On the analyzability of stories by children. *In* Directions in sociolinguistics: the ethnography of communication. J. J. Gumperz and D. Hymes, eds. Pp. 325–345. New York: Holt, Rinehart and Winston.
Spivak, G. C. 1988. Can the subaltern speak? *In* Marxism and interpretation of culture. C. Nelson and L. Grossberg, eds. Pp. 271–313. Chicago: University of Illinois Press.
Stoler, A. 1997. On political and psychological essentialisms. Ethos 25(1):101–106.
Swigart, L. 2001. The Limits of Legitimacy: Language Ideology and Shift in Contemporary Senegal. Journal of Linguistic Anthropology 10(1):90–130.
Tajfel, H. 1981. Human groups and social categories. Cambridge: Cambridge University Press.
Tajfel, H. and J. P. Forgas. 1981. Social categorization: Cognitions, values, and groups. *In* Social cognition: Perspectives on everyday understanding. J. P. Forgas, ed. Pp. 113–140. London : Academic Press.
Thiam, N. 1992. Nouveaux modèles de parlers et processus identitaires en milieu urbain : le cas de Dakar. *In* Des langues et des villes, actes du colloque de Dakar. E. Gouaini, and N. Thiam, eds. Pp. 495–512. Paris: Didier Erudition.
Van Binsbergen, W. 1998. Globalization and Virtuality: analytical problems posed by contemporary transformation of African societies. Development and Change 29:873–903.

Versluys, E. 2010. Langues et identités au Sénégal. Paris : L'Harmattan.

——— 2007. The notion of exclusion in the language attitudes of young Dakar urbanites. *In* Multilingualism and exclusion. T. du Plessis, P. Cuvelier, M. Meeuwis, and L. Teck, eds. Pp. 274–286. Pretoria: Van Schaik.

——— 2005 Challenging power: language attitudes and pragmatism in contemporary Dakar. Lodz papers in pragmatics 1:223–241.

APPENDIX

Transcription codes

..	short pause
...	longer pause
<3>	pause during 3 seconds
-	truncation
TALK	emphasized talk
@	laughter
<@ talk @>	laughter while talking
( )	unclear word or group of words
(talk)	guess at an unclear word
?	rising tone
!	exclamatory tone
[...]	omitted part

5
A CRIPPLED BULA MATARI: A HISTORICAL ACCOUNT OF LABOUR, MIGRATION AND BORDERS IN THE RWANDESE/CONGOLESE BORDERLAND

Gillian Mathys

INTRODUCTION

The image of *Bula Matari*, initially signifying Henry Morton Stanley and his "rock crushing" activities, has become the embodiment of the all-encompassing Belgian colonial state by virtue of Crawford Young, who also used it to allude to the omnipotence of the African colonial state in general (Young 1994). Young (1994:24–25) characterizes the African colonial state as an autonomous and "free-standing entity" in which state and society (the subjects over which the state governs) are detached from each other: there is no relationship of cooperation or conflict between these two levels.

According to Bruce Berman (1997:563), however, this portrayal of the colonial state in Africa "is based on a generalization of the experience of the Belgian Congo, which probably most closely approximated in practice the irresistible force it [the colonial state] implied." According to Berman, this image is not representative for other colonial powers. Other authors have also pointed out the more complex relationships between "state" and "society" in colonial states, focusing on the mediation of colonialism and representing colonialism as a dynamic encounter (see Van Wolputte 2004, Likaka 2009, Cooper 1994).

This chapter argues that the image of the Belgian colonial state as a "free-standing" state, represented by the image of a hegemonic Bula Matari, is too simplistic. It needs to be amended to take account of the struggles over the mobility of the population and the role of chiefs.[1] The case discussed will depict a crippled Bula Matari, only able to limp when, and if, supported by African chiefs.

These African chiefs —both in Rwanda and the Belgian Congo— were curtailed in the way they exercised their power. Although Tutsi authorities in Rwanda were responsible for ruling the population, it was the Resident of Rwanda —and not the *mwami* (king) —who was responsible for nominating and discharging chiefs (Rumiya 1992, 172), and chiefs were constantly monitored with regard to their execution of the Belgian administration's policies (Rumiya 1992).[2]

Rule in the Belgian Congo operated in a similar —although not equal— vein. The Belgian administration disposed of chiefs that they regarded as unfit to govern or did not comply with their rule (Newbury 1986, 1987), and chiefs were also closely monitored for the way that they implemented colonial policies.

These *chefs indigènes* (indigenous chiefs) —across the whole of Belgian colonial territory— were responsible for delivering labour, collecting taxes, supplying agricultural produce and implementing colonial policy in general (Couttenier 2005:247; Rumiya 1992). As such, chefs indigènes were an important extension of state power. But, at the same time, it was in this arena especially that the power of the colonial state was limited, as the Belgian administration *had* to rely on forms of African governance in order to administer the territory under its control.

Consequently I will show that the problem of African agency cannot be simply explained away by conceiving the chefs indigènes, who occupied the bottom tier of the colonial administration, as *mere* extensions of state power. Chiefs and African elites often pursued their own political agendas, which were not necessarily in accordance with colonial objectives. Chiefs who were able to capitalize on these contradictions — balancing compliance with colonial rule whilst, at the same time, defending their own interests— were the ones who were able to wield the most power.

However, elites were not alone in shaping cross-border patterns of mobility. Their subjects too were monitoring the differences between political and cultural contexts, regimes of taxation, remuneration and access to land (especially in Rwanda's more densely populated regions) all of which were prevailing at opposite sides of the colonial border and did not hesitate, where opportunity permitted, to act in their own interest. In the face of important push-and-pull factors which encouraged migratory flows and determined their direction, the colonial state, as well as African chiefs, often found themselves unable to effectively monitor or police their spheres of influence and the lines which separated them from each other.

THE BANYARWANDA IMMIGRATION SCHEME (MIB)

In order to understand how chiefs and their subjects were carving out space to pursue their own interests with regards to (cross-border) mobility, this paper takes a closer look at the MIB (*Mission d'Immigration des Banyarwanda*), and, especially, the Gishari region.

This scheme needs to be understood with reference to the colonial plantation economy in the region around Lake Kivu. The installation of European settlers in the Kivu did not start until the question of Rwanda-Urundi was solved,[3] but it was not until the development of the coffee crop and the opening of new transport routes enabling economic exploitation that the European colonization of the region was really set in motion (Jewsiewicki 1979). The economic exploitation of the Kivu was entrusted to the *Comité National de Kivu* (National Comittee of Kivu, CNKi) which was created in 1928.[4] The Kivu region, with its fertile soil, was considered ideal for European agricultural colonization (Mendiaux 1956:803). The main crop in the Kivu was coffee, and in the 1930s cinchona (for quinine), pyrèthre (insect-repellant) and tea were also introduced in an attempt to diversify the plantation economy (Fairhead 1990:96).

In order to make these plantations profitable, *main d'œuvre* (manual labour) was necessary. However, agricultural labour was perennially lacking in the Kivu. In addition to a sparse population, manifold migrations to Uganda (e.g. from Rutshuru in Kivu) were draining the Kivu of its already strained labour reserve. The difficulties of obtaining labour in the Kivu became accentuated in the 1930s due to the growth of economic activities and the plunge in international coffee prices. Some people in the colonial administration dreaded that a labour shortage would provoke the end of economic activity, and thus of European settlement, in parts of northern Kivu. To the colonial administration it was clear that the region would be unable to supply sufficient labour for European enterprises that were yet to be established.[5]

Among the reasons for migration from the Kivu to Uganda were: the existing cultural and social ties between the populations of the two colonial territories; resentment towards colonial impositions; and, forced labour, or, simply, the search for better living conditions and higher wages in Uganda.[6] Inhabitants of Rwanda took similar routes in order to escape from the multiple exactions in their territory. Many Banyarwanda (both Hutu and Tutsi) migrated to Uganda, pushed from Rwanda, on the one hand, by the harsh rural conditions and especially the manifold demands enforced on the population by the chiefs, and, on the other hand, pulled to Uganda by the relative prosperity of the region and by higher wages (Newbury 1988; Richards 1957; Chrétien and Mworoha 1980). These Banyarwanda labourers also moved to the Rutshuru region in Congo. Indications are that they worked as temporary labourers in the Congolese territories during the period in which tax was levied in Rwanda, and returned to Rwanda once tax collection had ended.[7] In so doing, they and their counterparts from the Kivu, exploited the vicissitudes of the labour market and the discrepancies of the Rwanda/Congo/Uganda borderland to their own advantage.

Before the official launch of the scheme, the colonial administration undertook some attempts to stabilize these uncontrolled (or uncontrollable) migrations, which were felt mostly in Rutshuru territory. The colonial administration on both sides of the Rwanda-Congolese border attempted to intensify and consolidate movements of Banyarwanda labourers to Rutshuru through propaganda, the promise of land, and exemption from taxation and *corvée* (forced labour). These ad hoc measures had little impact in creating a steady and more permanent migratory movement to solve the labour shortage in Rutshuru.[8] The main factor contributing to this failure was the availability of other options. Inhabitants of the Kivu and of Rwanda had choices other than working for agricultural European settlers in the Kivu. Wages were higher across the colonial border in Uganda, thus more could be gained from working in British territory. Furthermore, many inhabitants of Rwanda and the adjacent territories in the Belgian Congo held social and cultural ties with people living across these national borders and in British territories.

It is in this context that the Banyarwanda migration and settlement scheme needs to be understood. Basically, the scheme was designed by the Belgian colonial administration to formulate a practical answer to what Freund (1984:2) calls "the most basic question of all concerning labour in Africa": how to get it. The way to attract labour was through a resettlement scheme: the dense population in Rwanda would be resettled in the Belgian Congo. The people transplanted in this way could then be employed as agricultural labourers on the European held plantations in North Kivu. It is estimated that in the wake of this scheme some 300,000 Banyarwanda settled in North Kivu (de Saint Moulin 1975), although it is necessary to be cautious with regard to citing numbers derived from colonial documents.

Two phases can be distinguished. The first phase (1937–1945) was a continuation of discussions held in the 1920s which focused on appropriating and stabilising labour through the migration and settlement of Banyarwanda migrants.[9] During this first phase, most of the attention was directed towards the practical organization of labour migration: discussions within the colonial administration focused on: incentives to attract migrants; where migrants should be settled; and, the political organization of their settlement and the composition of the group of migrants. The impression one gets from this first phase is that things were planned rather haphazardly. Illustrative in this regard is that there was no formal institution that surveyed the execution of this migration scheme. Only a handful of officials in Nyamitaba occupied themselves with overseeing the migratory movement (Mararo 1990:149).

In colonial discourse, emphasis was on the gains this scheme could bring to the colonial economy: as Bucyalimwe Mararo (1997:510) points out, humanitarian motives were mentioned but it seems that, at least initially, these altruistic motives (such as decreasing the population pressure in

Rwanda) were invoked to placate the League of Nations.[10] In reality, Rwanda was integrated as a labour reserve into Congo's economic sphere (Dorsey 1983:123–124).

During the second phase of the scheme (1948–1954), four important shifts can be discerned. First, and most importantly, the need for labour —which was pivotal during the first part of the scheme— was now no longer as pressing. Secondly, whilst during the first phase of the scheme the collaboration of Rwandan elites (mwami and chiefs) was indispensable, this was no longer the case during the second phase of the scheme. Thirdly, a more methodical and scientific mode of operation was adopted to address problems which had arisen during the first phase of the scheme (such as soil erosion). Fourthly, the colonial administration realized that in creating the MIB and in transplanting the required population from Rwanda to Congo, they had created political problems.

THE FIRST PHASE: MOBILITY, LABOUR AND BORDERS[11]

The border delineating the Belgian Congo from the German possessions in East Africa was only drawn in 1910 and demarcated on the ground in 1911 (Louis 1963:87–91; Jentgen 1957). Rwanda was, at that time, part of *Deutsch Ost-Afrika* (German East Africa). The Belgians invaded and occupied Rwanda in 1916, and, in 1924, Rwanda became a mandated area under Belgian tutelage, relegating the once “national” border to an internal one.[12]

The limited agency of Africans in drawing this international boundary (mwami Musinga tried to influence the German authorities to secure the territory he considered to be part of the central kingdom, but without much success[13]) stood in sharp contrast to the lived experience of the colonial border that was nowhere as rigid as its counterpart on the map, and which had divided Kinyarwanda-speakers who had cultural and social ties in Uganda, the Belgian Congo and Rwanda. Although the border between the Belgian Congo and Rwanda was an internal border after Belgium's take-over —in the sense that both Rwanda and Congo were Belgian territories, had the same currency, and formed a custom union— this does not mean that it had little relevance (see, for instance, Ferme 2004:84–85).

The failure of the ad hoc attempts to attract Rwandan immigrants to Rutshuru in 1935 and 1936 gave the colonial administration clearer insight into the reasons —or at least the influencing factors— for this exodus to Uganda. In the context of the resettlement scheme, in order to compete with higher wages in Uganda and to stimulate people to leave Rwanda for the Kivu for a longer period, incentives were to be put in place. These consisted of: giving "unoccupied" fertile land and pastures in the Kivu to Banyarwanda migrants; food provisions in the first month; and, the exemption from exactions and obligatory labour for two years.[14] In addition to this, the colonial administration pleaded for a more effective policing of the borders with Uganda.[15]

The discussions on organizing this labour migration and transplantation of Banyarwanda workers clearly indicated which goals the colonial state wanted to pursue. These are: firstly, redirect existing migration flows to Congo instead of towards the British territories; secondly, drain Rwanda of "excess" population; thirdly, establish migrants in the Kivu to provide the necessary labour, and, consequently, develop the Kivu by using its migrant labour.[16]

In trying to redirect migratory movements to Uganda, and to in order to invigorate existing migratory patterns to the Belgian Congo to fit the interests of the Belgian administration, the colonial administration was attempting to capitalize upon already existing patterns of mobility.

According to David Newbury (2005:255), the colonial

boundaries in western Rwanda (bordering the Kivu) were implemented in a region that was previously characterized by a high degree of mobility of families and individuals in search of marriage, pasture, commerce and (at times) refuge. This high degree of mobility did not cease to exist with the advent of colonial spatial organization, although this did impose (stricter) restrictions on cross-border movements (Newbury 2005:255). However, at the same time, new opportunities brought about by the creation of the border increased movement across it —as in many other cases of African borders (Nugent and Asiwaju 1996:2).

Thus, whilst this scheme was basically a colonial construct aimed at reinforcing the Belgian Congo's labour force, the existing patterns of movement and migration, coupled to newly-emerged opportunities resulting from the imposition of the border, also created possibilities to escape the power of the state. It is exactly this paradoxical nature of borders that created opportunities to escape the power of Bula Matari as the (variable) success of the scheme was largely dependent on a temporary alliance between the colonial administration at the one hand and the mwami and Rwandan chiefs on the other. In this way, the shape the scheme took can be seen as an illustration of Cooper's thesis that European policy was also a reflection of adaptation to African initiatives (Cooper 1994:1531).

ON THE IMPORTANCE OF ELITES

From 1937 onwards, the colonial government was able to set in motion a steady influx of migrants into Masisi territory, North Kivu. These migrants were settled into the independent Banyarwanda chieftaincy of Gishari, former Hunde terrritory.[17] In shaping and enabling the migratory movement as planned the colonial administration had to guarantee the acquiescence of the Rwandan court and elites. The administration's other consideration was to assure the accomplishment of their economic goals. These two aims were reflected in the discussion on who should be allowed to migrate. At the root of this discussion was the reconciliation of economic exigencies with concerns over (racial) political organization and the assurance of compliance by the elites. Arguments reflecting colonial ethnic discourse focused on the proportion of Hutu and Tutsi needed to make the scheme work. Hutu were seen as necessary to supply the much needed labour force (after all, this was the paramount reason for redirecting migration flows), but it was feared that migration of Hutu alone would result in anarchy.[18] Members of the colonial administration were convinced that Tutsi, because of their "intelligence and heredity," had better capacities to rule and govern than Hutu. Consequently, the migration of a small Tutsi elite was crucial for the *encadrement* (guidance) of the mass of Hutu peasants.[19] Furthermore, this migration of Tutsi was deemed necessary so as to set in motion the migration of Hutu, who were expected to follow their Tutsi chiefs. According to colonial officials, Hutu themselves would not accept separation from their Tutsi notables, as they had cattle contracts (*ubuhake*[20]) with these notables.[21]

Governor Jungers of Rwanda proposed other reasons why Tutsi could not be excluded from the migratory movement: it ensured that Hutu peasants would not feel their status to be reduced to that of mere wage labourers. Consequently, in his opinion, restricting Tutsi migration would result in no migration at all, and he cited a case where, after restrictions had been set on the migration of Tutsi and their cattle (see below), Banyarwanda from Mulera allegedly declared: "*On ne veut pas là-bas de nos Watusi et de leur vaches; vous voyez bien qu'on ne demande que notre travail*" (They do not want Tutsi and their cattle over there, you see, the only thing they want is our labour).[22]

Finally, preference was given to the migration of both Hutu and Tutsi; the former perceived as the peasant mass that would provide the necessary labour, the latter as their governing elite. In colonizing discourse, Tutsi were perceived as pastoralists, occupying a vast area of land *sans grande utilité* (without much use), without any intention of going to work or of enticing their children to do so.[23] This complex constellation of Hutu masses and Tutsi chiefs would thus be settled in Gishari.

In 1937, however, this did not result in the envisioned migration of a Hutu majority and a Tutsi minority. Instead there was an exodus of cattle, accompanied by their guardians (Hutu) or owners (Tutsi) and followed by Hutu-clients (*abagaragu*). In the first half of 1938, this resulted in a proportion of 72 per cent Tutsi and 28 per cent Hutu, quite the opposite of the goals set by the administration.[24] The evidence indeed suggests that, in the beginning especially, these richer livestock owners (including the mwami) did not hesitate to send their cattle across the border, hence using the border and the opportunities offered by the administration to expand their pasture outside the colonial boundaries of Rwanda. More modest cattle owners, whose cattle could no longer find pasture in Rwanda, followed this economic elite.[25]

The Belgian administration in Rwanda saw this last migration as a solution to the problem of overgrazing in Rwanda, but they were aware that such migration would not contribute to the solution of the labour problem. As an official in the administration in Rwanda stated: "This is not really labour, as all these emigrants are Tutsi pastoralists not keen to do any kind of manual labour."[26] As it was labour, and not cattle, that the colonial state in Congo was after, the migration of Tutsi and their animals was restricted. In the second half of 1938 the proportions were reversed:85 per cent Hutu against 17 per cent Tutsi (*sic*) migrated to Gishari.[27]

Discussions on the ethnic composition of the migrant flow before 1937 were not solely concerned with so-called ethnic attributions and characteristics. Although these discussions were a reflection of the well-known colonial ethnicising discourse on the Hutu/Tutsi divide, the inclusion of Tutsi in the migratory movement was largely a matter of pragmatics. It was the only way to secure the indispensable compliance of the Rwandan authorities. The necessity of the local elite's co-operation was even more pronounced in matters pertaining to the political organization of the Banyarwanda settlement in Gishari. Three alternative organizational forms were considered. A first option was to provide unoccupied hills in the Kivu to poor Tutsi or to Hutu notables. Hill chiefs would be appointed and placed at the same level as the existing clan chiefs and under the authority of the sub-chief or head-chief of the region. However, as it was assumed by the colonial administration that Tutsi did not want to be subordinated to a Hunde chief, this model was rejected. A second possibility then considered was to design a political organization where Rwandans were as independent as possible and where Congolese chiefs were able to retain their authority and their land rights, by organizing the Banyarwanda settlement as a sub-chieftaincy under the control of and dependent upon the chief of the region. This was also rejected with the same justification by the Rwandan authorities, as it would have required the subordination of a Tutsi chief to an "inferior" Hutu or Hunde.[28] In this regard, the Rwandan authorities were referring to the alleged former rights the Rwandan Kingdom had over this region.[29] As discussed before, due to the colonial ideology that gave preference to Tutsi as rulers, and because the acquiescence of the Rwandan authorities was necessary, the only solution regarding how to organize the group of Banyarwanda was the third option, namely to constitute the Banyarwanda settlement as a political unit consisting only of Banyarwanda, independent from Congolese chieftaincies, and with a Tutsi notable as head-chief. Only through this option would resistance from the Rwandan authorities be avoided. Or, as district commissioner Absil put it :

> With this political statute, [there will be] no more opposition by the indigenous authorities in Rwanda, who consider the new political entities as Rwandan colonies, with no links to the motherland except for race, name, and language. [my translation][30]

Although the formal dependence of Gishari on the Rwandan authorities was not established by this political organization, the payment of *ikoro* (tribute) established a nominal dependence.[31]

The power and influence of the Rwandan authorities, and especially of the court, also reveals itself in the build-up to the migration scheme. Both mwami Rudahigwa and chiefs and notables of Rwanda inspected and approved the lands that were being considered for the transplantation of the Rwandan migrants. With the official start of the migration, Tutsi elites indeed tried to implement control over the expatriated Banyarwanda settlement by influencing the choice of the chief and notables. The first chief of the Rwandan chieftaincy in Congo, Joseph Bideri, was appointed by mwami Rudahigwa.[32]

These (Tutsi) elites, however, were not all in agreement in their attitudes towards borders, nor did their attitudes remain unchanged throughout time. Whilst it can be argued that the Rwandan Court had some interest in this migration scheme — in terms of the expansion of its territory — in the initial phase of the migration, other indigenous elites, and especially chiefs, had different motives for encouraging or impeding this migratory movement.

Even before the official start of the migratory movement in 1936, chiefs in Rwanda were hampering their "subjects" migration to Rutshuru. In order to prevent Hutu from migrating across colonial boundaries, it was rumoured by the

Belgian colonial administration in Congo that Tutsi notables were placing Twa as sentinels at the border. The possessions of those who migrated were seized (or, at least, threatened), and family members that remained behind in Rwanda were harassed.[33] The colonial administration attributed this to the chiefs' contempt for "usurper" chief Ndeze, categorized by the colonial administration as Hutu, and that they did not to want their subjects to be placed under his authority.[34]

However, it seems that this is a simplified explanation of the attitude of Rwandan chiefs. After the start of the migration scheme in 1937, migrants settled in the autonomous Banyarwanda chieftaincy of Gishari in Masisi rather in Rutshuru under the authority of a Rwandan-born Tutsi-chief. Nevertheless the resistance of the chiefs persisted, indicating that not only "ethnic deliberations" towards Hunde or Hutu (and especially Ndeze) were at stake. Even after the 1942-1943 Nyirahuku Famine had severely worsened living conditions for many (poor) Rwandans and large numbers of Banyarwanda had flooded into both Rutshuru and Masisi.[35] Gishari notables claimed that some Tutsi authorities were impeding the departure of Hutu migrants. Migrants willing to leave were drawn into *palabres* (judicial conflicts) over the apportionment of cattle after the rupture of cattle contracts. Often they were redirected to indigenous courts that were mainly comprised of Tutsi notables, and their cases were consistently ruled against. Furthermore, to be able to legally leave Rwanda for Gishari, migrants needed to have authorization from their hill chief. In many cases this permission was denied or accompanied by humiliations for the migrant and his family.[36] Apparently this problem was severe: in 1944 Rwandan Resident Sandrart ordered the administration to give the Rwandan authorities and patrons who were resisting the departure of willing migrants an exemplary punishment.[37]

Still, however, the Rwandan chiefs were divided with regard to the border and the migration issue. Oral testimonies collected by Bucyalimwe Mararo point out that, during the Nyirahaku Famine, some local authorities encouraged people to leave. An inhabitant from Kibuye testifies that he and others were asked by the local chiefs to migrate in order escape the famine (Mararo 1990:140). Such accounts are reinforced by Pinxten and Bruyns (1952). According to these authors, some of the chiefs understood the precarious situation of their subjects even if they did not want their subjects to leave. To underline their argument, they quoted Chief Kamuzinzi from Bugoyi. "Although it [the migration] is disadvantageous for me, I cannot resist it, because I cannot let my people live in poverty" (Pinxten and Bruyns 1952:254).[38]

Testimonies from Kinyaga territory, in contrast, demonstrate how this migration was used as a means to get rid of subjects and to appropriate their land: Gishari is called "the place where chiefs sent people they didn't like" (Newbury 1988:144).[39] Oral testimony from the same region underlines this: one informant recalls how his father took him to live in Kabare territory (adjacent to Kinyaga in the Belgian Congo) in order not to be sent to Gishari; someone else recounted how auxiliaries (*abamotsi*)[40] plucked people from the fields under orders of the chief to send them to Gishari (Interviews Rusizi-territory, Rwanda, March 16 and 17 2011).

The argument that the Tutsi chiefs' efforts to sabotage the migration scheme and to contain their Hutu subjects within the borders of Rwanda had less to do with ethnic preference than with other considerations is further reinforced when looking at the situation in Rwanda itself. Catharine Newbury (1988), for instance, points out that chiefs in Kinyaga were reluctant to provide labour to Europeans and that life was made extremely difficult for people who accepted such work. The reasons for this reluctance had to do with the economic independence achieved by wage labourers, which could ultimately lead to autonomy from the chiefs. In the case discussed here, this autonomy became even more pronounced as dependents began to settle permanently outside the reach of their (former) chiefs. Furthermore, it drained rural manpower that was required, for instance, to cultivate the lands of the chief (Newbury 1988:168). Permanent migration not only implied the permanent loss of labour but also of tax revenues; at the same time it reinforced the relative power of rival Hutu, Hunde or Tutsi chiefs. Colonial correspondence testifies to the fact that Belgian administrators were aware of these motives:[41] in order to avoid systematic opposition against the migration scheme by Rwandan authorities the loss of traditional resources (i.e. the departure of their subjects) was compensated for financially.[42]

THE EMERGENCE OF NEW/RENEWED SPACES OF CRITIQUE?

The examples above clearly illustrate that, for various reasons, different chiefs adopted different stances towards the migration of their subjects and, hence, towards the Rwandan-Congolese border. Next to these personal motivations, there are also indications that the power play between the mwami, the colonial administration and disgruntled elites was influencing the chiefs' attitudes.

According to Spitaels (1953:111), after initial support for the migration of Banyarwanda —in the preliminary stages, as discussed above— the Rwandan authorities and the mwami withdrew their formal support for the migration after they realized that the presence of Banyarwanda in the Kivu did not establish Rwandans' rights over this region.

This was probably at the beginning of the 1940s. In 1940 the mwami stated: “It is necessary that I as mwami have the same powers here [Gishari] as in Rwanda, in all matters, political and judiciary” (my translation).[43] According to the mwami, all Banyarwanda had to consider Gishari some years as a prolongation of Rwanda, at least for the years to come. He repeated a similar comment in 1941.[44]

When Wilfried Bucyanayandi,[45] one of the mwami's adversaries, replaced Joseph Bideri as chief of Gishari, this rift deepened. It is important to highlight this rift because it illustrates the power of local elites *vis-à-vis* colonial policy. Moreover, it also shows that border crossing can lead to the emergence of alternative spaces of critique. German, and later Belgian, colonial rule enabled the mwami and chiefs to expand and consolidate their power. The royal court sacrificed some of its former power, especially with regards to divine rule, but, in exchange, the elite gained new and more effective forms of power. The power of the royal court was perpetuated in alliance with the Belgian colonizers. The latter aimed to bolster their indirect rule through their manipulation of the (outward) status/prestige of the mwami —one of the central elements in their understanding of indirect rule (Lemarchand 1970:66; 1977). The case of Chief Bucyanayandi shows that this concept of maintaining the "outward prestige" also had its ramifications for intra-elite competition. The Belgian colonizers could not tolerate any overt challenge to the power of the mwami. The antagonism between mwami Rudahigwa and Bucyanayandi, then chief of the Ndara province, is illustrative in this regard. The latter was made to leave the country after a conflict with the mwami had escalated. It is not clear what caused the conflict (both Bucyanayandi and the mwami give different reasons for their hostility),[46] but colonial correspondence makes it painstakingly clear that Bucyanayandi —referred to as a "good" chief— was sacrificed on the altar of indirect rule. He was dismissed from his position and expelled from Rwanda because he managed to mobilize followers to challenge and ignore the mwami and, as such, jeopardized the political organization of the country under Belgian rule. The available accounts of this event disagree on two points: whether or not Bucyanayandi was expelled (or chose to leave);

and whether or not the mwami or the colonial administration appointed Bucyanayandi as chief of Gishari.[47] More important, however, is that, according to the administration, after Bideri's resignation mwami Rudahigwa would regard leaving Rwanda to join Buchyanyandi as an act of dissidence. Hence, leaving Rwanda to join Buchanyandi became a risky business,[48] and it was feared that Bideri's resignation would be a "mortal blow" to the migration scheme.[49] Bideri returned to Rwanda followed by some of his subjects and the number of immigrants in Gishari remained constant (influx equaled outflux).[50] However, it is impossible to say how Bideri's resignation affected immigration to Gishari, as his departure coincided with the Nyirahuku Famine of 1942–1943, which brought about a massive influx of migrants, not only in Masisi, but also in Rutshuru territory.[51]

For Bucyanayandi, though, and regardless of whether he was forced to leave or not, becoming chief in Gishari was an opportunity for him to develop a political (and economic) stronghold outside of the confines of Rwanda and beyond the reach of the mwami. Bucyanayandi was not the only one to arrive at this conclusion. As White Father M. Reyners (1954:344) puts it: "Since the time of Bucya [Bucyanayandi] Gishari also became the refuge for sinners from the higher echelons in Rwanda." Thus the existence of a Rwandan enclave across the Congolese border allowed dissident and politically marginalized (Tutsi) elites to develop and maintain an independent power base and escape political marginalization: a development that the mwami disapproved of, as he perceived it as undermining of his position.[52] This disapproval was not only made known to the colonial administration, it was also accompanied by direct action, and it seems that the authorities did everything within their power to stymie influential office-holders wanting to leave for the Gishari chieftaincy.[53] This suggests that the royal court could not accept Gishari as an asylum for dissident elites who could develop a political and economic power base independent from the mwami, but still within the periphery of his territory. Also, it signifies that the Royal Court in Rwanda started to lose its grip over the social and political organization of the Banyarwanda settlement in the Kivu. As a result, they attempted to maintain the colonial border and thwart the departure of disgruntled elites.

It was not only members of the elite who were using this exit option to escape the power of the royal court. Although it was the explicit intention of the first phase of the migration scheme to settle migrants in the autonomous chieftaincy of Gishari in the Masisi region, this was not always the case. An unanticipated effect of the migratory flow to the Kivu was the disorganized migration and settlement of Banyarwanda to other regions in Masisi. A substantial number of migrants settled in the Hunde chieftaincy, outside the influence of Gishari, even if this meant they missed out on some of the "privileges" (such as exemption from mandatory labour and exactions) the colonial administration had reserved for the inhabitants of Gishari. At present, it is not entirely clear how land entitlements were made to these "illegal" migrants, although Bucyalimwe Mararo (1990:166) states that land was distributed directly from the Hunde chiefs in exchange for some goods. But why was it considered more favourable to migrate into these Hunde chieftaincies? Maybe part of the answer lies in the history of the Rwandan Kingdom itself. Maybe this migration was a continuation of earlier precolonial patterns of escaping the expansion of the Rwandan state? Migrants who settled in Hunde *chefferies* (chieftainships) used the migration scheme as an exit-option[54] to escape the power of the Rwandan Royal Court. According to a local administrator, Hutu in the Hunde chieftaincy would first identify themselves as Hunde when interviewed because they no longer wanted to be compared to Hutu still complying with the power of Rwandan chiefs.[55] For them, labour migration (made possible by the existence of different labour markets and political and economic spheres), was a means to escape the imposition of state power by both the Rwandan elite and the Belgian administration.

THE SECOND PHASE AND THE END OF AN ERA

The second phase of the transplantation was essentially an attempt to respond to the problems encountered during the first phase, and an adaptation to the changing context after the Second World War (WWII). The end of the (official) migration to Gishari was proclaimed in 1945 because of problems of oversaturation and soil deterioration in the region. The administration considered other migration destinies (both inside and outside Masisi), but even after migration to the Kivu was declared *au point mort* (at a dead point)[56] it still continued, this time, more pronounced, to Rutshuru.[57] As the evidence illustrates, colonial policies were unable to completely monitor, let alone steer, force or forbid migration. Still, they attempted, with more vigour than before, to restrict it.

This second phase took off in the second half of the 1940s, and was shaped by the MIB (created in 1948) and the *Mission Anti-Erosive* (MAE). The MIB represented a marked departure from the first phase of migration. Most significant was the raised level of colonial planning and the increased attention paid to the humanitarian aspect of draining overpopulated areas. Linked to this new approach was a change in the way the Belgian administration perceived the mobility of labour across borders, both within the Belgian territories and across the border with its British counterpart. Firstly, even though the colonial administration was still unable to effectively monitor its internal and external borders, it seems that labour migration into Uganda was no longer regarded as an economic loss (at least not to the extent that it was in the 1930s), probably because of the diminishing need of labour brought about by increased mechanization after WWII (Tegera

2009:207). At the same time, political and economic changes that affected both Rwanda and Uganda caused Banyarwanda migration towards Uganda to drop considerably after 1948.[58]

Secondly, after 1945 the scheme became more restrictive with regard to whom was preferred or allowed to cross the internal border between Rwanda and the Belgian Congo. These efforts at controlling the movement of people more closely is reflected in the foundation of the MIB, which was entrusted with organizing the migration and settlement of Banyarwanda. Whilst in the first phase complaints about the "low quality" of the migrants abounded, preliminary measures during the second phase were aimed at establishing a core of "reliable" migrants. Suitable migrants were transported by trucks towards Goma (North Kivu), where they were medically examined (Spitaels 1953:113). Yet, as in the first phase of migration, colonial policies did not necessarily correlate to reality and many Banyarwanda migrated to the Kivu and settled outside the control of the MIB. These attempts at tighter control were linked to the status of Rwanda as a mandated territory, with an increasing emphasis on the humanitarian aspect of the migration scheme (see above). This can be partly explained by the changes on the international stage after 1945 and by the visit of the UN mission to Rwanda in 1948. But, moreover, the Kivu too was witnessing a population boom in the course of the 1940s and 1950s. Also, finally, the development of a *paysannat indigène* (an indigenous peasantry) came to play an important role (see, for instance, Jewsiewicki 1980). In addition to overpopulation in the Kivu, initial rejection of pastoralists into the zones of settlements became even more restrictive.[59] In the 1950s, for instance, any Tutsi owning more than 10 head of cattle were no longer allowed within the zones of settlement.[60]

Therefore, and because of legal problems concerning the nationality of Banyarwanda, the then Minister of Colonies Auguste Buisseret ordered a stop to the *systematic* and *organ-*

ized transplantation to the Kivu in 1954.[61] As uncontrollable incursions of Banyarwanda migrants only added to the problem of overpopulation, the MIB was renamed *Mission d'Installation Banyaruandais*. Also, it changed its character as its aim was no longer to encourage, but to guide and control (i.e. discourage) spontaneous migrations to the Kivu.[62] Despite this change of course, however, and despite the absence of official propaganda, Banyarwanda continued migrating to the Kivu. At the same time though, the colonial administration deemed it unwise to completely preclude migration towards the Kivu: this, it thought, would lead to uncontrolled settlement, further erosion of the soil, and provoke conflicts over land. Furthermore, in view of its international obligations towards the mandated territory, the colonial government saw it as its responsibility to solve Rwanda's overpopulation problem by emphasizing their international obligations towards the mandated territory. Therefore, it judged it not opportune to completely outlaw Banyarwanda migration.[63] To counteract the overpopulation in the Kivu, plans were then established for *internal* transfers of population *within* the Kivu. However, the "unoccupied" land to which this internal transfer was directed had already been delineated for the settlement of Banyarwanda. Now this land had to be reserved for the Congolese migrants rather than for Banyarwanda.[64] Thus, on the eve of independence, the emphasis was no longer solely on the migration of Rwandan labour towards the Kivu. Instead, overpopulated regions of the Kivu were turned into labour reserves.

A final element that influenced the more restrictive stance towards the border was a changed discourse on ethnic identity, as concerns over the nationality of the migrants were linked to the fear of Tutsi irredentism. Possibly this change in attitude towards Tutsi was related to changes in Rwanda itself: since the end of the 1940s, Tutsi were no longer seen as the sole group able to take up administrative, legal and ruling positions; a Hutu contra-elite was formed, and the "Bahutu-Tutsi complex" came to be thought of as a political danger[65] (Reyntjens 1985).

It is clear that, at this stage, the compliance of mwami Rudahigwa and his counterparts was no longer deemed necessary. Moreover, the alleged pursuit of an expansion of Rwanda became an argument by which to exclude Tutsi from the migratory movement: only Hutu were allowed to migrate, and they needed to be organized under the authority of the Congolese chiefs.[66]

In 1957 the suppression of the Gishari chieftaincy was ordained and it was integrated into the Hunde-chefferie (Mararo 1997:513); in 1959 migration to Masisi stopped completely.[67] Ironically, 1959 is the year in which the "revolution" in Rwanda broke out, setting in motion an exodus of (mainly) Tutsi refugees ("Fifty-niners") towards the eastern Congo and other neighbouring countries.

CONCLUSION

Without denying the power of the Belgian colonial state and the larger structural coercion engrained in the colonial system, the Banyarwanda resettlement scheme also clearly shows the weaknesses of that same state. The scheme discussed here illustrates how the Belgian colonial administration was not only seeing "[…] themselves as far smarter and farseeing than they really were and, at the same time, regarded their subjects as far more stupid and incompetent than they really were." (Scott 1998:343), but also that the Bula Matari needed the cooperation of the chiefs in order to obtain the necessary labour for the ailing plantations in the Kivu.

But it was not only chiefs who were needed to set the migratory movement in motion. The chiefs' subjects also tapped into the differences between political contexts, labour markets and tax regimes brought about by the imposition of the colonial border. Although their mobility was severely restricted as a result of the encroachment of the colonial administration (e.g. with the introduction of laws curtailing their mobility), neither the colonial state nor the chiefs were ever able to completely control the mobility of their subjects.

This meant that the colonial administration, in order to regulate the mobility of people, had to take important push and pull factors into account when designing the resettlement scheme. As such, their policies were not merely an extension of their interests, but a *marriage de raison* between what they wanted to obtain and the need to find an answer to the strategies of their subjects.

The permeable boundaries between the Belgian Congo and Rwanda were, at least in the first phase, instrumental in serving colonial interests. Yet, the Belgian colonial administration was unable to curb migration labour flows away from Uganda, at least (from its point of view) not to a sufficient extent. The acquiescence of local elites was crucial in enabling Belgian efforts at organizing (or tapping) labour migration. These elites, however, were divided in their attitudes towards the border and towards the relocation of Banyarwanda. One section of the elite used the colonial state's desperate need for labour as a means by which to acquire pasture for their herds, and to obtain political influence in neighbouring territories. Others interpreted the permeability of the borders as a threat to their position, which resulted in attempts to restrain the mobility of their subjects through the use of, for example, legal struggles over cattle contracts.

From the 1940s on Gishari developed into a Rwandese enclave outside the control of the mwami, a home for both disgruntled elites and Rwandan peasantry, which provoked the withdrawal of the mwami's support. However, in the second half of the 1940s, the collaboration of the court was not as crucial as it was during the first phase, nor was the need for labour as pressing as in earlier stages. These developments, and the fear of what was called "Munyarwanda irredentism" resulted in the rigidification of the Congo-Rwanda border. Whereas at first the Belgian administration perceived the permeability of this border as an economic asset, the opposite was true during the second phase of the migration scheme. But even towards the end of the Belgian colonial endeavor, the Belgian administration was still not completely able to monitor and police this "internal" border. This reality defied the image of Bula Matari as a "freestanding" entity, as it constantly had to adapt its policy to the cooperation and agency of its subjects. In the case of the Congo-Rwanda borderland it was the availability of other options across the lines separating colonial territories which crippled the Belgian colonial state.

ACKNOWLEDGEMENTS

This paper is based on extensive archival research in the African Archives, Ministry of Foreign Affairs, Belgium (African Archives Brussels, AAB) and on interviews in both the Kivu and Rwanda (May–July 2010 and January–April 2011) in the context of an ongoing Ph.D. project. I would like to thank the anonymous reviewers and Steven van Wolputte for their comments and Baz Lecocq, Johan Pottier, Jim Brennan and especially Aldwin Roes for their comments on earlier drafts of this work. Nevertheless, the normal disclaimer applies to this work: all mistakes are my own.

NOTES

[1] Of course, states are no monolithic blocs and also consist of many different actors, competing factions, and so on. Lack of space, however, prevents me from elaborating this important point (see, for instance, Van Wolputte 2004, 2007).

[2] *Bami* (pl., sing. mwami) institutions were found in several ancient kingdoms in the Great Lakes region, such as Rwanda, Bushi etc. In the Kivu, local 'customary' chiefs are still called mwami, e.g. the current mwami Daniel Ndeze of Rutshuru. In this paper I am mainly referring to mwami Mutara Rudahigwa of Rwanda who ruled between 1931 and 1959.

[3] Belgium invaded and occupied Rwanda (until then controlled by Germany) in 1916. It was not until 1924 that Belgium officially took the mandate over Ruanda-Urundi.

[4] The CNKi started out as a parastatal but was de facto dependent on private capital and closely resembled a private enterprise. It played an important role in allocating the land for the settlement of Banyarwandan immigrants in the context of the MIB. For more on this subject, see the work of Bucyalimwe Mararo (1990, 1997).

[5] African Archives Brussels (AAB), Rapports Annuels/Affaires Indigènes et Main d'Oeuvre (RA/AIMO), 163, Rapport Annuel (RA) Rutshuru 1933. The territorial administration even expressed fears that indigenous life might "disappear" completely.

[6] AAB, RA/AIMO 163, RA Rutshuru 1933. For a more complete picture of reasons why Banyarwanda chose to migrate towards Buganda for shorter or longer periods, see Fortt 1957: 77–118; Richards 1973:119–140.

[7] AAB, RA/AIMO 163, Rutshuru 1934 and 1936.

[8] See AAB, RA/AIMO 163 Rutshuru and AAB/Ruanda-Urundi (RA/RU) 96 Ruhengeri for the 1930s.

[9] See AAB, RA/AIMO, 112, Rapport Politique (RP), 1924.

[10] See AAB, AI, 4378, Letter to the Minister of Colonies, January 7, 1926.

[11] This is not the first publication dealing with the MIB. Bucyalimwe Mararo (1990, 1997) focuses primarily on land conflicts and contemporary ramifications, whilst Aloys Tegera (2009) concentrates on the financial and economic dimension. This chapter is concerned with the practice of colonialism and the importance of borders.

[12] The Belgian Congo and the mandate Ruanda-Urundi were administratively unified and formed a *vice-gouvernement general*. The mandate Ruanda-Urundi consisted of two *residences:* Ruanda and Urundi (Delvaux 1945:65). This, however, does not mean that Ruanda-Urundi and the Belgian Congo were administered in the same way. When I refer to Rwanda I am referring to the territory contained in the Rwandan Residence.

[13] AAB, RU 5156, Jahresbericht Rwanda 1911, p. 3.

[14] See correspondence and reports in AAB, AI (4378).

[15] AAB, AI (4738), G. Mortehan, 'Transplantation des Banyaruanda,' 1937.

[16] AAB, AI (Affaires Indigènes), 4378, M.G. Mortehan (Royal Inspector), 1937. Transplantation des Banyaruanda au Kivu, p. 5.

[17] In 1937 the land was officially relinquished from the Hunde-community for the settlement of Banyarwanda for the price of 30,000 francs, which was paid to Hunde chief Kalinda. Although Kalinda benefited financially from selling this land, his state of mind seemed to be "somewhat influenced" (*cependant quelque peu influence*) by the plans for creating an independent Banyarwandan chieftaincy in the future (AAB, RA/AIMO 142, RA Masisi, 1938). Furthermore it seems that not all Hunde notables had the same perception of this relinquishment (see AAB, RF 4609, Gerday, O., Candidate Territorial Administrator, September 11, 1937. Procès Verbal d'enquête de terres). Bucyalimwe Mararo (1990, 1997) sketches these events in more detail and also pays attention to the aftermath of these land relinquishments.

[18] AAB, AI (4378), M.G., Mortehan, June 9, 1937, Transplantation des Banyaruanda au Kivu, p. 11. Morthehan reacts to the Commissary of the Kivu-District Hackars, who wanted to exclude Tutsi completely from this migration.

[19] AAB, CP (1536), Gouverneur of Rwanda-Urundi Marzorati to Governor General, Usumbura, December 29, 1927.

[20] *Ubuhake* was a form of clientship existing in Rwanda, entailing the transfer of a cow from a patron to a client in exchange for *ubuhake* services. For a thorough discussion on *ubuhake* and misperceptions, see Newbury 1986, 135–136.

[21] AAB, AI (4378), Avis du commissaire de district Hackars, Transplantation de Banyaruanda au Kivu, 1928. However, it should be noted that in earlier discussion the colonial administration was divided on this subject. See for instance AAB, AIMO (1999), Letter of Governor Moeller to the Governor General, Irumu, March 18, 1928; Letter from Affaires indigènes et main-d'oeuvre (s.n.) to the Governor General, Stanleyville, January 21, 1928.

[22] Letter of Governor Jungers of Rwanda to the Governor General and the Minister of Colonies, Usumbura, November 7, 1938.

[23] AAB, AI (4378) Letter n° 5082/AO/403/VC.3 from the Governor General Ryckmans to the Governor of Rwanda-Urundi, Léopoldville, May 18, 1938.

[24] AAB, RACB (Rapports Annuels Congo Belge) (120bis), RA Kivu, 1938.

[25] AAB, AI (4378), s.d. 'Transplantation des Banyaruanda.'

[26] „Il ne s'agit pas proprement parler de MO [main d'oeuvre], tous ces émigrants étant des pasteurs watutsi ne s'adonnant à aucun genre de travail manuel." AAB, RA/RU 96 (12), RA Ruhengeri 1937. Members of the church (White Fathers) also adhered to this prejudice. As one of them stated: "The Batutsi form an economic problem. Like the Bahutu are agriculturalists, they are pastoralists. A real Mututsi will not take a shovel in its hands if it is not necessary. He lives for and with his cows" (Reyners M. 1954: 346).

[27] AAB, RACB (120bis), RA Kivu, 1938.

[28] AAB, AI (4378), Absil, D. (District Commissar), 1936. Transplantation de population Banya Ruanda dans le district du Kivu, October 6, 1936, pp. 1–2.

[29] In the context of the conflicts in eastern Congo, discussion often surfaces about the limits of the pre-colonial Rwandan kingdom (Vansina 2004). See Newbury (1997) for a discussion of this discourse and its fallacies.

[30] "Avec ce statut politique, plus d'opposition de la part des autorités indigènes du Ruanda qui considèreront ces nouvelles entités politiques comme des colonies du Ruanda, sans autre attache avec la mère patrie qu'une communauté de race, de nom et de langue." AAB, AI (4378), Absil, D. (District Commissar), 1936. Transplantation de population Banya Ruanda dans le district du Kivu, October 6, 1936, pp. 1–2.

[31] AAB, AI (4378), Absil, D. (District Commissar), 1936. Transplantation de population Banya Ruanda dans le district du Kivu, October 6, 1936, p. 2.

[32] AAB, AI (4378) Letter n° 42B/AO/202/VC.3 from Governor General Ryckmans to the Minister, Léopoldville, February 23, 1938.

[33] AAB, RA/AIMO 163, RA Rutshuru, 1936.

[34] AI (4378) Mortehan, M.G., Transplantation des Banyaruanda au Kivu. Léopoldville, June 9, 1937.

[35] AAB, RA/AIMO 143 Masisi and RA/AIMO 163 Rutshuru, 1942 and 1943.

[36] AAB, RA/AIMO 143, RA Masisi, 1943. The evidence that indigenous courts were indeed used as a means to hinder the departure of migrants is abundant and was clearly an important worry of the colonial administration. Multiple indications of this can be found in AAB, RWA 353 and

RWA 354.

[37] AAB, RWA 354, Resident Sandrart to Governor, informing him of communication he had with Territorial Administrators, Kigali, October 3 1944, letter n° 1486/A.I.4.

[38] Kamunzinzi might have been exaggerating his benevolent role in the migration. In a Kinyamateka article from 1944 he is accused by a certain K.M. that he was forcing people to migrate to Gishari. AAB, RWA 353, translation of Kinyamateka article (Kinyamateka no. 146, December 1944).

[39] See also AAB, RWA 353, Territorial Administrator Collinet to Resident, No.17/Imm., Nyamitaba, November 20, 1940.

[40]*Abamotsi* was the term informants used to refer to the auxiliaries of *chefs* or *sous-chefs* (Interviews January–April 2011). These *abamotsi* or *ibirongozi* (as they are also referred to) were the bottom tier of the colonial administration. They were often Hutu and had to perform unpopular tasks such as collecting taxes and assuring *prestations* (labour) and services for the chiefs (see Newbury 1986:115).

[41] AAB, AI (4378), s.n., Note au sujets des immigrations de Banyarruanda vers le Kivu, April 1, 1957

[42] AAB, AI (4378), Letter no. 145/VE/VII.C.3 from the Governor General to the Minister of Colonies, Léopoldville, March 13, 1955.

[43] [I]l faut que moi le mwami, j'aie exactement les meme pouvoirs ici qu'au Rwanda, en toute matière, politique et judiciaire […]." AAB, RWA 354, Paradis, Resident of Rwanda, L'immigration dirigée des Banyarwanda au Gishari, February 25, 1941, paraphrasing the mwami.

[44] AAB, RWA 354, Dessaint, Delegate of the Resident of Rwanda to Resident, Nyanza June 9 1941, Letter no. 489/AI/VIII

[45] Bucyanayandi was chief of the province of Ndara since 1934 and was appointed chief of Gishari in 1941.

[46] Extracts from letters from mwami Rudahigwa and and Buchanyanda are cited in AAB, RWA 5, letter from territorial administrator Houben to the Residence of Rwanda (confidential), July 29, 1941, letter from the delegate of the Resident, Dessaint, August 26, 1941; letter from Bucyanayandi to the resident August 11, 1941, Territorial Administrator Houben in his correspondence with the Resident; AAB, RWA 5, letter from territorial administrator Houben to the Resident, July 29, 1941.

[47] AAB, RWA5. It is not entirely clear what the fact of the matter with Bucyanayandi's dismissal is: Bucyanayandi declared *he* had asked permission to leave Rwanda because of his strained relation to mwami

Rudahigwa (AAB, RWA 8, Letter of W. Bucyanayandi to the local administrator, December 20, 1947), whilst the mwami gave the impression that his dismissal was a disciplinary measure (Letter of the delegate of the Resident close to the mwami Dessaint to the resident of Rwanda, October 17, 1941). That the latter could be the case is echoed by Muyaneza's oral testimony stating that Bucyana [Bucyanayandi] was expelled to Gishari because he committed a crime against the mwami (see Codere 1973: 211). Elsewhere it is argued that the mwami had proposed another candidate to succeed Joseph Bideri, but that the colonial administration had not approved of the mwami's candidate (Reyners M. 1953: 343).

[48] AAB, RA/AIMO Masisi 142, 1942.

[49] AAB, RA/AIMO 142 Masisi, 1941.

[50] RWA 354, Letter No. 3332/AO/157/VC3a, Gouverneur Générale Ryckmans to Gouverneur de Costermansville, March 9, 1942.

[51] To indicate how severely famine intensified migration we can state some figures from the influx of migrants in Gishari. Whilst in 1942, 7,432 immigrants are recorded, in 1943, 15,309 migrants are recorded. In 1944 there were 24,493, tripling the number of immigrants over the course of two years. Until 1951 this number stays more or less stable. Next to Gishari, Jomba (Rutshuru) also witnesses a large influx of migrants. Estimates are around 8,000 in 1943 (AAB, RA/AIMO 163 Rutshuru, 1943). However, both the estimates for Gishari and Jomba are no more than estimates: the administration is well aware that many migrants left without informing the authorities, and outside of the known areas of settlement (Gishari and Jomba), the administration thinks that many of them settled in neighbouring regions (AAB, RWA 353, Letter of Territorial Administrator Vauthier to the resident, Territoire Ruhengeri, n° 269/Gishari, April 28 1944).

[52] AAB, RWA5, Letter of the delegate of the resident Dessaint, October 17, 1941.

[53] AAB, RA/AIMO 142 Masisi, 1944.

[54] Asiwaju was the first to coin this term (Asiwaju 1976).

[55] AAB, RA/AIMO 142, Masisi 1948.

[56] AAB, AI (4378), Letter n° 473B/2485/AO/2916/VC/3a from Governor General Jungers to Minister, Léopoldville, December 30 1946.

[57] The annual reports from Masisi indicate a more pronounced migration towards Muvunyi and Washali-Mokoto (Hunde chieftaincies) in Masisi instead of Gishari after 1945. In 1947, a large number of migrants is reported in Rutshuru, migrating towards Busanza, Mushari and Jomba.

(AAB, RA/AIMO 143, RA Masisi, 1947).

[58] For an indication of the reasons of this drop: AAB, RUDI (82) 581, "PV de la conférence qui s'est tenue a Kisenyi le 24 et 25 novembre 1948 relative a la MOI du RU employé au Tanganyika et en Uganda.," and the other reports on these meetings in AAB, RUDI (82) 581.See AAB, RUDI (82) 581 and especially "PV de la conference tenue à Masaka le 31 mai 1950 entre les representants de RU, Tanganyika et Uganda sur la MOI immigrante," which states economic development in Ruanda-Urundi resulting in higher wages, the replacement of unpaid labour for the chief and road works by salaried main d'oeuvre, decreasing wages in Uganda as a result of devaluation, stabilization of the coffee prices.

[59] AAB, AI (4378), Letter n° 473B/2485/AO/2916/VC.3a from the Governor General Jungers to the Ministry of Colonies, Léopoldville, December 30, 1947.

[60] AAB, AI (4378), s.n., Note sur les déplacements de populations Banya-Ruanda vers le Congo Belge. Etat de la question au 1re Mai 1951. May 1, 1951.

[61] AAB, AI (4378), RF (4609), RUDI (165) 1321, Brebant, V., 1953. Problème foncier indigène au Kivu. Letter no. 21/3697/II.L/1a, Léopoldville, December 3, 1953.

[62] Banyarwandan migrants who came to Goma were now denied access to the means of transportation by which they were before brought into the rural areas of the settlement, in order to discourage them to migrate (AAB, GG 5915, Lettre from J. Bomans to the Governor General, December 28, 1956).

[63] AAB, AI (4378), Note pour Monsieur l'administrateur général des colonies from Minister Buisseret to the Administrator General of the Colonies, Brussels 9th August 1954. AAB, RUDI (165)1327, Letter no. 211/432/III-J.8, Letter from Minister of Colonies (signed by Administrator General Van den Abeele for the Minister) to the Governor General, Brussels, September 30, 1954.

[64] AAB, AI (4378), Note pour monsieur l'administrateur général des colonies from the Ministry of Colonies, s.d.

[65] For a discussion, see: AAB, GG 5915, 'Letter from the province Governor G. Schmidt to the district commissary of North Kivu,' November 19, 1956.

[66] See AAB, RA/AIMO 143, RA Masisi.

[67] AAB, RACB (121bis) 7, RA Kivu, 1959.

REFERENCES

Asiwaju, A. I. 1976 Migration as Revolt: The Example of the Ivory Coast and the Upper Volta Before 1945. Journal of African History 17 (4):577–594.

Berman, B. J. 1997. *Review of* The African State in Comparative Perspective: The Perils of Bula Matari: Constraint and Power in the Colonial State. Canadian Journal of African Studies 31(3):556–570.

Bruyns, L., and K. Pinxten. 1952. De Geleide Immigratie Van de Banya Ruanda in Kivu. Zaïre: Revue Congolaise (Mars):251–271.

Chrétien, J.-P., and E. Mworoha. 1980. Les Migrations du XXe Siècle en Afrique Orientale. Le Cas de l'Emigration des Banyarwanda et des Barundi vers l'Uganda. *In* Les Migrations Internationales de la Fin du XVIIIe Siècle à Nos Jours. Commission Internationale d'Histoire des Mouvements Sociaux et des Structures Sociales, ed. Pp. 643–680. Paris: Editions du Centre Nationale de la Recherche Scientifique.

Cooper, F. 1994. Conflict and connection: rethinking colonial African history. American Historical Review 99(5):1516–1545.

Couttenier, M. 2005. Congo tentoongesteld: een geschiedenis van de Belgische antropologie en het museum van Tervuren (1882-1925). Leuven: Acco.

De Saint Moulin, L. 1975. Movement récents de population dans la zone de peuplement dense de l'est de Kivu. Etude d'Histoire africaine 7(special issue: L'Afrique des Grand Lacs). Kinshasa: Presses Universitare de Zaire.

Dorsey, L. 1983. The Rwandan colonial economy, 1916-1941. Unpublished dissertation, State University of Michigan.

Fairhead, J. 1990. Fields of Struggle: Towards a Social History of Farming Knowledge and Practice in a Bwisha Community, Zaire. Ph.D. dissertation, SOAS.

Ferme, M. 2004. Deterritorialized Citizenship and the Resonances of the Sierra Leonean State. *In* V. Das and D. Poole, eds. Anthropology in the Margins of the State. Pp. 81–115. Santa Fe: School of American Research Press.

Fortt, J.M. 1957. The Distribution of the Immigrant and Ganda Population within Buganda. *In* A study of Immigrant Labor in Buganda, A. I. Richards, ed. Pp. 77–118. Cambridge: W. Heffer and Sons Ltd.

Freund, B. 1984. Labor and Labor History in Africa: A Review on the Literature. African Studies Review 27(2):1–58.

Jentgen, P. 1957. Les frontières du Ruanda-Burundi et le regime international de tutelle. Bruxelles: Académie Royale des Sciences Coloniales.

Jewsiewiecki, B. 1980. African peasants in the totalitarian colonial society

of the Belgian Congo. *In* Peasants in Africa. Historical and contemporary perspectives. M. Klein, ed. Pp. 45–73. London: Sage Publications.
——— 1979. Le colonat agricole européen au Congo-Belge, 1910–1960: Question politiques et économiques. Journal of African History 20(4):559–571.
Lemarchand, R. 1977. Rwanda. *In* African Kingships in Perspective. Political Change and Modernization in Monarchical Settings. R. Lemarchand, ed. Pp. 67–93. London: Frank Cass and Co. Ltd
——— 1970. Rwanda and Burundi. London: Pall Mall Press.
Likaka, O. 2009. Naming Colonialism. History and Collective Memory in the Congo, 1870–1960. Wisconsin: University of Wisconsin Press.
Louis, R.W. 1963. Ruanda-Urundi 1844-1919. Oxford: Clarendon Press.
Mararo, B. 1997. Land, Power and Ethnic Conflict in Masisi (Congo-Kinshasha), 1940–1994. International Journal of African Historical Studies 30(3):503–538.
——— 1990. Land Conflicts in Masisi, Eastern Zaire: The Impact and Aftermath of Belgian Colonial Policy. Ph.D. dissertation, Department of History, Indiana University.
Mendiaux, E. 1956. Le Comité National du Kivu. In Zaïre, vol. 10.
Newbury, C. 1988. The Cohesion of Oppression: Clientship and Ethnicity in Rwanda, 1860–1960. New York: Columbia University Press.
Newbury, D. 1987. Bunyabongo: The western frontier in Rwandan History. *In* The African Frontier: The Reproduction of Traditional African Societies, Igor Kopytoff, ed. Pp. 164–192. Bloomington: Indiana University Press.
——— 1986. From 'Frontier' to 'Boundary': Some Historical Roots of Peasant Strategies of Survival in Zaire. *In* The Crisis in Zaire: Myths and Realities, G.N. Ntalja, ed. Pp. 87–97. Trenton: Africa World Press.
Nugent, P. and A. I. Asiwaju. 1996. Introduction. The Paradox of African Boundaries. *In* African Boundaries, Barriers, Conduits and Opportunities, P. Nugent and A. I. Asiwaju, eds. Pp. 1–17. London: Pinter.
Reyners, M. 1954. Een Land Wordt Geboren. Nieuw Afrika 70:339–351.
Richards, A. I. 1973. Methods of Settlement in Uganda. *In* A Study of Immigrant Labor in Uganda. A. I. Richards, ed. Pp. 119–140. Cambridge: W. Heffer and Sons Ltd.
Rumiya J. 1992. Le Rwanda sous le régime du mandat belge (1916–1931), Paris, L'Harmattan.
Scott, J. 1998. Seeing like a state. Why certain schemes to improve the human condition have failed. New Haven: Yale University Press.
Spitaels, R. 1953. Transplantation de Banyaruanda dans le Kivu-Nord. Problèmes d'Afrique Centrale 19-22:110–116.
Tegera, A. 2009 Les Banyarwanda du Nord-Kivu (RDC). Analyse Historique et Socio-Politique d'un Groupe Transfrontalier (1885–2006). Un-

published Ph.D. dissertation, Université de Paris 1, Panthéon Sorbonne, Paris.
Vansina, J. 2004. Antecedents to Modern Rwanda. The Nyinginya Kingdom. Wisconsin: The University of Wisconsin Press.
Van Wolputte, S. 2007. Cattle works: livestock policy, apartheid and development in Northwest Namibia, c. 1920-1980. African Studies 66(1):103–128.
——— 2004. Subject Disobedience. The colonial narrative and Native Counterworks in Northwestern Namibia, ca 1920-1975. History and Anthropology 15(2):151–173.
Willame, J.-C. 1999. Conflits et Guerres au Kivu et dans la Région des Grand Lacs: Entre Tensions Locales et Escalade Régionale. Paris: L'Harmattan.
Young, C. 1994. The African State in Comparative Perspective. New Haven: Yale University Press.

6

FENCED FRONTIERS AND MURKY BOUNDARIES. TWO CASES FROM KAOKO, NORTHERN NAMIBIA

Steven Van Wolputte, Els Hoorelbeke and Laura Bleckmann

INTRODUCTION

It was early January in 1969, in a small and dusty administrative outpost in the northern Kunene Region, Namibia. In this mountainous and arid borderland, often referred to as Kaoko, the short rainy season had —again— passed without a drop of rain, and the situation had become critical for the mostly pastoral population. As their livestock was succumbing to thirst, starvation, and disease, the elders in the Kaoko Tribal Council petitioned the colonial administration to allow emergency grazing across the fence that, at the time, separated Kaoko from the Etosha Game Reserve.[1]

The Chief Bantu Affairs Commissioner in Windhoek, however, turned down their request. A few days later, though, he received a note by Johan S. Malan, a civil servant working in the region. Malan (also one of the first ethnographers on Kaoko) pointed out that some thousand head of cattle had already crossed the fence. He mentioned that huge livestock losses compelled the inhabitants of Kaoko to demand immediate action, "regardless whether or not it is in accord with existing laws and regulations."[2]

Attached to Malan's note were two short letters by eminent members of the Tribal Council. The one by Joel Tjiyahura (from Otjondeka) read:

> I heard emergency grazing is not yet allowed. … You should come and see for yourself, please. I will not rest as long as my animals are dying, and I will not give you peace. … We inhabit the area adjacent to the game reserve and our animals see the grass beneath the fence.[3] [Our translation]

The other letter, signed by Kephas Muzuma (from Otjokavare), alluded to the common practice of dealing with African-owned animals trespassing into the cattle-free zone: "If the government cannot help, they should bring bullets to shoot my animals in the game reserve, because I will not leave from there."[4] The desperation in these letters was unable to convince the Chief Bantu Commissioner in Windhoek. After these events, though, Tjiyahura and Muzuma changed tactics. Instead of opposing an apartheid livestock policy —as the Tribal Council had done— they decided to cooperate with the South West African Administration (SWAA) and its veterinarians.[5]

This decision acted as a catalyst for the historical tensions within the Kaoko Tribal Council to erupt, and in the months that followed Tribal Council fissioned into a "small group" (*okambumba,* around Tjiyahura and Muzuma), supported by the colonial administration but ostracized by the other headmen and councillors in the Tribal Council who were referred to as the "big group" (*otjimbumba*). This fission would later, in the 1980s, lead to the establishment of two traditional authorities in Kaoko: the Vita Thom Royal House Traditional Authority and the Otjikaoko Traditional Authority that exist until today (even if they were recently, in 2010, joined by a third competitor, the Kakurukouje Traditional Authority).[6]

These past and present rivalries and tensions are at least partly a result of the colonial administration's efforts at drawing boundaries, which in the case of Kaoko should be taken quite literally as the colonial administration went through great trouble to have the region fenced. More than half a century after they were constructed these "real" and "symbolic" fences still cast their shadow over contemporary public discourse and daily life in Kaoko. Therefore, this essay focuses on the effects colonial boundaries had (and still have) on life in the borderland between Namibia and Angola, with the period considered being roughly the five decades between 1920 and 1970.

To do so, the analysis presents two case studies. The first one, on the ethnographic category of "Dhimba," illustrates the *uncertainties* of colonial gerrymandering by looking at a group that fell between the lines of the colonizing, "ethnogracizing," grid (Wilmsen 1989: vii; also see Roque, Breusers, this volume). The second one, on former Herero contract labourers, looks at the *ambivalence* of how people experienced these once colonial boundaries. The fences around Kaoko, obviously, imposed strong restrictions on the mobility of people and animals, and hence on trade and livestock management. Yet, they also opened opportunities in that they allowed the migrating Dhimba families to escape the violence and (labour) exploitation that existed under Portuguese rule, or offered young Herero men the possibility (or, at least, the promise) of climbing the social ladder faster than traditional kinship or the unfavourable circumstances would otherwise permit (Bollig 1998a; also see Werner 1998).

FENCING

Kaoko was created as a buffer zone to shield the rest of Namibia (and hence, South Africa) from the danger posed by Transboundary Animal Diseases (TADs, such as Contagious Bovine Pleuropneumonia and Rinderpest) (see Van Wolputte 2007). In the 1930s, this threat legitimated the building of a fence that cross-cut Namibia from east to west. This Veterinary Cordon Fence, or "Red Line" (*omukoka omuserandu*) divided Namibia into the northern Communal Areas, and the Police Zone in the centre and south of the country (see Miescher 2010:219). This Red Line, however, was built not only to control the flow of livestock, but also (or even primarily) to control the movements of people: it restricted Africans' access to the official livestock market, and was instrumental in creating an African labour reserve for the commercial farms and industry in the Police Zone (see Silvester 1998; Bollig 1998a,b; Rizzo 2007; Van Wolputte 2004).[7] In the 1960s then, construction commenced on a fence that separated Kaoko from the North-Central Regions (Miescher 2010:326). Hence, Kaoko was hemmed in by fences towards the south and east; by the Kunene River in the north, and by the Skeleton Coast in the west. In the north, east, and south, cattle-free zones were declared. These boundaries, once in place, were a cause for continuing concern by the South West African Administration (SWAA): despite their "facticity," these boundaries were relatively fluid and permeable, and needed to be continuously negotiated (see Miesscher 2010, Van Wolputte 2004).[8]

Besides being a borderland, Kaoko was also a frontier. At least until the mid-1970s, colonial control was uncertain, and the local administrators faced a continuous lack of manpower and means to supervise a vast, rough, and scarcely populated region such as Kaoko. At least during the period concerned, colonizing activity was mainly centred along Kaoko's main road (see fig. 6.1). This road functioned as the main artery of colonial control; South African rule in the

Fig. 6.1. Main road in Kaoko, view from Opuwo. Photo by Steven Van Wolputte, April 2012.

northern Kunene Region can, therefore, be characterized as arterial (as opposed to capillary, see Van Wolputte 2007): so, whilst it is true that the colonial presence had a tremendous bearing on life in Kaoko, at the same time, it was unable to penetrate the total social fabric. In view of its limitations, colonial rule focused primarily on those villages that were "visible" from the main road, and was less pervasive and ubiquitous than the colonial administration wanted and presented itself to be (Van Wolputte 2004; 2007, see Cole 2001).

Georg Steinmetz (2007) recently demonstrated that it is counterproductive to consider colonial rule as a national policy: a comparison of German colonialism in Qingdoa (East China), Samoa (Oceania), and Namibia (southern Africa) reveals that these three contexts resulted in as many variants of "German" colonialism, ranging from genocidal (Namibia), paternalistic (Samoa), to segregationist and integrationist (Qingdoa). Something similar can be said about South African colonialism in Namibia. In Kaoko, for instance, colonial rule and state supervision (or "administrative development") was less omnipresent and compelling than in the rest of the country, at least until the early 1970s. What played a role, too, was that indirect rule was less equipped to deal with an acephalous political organization, as was the case in this region. Finally, colonizers' attitudes towards the Herero in general, and towards the inhabitants of Kaoko in particular, were more ambivalent than towards other groups in Namibia. As from the 1930s, Herero were increasingly depicted as "a true master nation with many good qualities and all the bad qualities that go with it" (Vedder 1991:45).[9]

But also within Kaoko, colonial perceptions and attitudes-cum-policy toward the different groups varied considerably. In the course of the 1950s, especially Himba from Kaoko— "conservative people who hardly fit in with today's world" (Bruwer 1968:15)[10]— were singled out as archetypical "noble savages" inhabiting a pristine and untouched, authentically African landscape, a questionable reputation they shared with, for instance, the San-speaking groups of the Kalahari (see Gordon 1992). This culminated in the plans to divide Kaoko into a southern ("Herero") and northern ("Himba") Homeland in the 1960s. Even though these plans never materialized, people from southern Kaoko were generally considered "good," "obedient," or "civilized" subjects. Those from northern Kaoko were seen as both "proud" and "stubborn," "conservative by nature" and "authentic" (Malan 1995:80). Worth noting is that the Herero from southern Kaoko played an important role in spreading and maintaining this stereotypical portrait.

What —besides colonial imagery— also explains these perceived differences was the fact that many southerners had migrated from central Namibia and Angola in the 1910s and 1920s. They had often received a missionary education, were Christianized, and spoke English and Afrikaans. Though of mixed background, the SWAA grouped them together as

Fig. 6.2. The Veterinary Cordon Fence at the gate in Werda, southern Kaoko. Photo by Steven Van Wolputte, August 2002.

"Herero." Affiliated to Vita Thom —a local warlord who enjoyed the sympathy of the local Bantu Affairs Commissioner — they became the privileged partners of the SWAA (see Friedman 2005:24–25) and, under the system of indirect rule, became the first officially appointed headmen of Kaoko, at the expense of other local (so-called Himba and Tjimba) leaders. Even though Himba and Tjimba headmen and councillors also became part of the Tribal Council in the course of the 1950s, tensions between the two groups would remain, and later culminate in the fission between the OtjiKaoko Traditional Authorities, and the Vita Thom Royal House Traditional Authority (see above).[11]

Finally, most of these southern villages were located near Kaoko's main road, hence greatly enhancing their visibility and proximity. This made these villages easier to supervise and control (which was why the colonial government encouraged, and sometimes forced, people to move there). It also made them easier to reach for the few licensed traders operating in Kaoko (see below). This road thus acted as a boundary, in a very literal sense, as the SWAA planned to delineate the road by erecting a double fence alongside it. It also acted as a boundary in a more metaphorical sense, as it marked the distinction between "good" and "bad" colonial subjects, between "known" and "unknown," but also, later, between "civilized" and "authentic." In that sense, this main road functioned both as a symbol and as a border of the colonial administration (see the introduction to this volume).

Like all boundaries, this main road created impediments: devised to supervise and control, it —paradoxically — restricted the mobility of people and herds. At the same time, though, the road also created opportunities, such as easier access to commodities and the labour market, enhancing the mobility of those without herds, especially youngsters. We turn to them in our second case study. First, however, we take this main road to northeast Kaoko, to the area around Ruacana. This area is situated along the border with Angola, and along the border between Kaoko and the North-Central Regions of Namibia. Since the early 20th century, it has been this border region that Dhimba refer to when talking about "home."

FOLKS OF NO CONSEQUENCE

The South African policy of divide and rule resulted in a rigid consolidation of existing, but flexible, ethnic boundaries (Van Wolputte 2004, Wallace 2011) between Himba, Tjimba, and Herero.[12] This, in its turn, would later give rise to the opposition between northern (Himba and Tjimba) and southern Kaoko (Herero), and between the two main traditional authorities in Kaoko. This policy was backed by ethnography. In 1951, for instance, government ethnologist N.J. van Warmelo published his "Notes on the Kaokoveld and its people," in which he distinguished the three groups. This booklet became an

Fig. 6.3. Concrete remnants of the fence that once surrounded Opuwo, then still a garrison town. Photo by Steven Van Wolputte, November 2006.

important tool: it was, for instance, mandatorily present in the office of the Bantu Affairs Commissioner.[13]

This threefold division was not uncontested, though. In 1962, during a meeting of the Tribal Council, Joel Tjiyahura (whom we already encountered in the introduction) objected to the Native Affairs Commissioner's use of the names Himba, Tjimba and Herero, claiming they were all Herero. The commissioner responded by reading from van Warmelo's book before stating, "You see now that you are three tribes."[14] Of interest here, however, is the fact that van Warmelo (1962:20) recognized the existence of other groups in Kaoko, but also dismissed them as "folk of no consequence."

One such inconsequential group were the Dhimba. Many of them had already settled in northern Kaoko prior to the 1940s. After 1940, however, Dhimba efforts to escape Portuguese colonialism and the violence of the Kuvale War in Angola led to a major migration wave into Namibia. This relatively large group were neither the first nor the last Dhimba migrants who settled in Kaoko. They did so only twenty years after Herero settlers occupied the south, and by the time van Warmelo wrote his *Notes*, Dhimba communities were well-established in northern Kaoko, mainly in Okangwati and Ruacana (see, for instance, Mans 2004:19). Yet they are not mentioned in his overview.[15] Also, the ethnography by Johannes Malan hardly mentions them, except as "magico-religious specialists and medicine-men" who "have not congregated in any single space but live dispersed among the Himba" (Malan 1974:116).[16]

As in Malan's (1995, 1974, 1973) work, Dhimba usually appear in the margin of anthropological and historiographical accounts on Kaoko and the Namibian-Angolan borderland (see for instance Gewald 1999:12; Bollig 1997:xi; Friedman 2004:32). The most notable exception is Carlos Estermann, a Catholic missionary who arrived in southern Angola in 1923. He compiled his ethnographic writings (Esterman 1981, 1979, 1964, 1954, 1950, 1944, 1935) in a three-volume monography on the peoples of the region.[17] Even though, during the first years of his stay, Estermann was clearly in doubt as to whether or not Dhimba belonged to the Herero cluster, his tome on Herero is heavily based on his experiences with Dhimba, whom he regarded as exemplary for all the Herero-speaking peoples in the region (including Himba, Tjimba, Tjavikwa, Hakaona, Kuvale, and others) (Estermann 1981: vii; but see Estermann 1935:46; 1944:136; also see Redinha 1962; Van Wolputte 2011:65).

To other authors as well, Dhimba posed a problem of classification: among other things, their extensive use of agriculture seemed to contradict their apparent belonging to the "Herero cattle complex" (see Marquardsen and von Stahl 1928; Baumann and Westermann 1948:117; Baumann 1974:484–485; see Heintze 1999:116). In an unfinished draft, Gordon D. Gibson, an American anthropologist who worked on the Namibian-Angolan border region in the early 1970s, formulated it as follows: "the semi-nomadic pastoral groups having a dual descent social organization, with both matrilineal and patrilineal clans, while the settled people practicing a mixed economy having only matrilineal clans."[18]

Gibson was taken aback by the multiethnic reality he experienced whilst on fieldwork. He noted, for instance, how his Dhimba translator Nicolau could not understand an informant talking a cross between Otjitjavikwa and Otjihimba.[19] So Gibson raised questions regarding Estermann's and other experts' working classifications. He regarded the "shared" use of the Herero language as the main ground for Estermann's and others' suppositions. This stimulated him to start an assessment of the degree of relationship between Oludhimba and Otjikuvale languages, on the one hand, and Otjiherero on the other. Regrettably, however, he never finalized his analysis nor arrived at a satisfactory answer.

More questions are raised in the field of linguistic studies. Here, also, Dhimba occupy an in-between position, the main classificatory question being whether Oludhimba is a dialect of Otjiherero or Oshiwambo (Oshindonga), or a language of its own. Zimmerman (1982), for instance, listed the language as a Oshiwambo (Oshindonga) dialect,[20] but in an unpublished paper Kavari and Ohly (1991:1,7) argued that Oludhimba is a proper language that originated in Angola, one that borrows extensively from both Otjiherero and Oshiwambo (Oshindonga) and, in its turn, has considerably influenced both other languages (Kavari and Ohly 1991:16–17). These authors not only challenge the dialect status of Oludhimba; they also argue against the common view of Otjiherero as a homogenous unit. Kavari and Ohly, say that Oludhimba is probably in the process of being transformed from a migrant language into a Herero dialect. Biddulph (1992), in contrast, aimed at highlighting similarities between Otjiherero, Oshindonga, and Oludhimba, and never questioned the status of Oludhimba as a separate language. Then, in 1995, Raimund Ohly (1995:5) published an article in which he wanted to "establish the linguistic position of Dhimba in relation to Herero and Ndonga." Apparently, Ohly had shifted his position, and no longer doubted that Oludhimba constituted a Herero dialect. To some extent, this conclusion is corroborated by Cameron and Kunkel (2002). These authors observed that the understanding of both Otjiherero or Oshindonga by Dhimba speakers rose with their level of education and that "only those Dhimba-speakers with education have any significant levels of understanding Herero or Ndonga" (Cameron and Kunkel 2002:23). As their aim was to investigate whether a Dhimba Bible translation was necessary, they concluded that "a high proportion of Dhimbas do not adequately understand Herero or Ndonga [...] to use the Scriptures in those languages [sic]" (Cameron and Kunkel 2002:4). This points at "a general low level of inherent mutual intelligibility between Dhimba and Ndonga, and between Dhimba and Herero" (Cameron and Kunkel 2002:23), an indication that Oludhimba constitutes a language of its own.

What emerges out of these examples are doubts, confusion, and the lack of unanimity with regard to the ethnographic and linguistic categorization of Dhimba. As Ohly (1995:49) remarks, "Dhimba-speakers are often *trilingual*, i.e. fluent in Herero and Ndonga. Therefore, Dhimba remains a strong means of ethnic identification" (emphasis added).

At stake here is the equation between language and identity, and the validity of *ceteris paribus* models. At the level of academia, linguists often build their argument on the presumption of ethnic-bound "speech communities" (see Le Page and Tabouret-Keller 1985:243). Anthropologists, in contrast, question identity, but assume that languages are "unproblematic indicators of social boundaries" (Gal and Irvin 1995:3; also criticized by Barth 1998; Fabian 1983; Mahmood and Armstrong 1992; Maho 1998; Mudimbe 1988; Said 1978). Language, indeed, is perhaps less a linguistic category than a political one (see, for instance, Barth 1998:11, Chambers and Trudgill 1980:5; Maho 1998:20; Gal and Irvin 1995:15). Also, the distinction between language and dialect is political, and it is probably no coincidence that two local academics (Kavari and Melo) have argued against the overarching ethnographic-cum-linguistic categorizations of their European counterparts (Ohly and Estermann). Kavari (1991), for instance, maintains that the different speeches found in northern Namibia and southern Angola cannot be subsumed under the header of Otjiherero (see above). Also Rosa Melo (2007:45–46) argued against colonizing categories that were geared towards aggregating distinct groups under the broadest possible header. These categories, says Melo, are artificial and external, as local "dialects" often experience "related languages" as completely foreign, both in a linguistic and an ethnic sense (Melo 2007:25–26, 49). As Gordon Gibson noted in his draft:

> The only evidence that Estermann presents that the people of the Dhimba, Kuvale, and other settled peoples of southwest Angola spoke the Herero language is his statement that they did not object when he referred to their language as Herero. At the same time, though, Estermann (1981:2) himself noted that the word Herero probably means "lowland," and thus refers primarily to a region rather than to a people or a language.[21]

Throughout their recent history, Dhimba have indeed occupied a position in between clusters or categories, hovering between pastoralist and horticulturalist, language and dialect, Otjiherero and Oshiwambo, or even Angolan and Namibian. In more than one sense, they live on the border of what itself is already a borderland. This position betwixt and between is a major concern for a newly emerging Dhimba elite wanting to carve out a proper Dhimba niche in the postcolonial landscape by codifying a proper Dhimba cultural and historical heritage, and by attempting to gain official recognition of traditional Dhimba leadership. What their case illustrates is that boundaries are constructed and are politically, ideologically or economically motivated and, by consequence, that it becomes increasingly difficult to consider boundaries as continuous lines of difference (Bashkow 2004:450–453). In what follows, we propose an understanding of boundaries that, besides acting as markers of such difference, also regards them as interactional, processual and relational. As the Dhimba case illustrates, boundaries do not simply divide; they also relate and connect (Brubaker and Cooper 2000:21; Lamont and Molnar 2002; also see Amselle 1998:146; Barth 1998; Kopytoff 1987). It also illustrates that western scholarship has encountered difficulties in accounting for, or dealing with, this ambivalence.

MOVING BEYOND THE FENCE

Kreike (2004:62) pointed out that the colonial divide between Angola and Namibia, which until the 1950s determined not only the political but also the natural landscape east of the Kunene, was as much the product of Portuguese and South African colonial rule, as it was the result of migrations trying to escape the taxes, violence and forced labour in Angola. "Ironically," Kreike wrote:

> The proximity of the colonial border opened up more opportunities than it closed. […] Because the border cut across the floodplain, […] colonial subjects could escape the Portuguese exactions by simply stepping over an imaginary line […]. Yet, once refugees from the north

> had crossed the line into the South African colony, the border became an insurmountable barrier to the Portuguese colonial police. South African officials actively (though clandestinely) encouraged and sponsored in-migration from Angola to increase their migrant labor pool. [Kreike 2004:70–7]

Other than in the region described by Kreike, contract labour recruitment in Kaoko as a whole remained rather low. In 1952, for instance, the South West Africa Native Labor Association (Pty.) Ltd. (SWANLA) interviewed young men in (mainly southern) Kaoko about whether they were prepared to do farm labour; only one out of 163 interviewees answered in the affirmative.

> Notwithstanding the attitude adopted by the OvaHimba's, it is felt that most of our labor will be recruited from amongst them. Recruiting can almost be described as a full-time job. Most werfs [homesteads] cannot be reached by car as they are situated between or against mountains and away from any existing road. The inhabitants have been instructed to remedy this matter and to either build roads leading to their werfs or to move to localities near the road (...). As soon as this has been completed it is intended launching an intensive recruiting campaign throughout the Kaokoveld and Zessfontein, visiting each werf and interviewing each and every able-bodied young native who, in my opinion, should be working.[22]

The SWANLA report attributed the unwillingness to accept *mutete* (contract labour) to the conservatism of the

Himba, the mountainous landscape, and the lack of infrastructure in Kaoko; state ethnologist van Warmelo (1962:34) mentioned the "prevalence of dysentery and venereal disease" as a major reason. Employment numbers in Kaoko, indeed, remained quite low until the mid 1970s, when the contract labour system was abandoned and a relatively large group of young men voluntarily or involuntarily, joined the South African military and police forces to escape the combined consequences of violence and drought.

There are, however a few elements that provide a more sound explanation for this overall lack of labour recruitment. First of all, Kaoko was purposely isolated from the rest of Namibia (see this chapter's introduction), and within Kaoko, employment opportunities were very few. Secondly, the marginalized character of the region —its remoteness and lack of infrastructure— meant that investment costs to find new labourers were rather high (see Friedman 2004:67). The SWAA, moreover, was reluctant to invest means and manpower in the region, at least until after the outbreak of the conflicts in Namibia and Angola: a hospital and local post office were built only in the early 1970s (see Van Wolputte 2007). From 1926 —when white settlers were expelled from Kaoko and resettled around Outjo— until the late 1960s, early 1970s, the colonial presence in Opuwo amounted to a handful of officials, whose stay in Kaoko was just a temporary assignment. Finally, the Kaoko Tribal Council also resisted the contract labour system, even if their objections mainly focussed on the long term (18 to 24 months) labour contracts, rather than on the idea of contract work itself.

This, however, does not tell the entire story, and, when it came to contract work considerable differences existed between the northern and southern part of Kaoko. Despite the overall low recruitment numbers, in the period between the 1950s and 1970s quite a number of young men were persuaded to engage in contract labour on the farms, in the cities, and in the mines in the Police Zone. Most of these young men came from southern Kaoko, usually from villages near the main road (such as Sesfontein, Oruvandji, Otjozongombe, Ombombo, Kaoko Otavi, Okorosave).

Our interviews also suggest that these young men were not recruited in Kaoko. In 1954, SWANLA stopped its operations in the region due to its limited success and the civil administration (SWAA) took charge of recruitment and the transporting the workers to the SWANLA office in Ondangwa, Oshana Region (Bollig 1998b:525).[23] However, as the SWAA truck only left occasionally for Ondangwa, most former contract workers made their way to the SWANLA office on foot. Once there, they were registered as "Ambo." The actual number of contract workers from Kaoko was, hence, probably higher than colonial statistics indicate.

Most contract workers in Namibia and South Africa were forced to move from one contract to the next. The contract workers from southern Kaoko, however, only went on *mutete* once or twice during their lifetime. In their accounts, going on contract was primarily perceived as a transition ritual, from *omuzandu* (boy) to *omurumendu* (man), which implied a move to and fro between *ehi indi* (this world or land), and *ouye warwe* or *ouye oupe* (the "new" or "other" world behind the fence).

> Long ago when people went on contract, they were going there on foot. They went from here to Ondangwa. When you arrived at Ondangwa you got a health check, they checked in different ways, some (of the methods) were that bad that I can't mention them. They checked whether you had gonorrhea, they checked your eyes, and whether you had ever broken your arm (…). From Ongandwa, the contract workers continued to Otjivanda (Grootfontein).

> There they were assigned to the different jobs, to farms, to mines, to work in towns, it was like that (…). The day they took you from Ondangwa, they gave you grey shorts and a shirt —like a uniform, so that everybody looked the same. They also gave you a metal tag you carried around your neck, so that everywhere, people could check your tag and know where you were sent to [Interview with Christoph Kavari by L. Bleckmann, February 2008]

As Cristoph Kavari testifies, these young men's itineraries —a common trope in Herero memory practices— implied a number of border crossings. Besides legally or illegally crossing the administrative divides with the Police Zone and with the North Central regions prospective labourers had to overcome linguistic and cultural, not to mention political boundaries. However, it was in the SWANLA camp that the fundamental boundaries of body and self were transgressed, as workers underwent a humiliating medical check to be classified (or commodified) into different categories of physical aptness (also see Gordon 1977:95; Kreike 2004:93; Silvester 1998:139). Their hair was cut and they received the khaki camp uniform and a Christian name; many interviewees remembered how they were addressed and registered as Ambo labourers. From the camp they were then taken to the farms, mines, industries, and cities in the south. This transition —from Kaoko to the SWANLA camp in Ondangwa and from there to the Police Zone— also signalled the transition into a different political and moral landscape.

Most contract workers regarded apartheid (translated as *ombangu*, the first —general— meaning of which is "difference" or "distinction") as something from the outside or other world, a point also underscored by John Friedman (2004:67): "For the majority of Kaokolanders, apartheid was something that was to be experienced most profoundly elsewhere." Partly, this can be attributed to the limited and "arterial" character of the South African presence in Kaoko during the period considered (see above). Other than in the Police Zone, apartheid in Kaoko percolated only very slowly into the minute particulars of everyday life.

But the notion of apartheid solicited different and often contradictory meanings. In the context of contract labour, former contract workers experienced ombangu (in the sense of apartheid) not as a characteristic of a system of racial segregation, but as a personal trait: some employers *had* ombangu, others did not. When discussing contract labour, our interviewees usually understood ombangu (in the primary sense of "difference") as inherent to the hierarchy of the work setting. Only very few recollections questioned this hierarchy, and most considered it a normal outcome of the employer-employee relationship, rather than as an outcome of a systematic policy — the expropriation and creation of deprived so-called Homelands to force the African population into migrant labour (Gordon, 1977). Instead, most contract workers regarded it as obvious that their *omuhona* (employer) enjoyed a privileged and dominant position from which to give orders and, even, to punish. At the same time, though, they also expected a certain degree of care and protection, in line with the existing institution of "big men" or patron (also translated as *omuhona*) in Herero society (see Van Wolputte 2011).

"Real" *ombangu* (apartheid) started only after work, when the workers went to their compound, and their *baas* (boss, omuhona) to his house. However, even more compelling than this spatial segregation were the many and rigid rules that governed daily life both in the public and private sphere. These kind of differences made people "experience apartheid":

> Sometimes, the moment you got out of the shop with your white bread, like the one you

> tasted at your boss's place, you met with the police. They would ask you "who is the owner of the bread?" and you reply "I am." Then they would ask, "who gave you the permission to eat this bread?" and put you in prison. Then I had to buy a brown bread, that used to be eaten by blacks. When you bought a white bread, you had to hide it. Into those shops of the whites, blacks were even not allowed to enter, only when your boss had sent you to buy his groceries. [Interview with Karunambota Nderura by L. Bleckmann, July 2008]

"Difference" was part of common demeanour and comportment; as Gordon already noted:

> In order to "stay out of trouble" a Black must behave with proper demeanor and show the required deference to Whites. Under all circumstances his language should be politely toned, honorific and appreciative of the smallest favor or even non-favor. The same applies to his comportment and features. [Gordon 1977:122]

Yet, former contract workers played down the impact apartheid had on them, for instance by stating that corporeal punishment was "part of the job"; they, in contrast, emphasized that leaving for contract was an initiation into adulthood, a rite of passage that led into the unknown "other" world and from where one would return with cash and with commodities that, in Kaoko, were expensive and hard to get. Leaving for contract work in the outer world held the promise one would return as a *omuhenendu*, a "somebody," epitomized in the trendy *pantsula* style that had originated in the South African townships, and was reflected in the hats, suits, shoes, and other commodities (such as cloth, Singer sewing machines, …) returning contract workers brought home. As Sam Herunga from Okahwa testified, "When I went to do contract work, I was becoming a young man. I wanted to have my own clothes and my own cattle, that's why the idea crossed my mind that I should go" (interview with Sam Herunga by L. Bleckmann, july 2008).

All in all, memories and attitudes towards contract work were highly ambivalent rather than univocally "bad." Many informants, for instance, switched to Afrikaans when recalling their time on contract —sometimes entire accounts were presented in the former "master" language. Also, in daily life, they turned to Afrikaans to curse (*Bliksem! Fok!*), or address their friends with an ironic *Ey kaffer!* or *Kartoffelschwein!* (potato pig). Such code-switching, and the mimetic use of derogatory terms, suggest that the experience of contract work was much more ambiguous than the public transcript of these experiences suggests (see Gordon 1977: Scott 1990; Taussig 1993).

This ambiguity also surfaces in former contract worker's nostalgia for colonial times, for instance when they deplore the loss of values such as "hard work" or "merit" and contrast them to today's "corruption" and "nepotism," or when they state that new forms of ombangu (apartheid) have replaced the former ones. These sentiments, however, need to be placed against today's socio-historical and political background. As Bissell formulated it:

> Nostalgia is shaped by specific cultural concerns and struggles; and as with other forms of memory practice, it can only be understood in particular historical and spatial contexts... [It is] a mode of social memory by emphasizing distance and disjuncture, utilizing these diacritics of modernity as a means of critically framing the present. [Bissell 2005:216]

Memories of contract work underline that when on contract work, there was (some) room for upward mobility, as long as one displayed the proper demeanor of a "good" and "obedient" colonial subject: one could enjoy favours (such as eating white bread), climb up the hierarchy, or even invest one's earning in cattle or commodities. This mobility, informants felt, is not offered by the customary system of inheritance (based on kinship), nor by the formal or informal economy in the Namibian post-colony. The young men who left Kaoko to go on contract, nowadays feel neglected by the post-colonial government, partly because:

> More and more often, the government is drawing its legitimacy from the moral weight of the nationalist past, especially from the heroics of the liberation struggle. The structures within the party are divided into ranks according to seniority, that is according to party members' involvement in the liberation struggle or their long-term commitment to party politics. [Fumanti 2007:169]

In popular imagination, people in Kaoko did not make part of this nationalist past: after the contract labour system was abandoned in the early 1970s, the outbreak of the armed conflicts in Namibia and Angola led to a militarization and (hence) monetization of the northwestern Namibian border region. This, combined with a severe drought between 1978 and 1981, pushed a relative high number of men into the South African military and police forces stationed in Kaoko. Also, due to the effects of South African propaganda and internal political struggle, after independence the Kaoko elite felt ostracized and excluded by the new postcolonial government. Nostalgic memories of colonial rule should hence be comprehended as, in the words of John Friedman (2004:46), a "Kaokoland critique" of postcolonial Namibia (also see Battaglia 2005; de Boeck 1998; Werbner 1998).

CONCLUSION

This chapter presented two case studies of border-crossing under colonial rule. They warn us that colonial rule was highly uncertain and ambiguous. Our first case, on Dhimba ethnicity, illustrated how changeable and mutable colonial categorizations were (and are). The second case, on Herero contract workers, illustrates to what extent these colonial boundaries had different meanings: despite Kaoko's status as a native reserve, and despite the fences that surrounded it, apartheid was seen as belonging to the "outside world." Also, despite memories of violence and racial segregation, apartheid was experienced mainly "after hours." The nostalgia that permeates these memories of colonial rule, however, should be understood as a contemporary commentary on modernism and postcolonial governance.

The cases of Dhimba in northern Kaoko, and of the contract workers from southern Kaoko draw our attention to the paradoxical and sometimes divergent meanings of "borders" in an African borderland. First of all, Kaoko was at the divide between two colonial regimes —a difference that had less to do with the supposed intrinsic characteristics of Lusophone versus Anglophone colonization than with the way these regimes responded to local and national political and economic contingencies. Secondly, Kaoko was made into a buffer zone between central and southern Africa, according to the SWAA to safeguard the latter from animal diseases that threatened the artificial white monopoly on the (legal) trade in animals and animal products. The creation of this buffer zone, thirdly, also implied that the first decades under South African rule witnessed a policy of, as Michael Bollig (1998:506) phrased it, "isolation and encapsulation." Efforts were made to close off the northern border (the Kunene River) to the "illegal" trafficking of livestock and people, and Kaoko's eastern border (with the North-Central Regions, Namibia) and its southern border (with the Police Zone) were fenced. The region was hemmed in by so-called cattle-free zones (on the map in van Warmelo's "Notes" indicated as "uninhabited areas"). Finally, the geographical gerrymandering also implied an ethnographic gerrymandering, in that distinctions between socio-economic groups and political factions within Kaoko were re-interpreted as constituting essential divides between ethnic groups.

Yet, colonial rule in Kaoko can best be described as arterial (as opposed to capillary), and colonial surveillance was limited to the view from the main road: if Kaoko was marginal to the South African state (at least when judged in terms of means and manpower invested in Kaoko's colonial administration), so was the colonial state situated in the margins of daily life in large parts of Kaoko. Hence it constitutes somewhat of a paradox that, in many regards, the impact of colonial gerrymandering was felt hardest in the post-colony. In the Kaoko Tribal Council, for instance, the conflict between the "big group" and the "small group" around Muzuma and Tjiyahura dated back to the tensions between two political factions in Kaoko in the 1910s, but only led to conflict and formal fissioning in the 1980s. Nowadays, the political landscape in Kaoko is dominated by the Otjikaoko Traditional Authority (the original "big group"), and the Vita Thom Royal House Traditional Authority (the original "small group"). This oligarchy, however, is challenged by smaller groups (such as the newly established traditional authority of Kakurukouye, or by Dhimba) who invoke ethnic identity and historical, sometimes linguistic, particularity to demand political representation and recognition as a distinct tradition. In that sense, it seems paradoxical that, under apartheid, political factions in Kaoko stressed their common origin and background, whilst after apartheid they insisted on their differences. In that sense, the grass is always greener on the other side of the fence.

ACKNOWLEDGEMENTS

Our research was made possible by the project *Beyond the border: the political ecology of the Kunene frontier, 1850-1950* (G.0251.07N), funded by the Research Foundation – Flanders (Fonds voor Wetenschappelijk Onderzoek – Vlaanderen), and by successive research grants by the same institution.

NOTES

[1] The three of us conducted extensive anthropological fieldwork in northern Namibia, in the rural settlements in western Kaoko and in Opuwo (Van Wolputte, 1995–present), southern Kaoko and Opuwo (Bleckmann, 2007–present), and in Ruacana (Hoorelbeke, 2007–present). Where possible, these findings were complemented by archival research.

[2] NAN BOP 34 4/17/2 J.S. Malan to Hoofdbantusakekommissaris Windhoek, *Noodweiding in Wildreservaat*, January 13 1969, our translation. In the early 1970s, J.S. Malan would become the author of a few influential ethnographic articles on the region and its inhabitants. His ethnography was based on his fieldwork as a civil servant in the northern Kunene Region (see Malan 1973, 1974).

[3] NAN BOP 34 4/17/2 Joel Tjihahurua. Letter to the Administrator of SWA and the Chief Bantu Affairs Officer of SWA, in J.S. Malan, Noodweiding in Wildreservaat, January 13 1969.

[4] NAN BOP 34 4/17/2 Kefas Mazuma, *letter to Sy Edele die Administrateur van SWA and die HBSK van SWA*, undated (prob. January 1969), in J.S. Malan, *Noodweiding in Wildreservaat*, January 13 1969. Our translation.

[5] See also Owen-Smith 2010:86–91, 135–136.

[6] The rivalry between these two (and, nowadays, three) political factions goes back to the end of the 19th century (Friedman 2004). These tensions have overshadowed local politics ever since; culminating in an open conflict after the events of January 1969.

[7] Miescher (2010:23) describes how this fence was conceived as an *Imperiale Barbarengrenze*, that demarcated the South Afri can empire from the wilderness.

[8] Pass laws were introduced following the so-called *Eingeborenenverordnung* in 1907; the Vagrancy Act of 1920 restricted the free movement of Africans within the Police Zone.

[9] "Ein echtes Herrenvolk mit vielen guten Seiten und allen schlechten Eigenschaften eines solchen" (Vedder 1991:45).

[10] "Konserwatiewe mense wat haas nie meer inpas bij die dinge van vandaag nie" (Bruwer 1968:15).

[11] For details on this aspect of Kaoko's history, see Bollig 1997:21–28 and, especially, Friedman 2004.

[12] After all, it concerns groups who lived intermixed, speaking mutually understandable languages, and sharing cultural backgrounds. Differences between these ethnic groups can largely be traced back to socio-economic stratification, a different pattern of consumption, and, more recently, political claims (see Bollig 1997:22, 1998; Van Wolputte 2004).

[13] NAN BOP N1/15/2, Hoofbantoekommissaris SWA (J. J. van der Watt), Wetgewing van toepassing op naturelle en naturellegebiede in SWA (1969).

[14] NAN BOP 5 N1/15/4/3, Administratief Beampte (B.J. Marais), Notule van vergadering met hoofmanne: Kaokoveld 20 tot 23 maart 1962 (March 24 1962), pp. 11–13.

[15] Personal communication of Van Warmelo with the official photographer of the Cape Town museum, Alice Mertens, in 1959, illustrates that he is unaware of any Dhimba presence near Ruacana. (NAN Van Warmelo, Personal Notes).

[16] Nowadays, most Dhimba designate the border land between North-West Namibia (Etunda, Ruacana, Etoto, Opuwo, and Okangwati) and South-West Angola (Chitado, Otchinjau, Cahama, Tchipelongo) as their "home."

[17] These three volumes (on Non-Bantu and Ambo, Nyaneka-Nkumbi, and Herero) were first published in Portuguese between 1956 and 1961. An

English translation, edited and translated by Gibson, appeared in 1981.

[18] Papers of Gordon G. Gibson, n.d., box 36: 4. Gibson left his archive, including field notes, ethnographic films, unfinished articles, and a draft of his unfinished book (on "Himba and related people of S.W. Angola and N.W. Namibia, Herero speakers of Angola") to the National Anthropological Archives of the Smithsonian Institute (Wang 2009).

[19] Papers of Gordon D. Gibson, box 46, Zimba notes for filing.

[20] Later, however, he omitted Oludhimba from his list of Oshiwambo dialects (Zimmermann 1982).

[21] Papers of Gordon D. Gibson, n.d., box 36: 4, last revision 1999.

[22] NAN SWAA 2515 A552/18/18, SWANLA, Report on a visit to the Kaokoveld, January 6 1952.

[23] NAN SWAA/1060, A 135/46. Application for Hawkers Licence: Simon Kaatendekua. 1 December 1951.

REFERENCES

Amselle, J.-L. 1998. Mestizo logics: Anthropology of identity in Africa and elsewhere. Stanford: Stanford University Press.

Barth, F. 1998 [1969]. Ethnic groups and boundaries: The social organization of culture difference. Illinois: Waveland Press.

Baumann, H. 1974. Die Südwest-Bantu-Provinz (inkl. Jägerreste SW-Angolas). *In* Die Völker Afrikas und ihre traditionellen Kulturen. Teil 1: Allgemeiner Teil und südliches Afrika. H. Baumann, ed. Pp.473–511. Wiesbaden: Steiner.

Baumann H. and D. Westermann 1948 Les peuples et les civilizations de l'Afrique suivi de les langues et l'éducation. Paris: Payot.

Bashkow, I. 2004. A Neo-Boasian Conception of Cultural Boundaries.

Battaglia, D. 1995. On practical nostalgia: self-prospecting among urban Trobrianders. *In* D. Battaglia, ed. Rhetorics of self-making. Pp. 77–96. Berkeley: University of California Press.

Biddulph, J. 1992. Meet me in Windhoek: Notes on four Bantu languages of Namibia —Herero, Ndonga, Kwanyama, Dhimba. Pontypridd: Biddulph Publications.

Bissell, G. 2005. Engaging Colonial Nostalgia. Cultural Anthropology, 20(2):215–248.

Baumann H. and D. Westermann. 1948. Les peuples et les civilizations de l'Afrique suivi de les langues et l'éducation. Paris: Payot.

Bollig, M. 1998b. The colonial encapsulation of the north-western Namibian

pastoral economy. Africa 68(4):506–536.
——— 1998a. Power and trade in precolonial and early colonial Northern Kaokoland 1860s-1940s. *In* Namibia under South African rule. Mobility and containment 1915–1946. P. Hayes, J. Silvester, M. Wallace and W. Hartmann, eds. Pp. 175–193. Oxford: James Currey.
——— 1997. "When war came the cattle slept." Himba oral traditions. Köln: Rüdiger Köppe Verlag.
Brubaker, R. and F. Cooper (2000). Beyond 'Identity'. Theory and Society 29:1–47.
Bruwer, J. P. 1968. Land van die swervende Himba. Die huisgenoot 26(1):12–15.
Cameron, B. and J. Kunkel. 2002. A sociolinguistic survey of the Dhimba language. Dallas: Lutheran bible translators. Electronic document. http://www.sil.org/silesr/2002/SILESR2002-070.pdf, accessed Jan. 14, 2012.
Chambers, J.K. and P. Trudgill. 1980. Dialectology. Cambridge: Cambridge University Press.
Cole, J. 2001. Forget colonialism? Sacrifice and the art of memory in Madagascar. Berkeley: University of California Press.
De Boeck, F. 1998. Beyond the grave. History, memory and death in postcolonial Congo/Zaire. *In* R. Werbner, ed. Memory and the postcolony: African anthropology and the critique of power. Pp. 21–57. London: Zed Books.
Estermann, C. 1981. The ethnography of southwestern Angola III: the Herero people. New York: Africana Publishing Company. Ed. by Gordon D. Gibson.
——— 1979. The ethnography of southwestern Angola II: the Nyaneka-Nkumbi. New York: Africana Publishing Company. Ed. by Gordon D. Gibson.
———1964. Les Bantous du sud-ouest de l'angola. Anthropos 59:20–74.
———1954. Culte des esprits et magie chez les Bantous du sud-ouest de l'Angola. Anthropos 49:1–26.
——— 1950. Le bétail sacré chez quelques tribus du sud-ouest de l'Angola. Anthropos 45:721–732.
——— 1944. A festa da puberdade em algumas tribos de Angola meridional. Portugal em Africa 2(1):340–351.
——— 1935. Notas etnograficas sobre os povos indigenas do distrito da huila. Boletim Geral das colonias, ano XI, n.115:41–69.
Fabian, J. 1983. Time and the other. New York: Columbia University Press.
Friedman, John T. 2005. Making politics, making history: chiefship and the post-apartheid state in Namibia. Journal of Southern African Studies 31(1): 23–51.
——— 2004. Imagining the post-apartheid state: An ethnographic account

of Namibia. Unpublished Ph.D. dissertation, Darwin College, University of Cambridge.
Fumanti, M. 2007. Imagining post-apartheid society and culture. Playfulness, officialdom and civility in a youth elite club in northern Namibia. *In* Transitions in Namibia. Which changes for whom? H. Melber, ed. Pp. 153–172, Uppsala: Nordiska Afrika Institutet.
Gal, S. and J. T. Irvin. 1995. The boundaries of languages and disciplines: How ideologies construct difference. Social Research 62(4):967–1001.
Gewald, J.-B. 1999. Herero heroes: A socio-political history of the Herero of Namibia 1890–1923. Oxford: James Currey.
Gibson, G. D. 1977. Himba epochs. History in Africa 4:67-121.
Gordon, R. J. 1977. Mines, migrants and masters. Johannesburg: Ravan.
Heintze, B. 1990. In pursuit of a chameleon: Early ethnographic photography from Angola in context. History in Africa 17:131–156.
Kavari, J. U. 1991. Dialects of Herero. Paper presented at the conference *Language ecology in Africa* held at the University of Namibia, Windhoek, September 1991.
Kavari, J. U. and R. Ohly. 1991. The Question of Herero Dialects. Unpublished paper.
Kopytoff, I. 1987. The African frontier: The reproduction of traditional African societies. Bloomington: Indiana University Press.
Kreike, E. 2004. Re-creating Eden. Land use, environment, and society in southern Angola and northern Namibia. Portsmouth, NH: Heinemann.
Lamont, M. and V. Molnar. 2002. The study of boundaries in the social sciences. Annual Review of Sociology 28:167–195.
Le Page, R. B. and A. Tabouret-Keller. 1985. Acts of identity: Creole-based approaches to language and ethnicity. Cambridge: Cambridge University Press.
Mahmood, C. K. and S. L. Armstrong. 1992. Do ethnic groups exist? A cognitive perspective on the concept of cultures. Ethnology 31(1):1–14.
Maho, J. F. 1998. Few people, many tongues: The languages of Namibia. Windhoek: Gamsberg MacMillan Publishers.
Malan, J.S. 1995. Peoples of Namibia. Pretoria: Rhino Publishers.
——— 1974. The Herero-speaking peoples of Kaokoland. Cimbebasia, ser. B, 2(4):113–129.
——— 1973. Double Descent among the Himba of South West Africa. Cimbebasia (B) 2 (3):81–112.
Mans, M. 2004. Discover musical cultures in the Kunene: A guide to the living music and dance of Namibia. Windhoek: Namibian Scientific Society.
Marquardsen, H. and A. von Stahl. 1928. Angola. Berlin: Dietrich Reimer.
Melo, R. 2007. Homem é homem, mulher é sapo: Género e identidade entre

os Handa no sul de Angola. Lisboa: Edições Colibri.
Miescher, G. 2010 Die Rote Linie. Die Geschichte der Veterinär– und Siedlungsgrenze in Namibia (1890er –1960er Jahre). Unpublished Ph.D. Dissertation, University of Basel.
Mudimbe, V. Y. 1988. The invention of Africa. Bloomington: Indiana University Press.
Ohly, R. 1995. Dhimba a Herero dialect. Studies of the Department of African Languages and Cultures 18:5–52.
Owen-Smith, G. 2010. An Arid Eden: A Personal Account of Conservation in the Kaokoveld. Johannesburg: Jonathan Ball Publishers.
Redinha, J. 1974. Etnias e culturas de Angola. Luanda: Ediçao do instituto de investigaçao cientifica de Angola com a colaboraçao do banco de Angola.
Rizzo, L. 2007. The elephant shooting: colonial law and indirect rule in Kaoko, northwestern Namibia, in the 1920s and 1930s. The Journal of African History 48(2):245–266.
Said, E. 1978. Orientalism. New York: Pantheon.
Scott, J. C. 1990. Domination and the Arts of Resistance: Hidden Transcripts. London: Yale University Press.
Silvester, J. 1998. Beasts, boundaries and buildings. The survival and creation of pastoral economies in southern Namibia 1915-1935. *In* Namibia under South African rule. Mobility and containment 1915–1946. P. Hayes, J. Silvester, M. Wallace and W. Hartmann, eds. Pp. 96–116. Oxford: James Curry.
Steinmetz, G. 2007. The devil's handwriting. Precoloniality and the German colonial state in Qindao, Samoa, and Southwest Africa. Chicago: Chicago University Press.
Taussig, M. 1993. Mimesis and Alterity.A Particular History of the Senses. New York: Routledge.
Van Warmelo, N.J. 1962 [1951]. Notes on the Kaokoveld (South West Africa) and its people. Ethnological Publications 26. Pretoria: Govt. printer.
Van Wolputte, Steven. 2011. Twins and Intertwinement. Ambivalence and ambiguity in northern Namibia. *In* Twins in Africa and diaspora cultures. Double trouble or twice blessed. P. Peek, ed. Pp. 61–78. Bloomington: Indiana University Press,
——— 2007. Cattle works: livestock policy, apartheid and development in Northwest Namibia, c. 1920-1980. African Studies, 66(1):103–128.
——— 2004. Subject Disobedience. The colonial narrative and native counterworks in Northwestern Namibia, ca 1920-1975. History and anthropology 15(2):151–173.
Vedder, H. 1991 [1934]. Das alte Sudwestafrika. Die Geschichte Sudwestafrikas bis zum Tode Mahareros 1890. Windhoek: Wissenschaftli-

che Gesellschaft.
Wang, L. 2009. Register to the Papers of Gordon D. Gibson. National Anthropological Archives, Smithsonian Institution.
Wallace, M. 2011. A history of Namibia. London: C. Hurst & Co.
Werbner, R. 1998. Beyond Oblivion: confronting memory crisis. *In* R. Werbner, ed. Memory and the postcolony. African anthropology and the critique of power. Pp. 1–17. London: Zed Books.
Werner, W. 1998. 'No one will become rich': economy and society in the Herero reserves in Namibia, 1915–1946. Basel: Schlettwein Publishing.
Wilmsen, E. N. 1989. Land filled with flies. A political economy of the Kalahari. Chicago: University of Chicago Press.
Zimmermann, W. 1982. Ondersoek an die onderwijs in SWA/Namibië. Windhoek: Star Binder and Printers.

7
ON THE BORDERS OF RACE, MISSION, AND STATE: AFRICAN AMERICANS AND THE AMERICAN PRESBYTERIAN CONGO MISSION

Ira Dworkin

Beginning in the late 1880s, William Henry Sheppard, an African American minister, repeatedly requested that the southern Presbyterian Church (US) send him to Africa as a missionary.[1] The church refused his application, as it had no existing African missions and was unwilling to appoint a black man to pioneer one. Eventually, the church found Samuel Norvell Lapsley, a white minister and son of a well-connected Alabama judge, who was willing to accompany Sheppard. In 1890 the two men co-pioneered the American Presbyterian Congo Mission (APCM) in the Kasai region of the Congo state (*l'État Indépendant du Congo,* Phipps 2002:11–13), which was, as a result of the 1884–1885 Berlin Conference, the personal dominion of King Leopold II of Belgium. Lapsley, however, died in 1892, leaving the mission under the leadership of Sheppard. Soon thereafter, Sheppard returned to the US on furlough and recruited four other college-educated African Americans to the APCM. These and subsequent African American recruits created the decade-long anomaly of a majority-black, racially-integrated African mission representing a racially-segregated US church.

This essay explores how American racial dynamics shaped the church's relationship with the colonial state, which remained under Leopold's rule until 1908, when international pressure forced him to cede control to the Belgian Government. Like other missions, the APCM served the colonial state in obvious ways by providing educational and medical services to its subjects. However, during the APCM's early years, Sheppard and his colleagues worked to develop an independent mission that, although it shared the central principles of the church, took concern for human rights and respect for African culture —including language— seriously. Furthermore, during the early decades of the APCM, when the mission was staffed by a substantial cohort of African Americans, the church did not see itself as beholden to the state's interests, a relationship that would change markedly with the whitening of the mission.

***

Sheppard, a 25 year-old Virginian who attended Hampton Institute, had, like many African Americans of his generation, a regnant desire to go to Africa. After attending seminary at Tuscaloosa Theological Institute (later renamed Stillman Institute) in Alabama, he actively pursued his dream. While the church, which had few African American members in its US congregations, was struggling to recruit whites (of varying qualifications and racial attitudes) to its ranks, the mission was under the effective direction of Sheppard, its senior member, for most of its first 10 years.

As the APCM was increasingly staffed by a group of highly-educated African Americans, there was an intense push by church officials to maintain white leadership in the field. The pages of the *Missionary*, an official organ of the southern Presbyterian Church, were littered with appeals for white missionaries in language indicative of US domestic racial politics

—which informed the work of the APCM. For example, in September 1895, under the headline "Help Needed for Africa," Samuel H. Chester, Secretary of the Committee of Foreign Missions for the Presbyterian Church (US), requested;

> four additional white men, one of these to be stationed at Matadi, one at Lukunga, one at Leopoldville, and one at Luebo. On account of "The State," with which we have relations of many kinds, it is desirable to have white men at all these points to represent the business interests of the mission. Outside of this, our policy is to reinforce the mission chiefly with colored men. More of these are offering than we are able to send, but at present no white man is offering for the African work. […] Dr. [De Witt] and Mrs. [May] Snyder ought to be brought home at once, to recuperate their strength but they *will not* come till their places are supplied. [Chester 1895a:398]

The candour of the *Missionary* draws attention to the centrality of race to the mission. Remarkably, the Presbyterian Church appears willing to sacrifice the physical health of two missionaries on an altar of white supremacy. The supposed "business interests of the mission" enabled the APCM to attribute its racial hierarchy to "The State," without ever claiming ownership of the policy.

One month later, Chester became less demanding in terms of the quantity and quality of missionaries needed. The only credential was that they be white:

> On account of relations with "The State," and for other reasons, it is absolutely necessary that we have one white man, and very desirable that we have a least two, in our mission work on

> the Congo. Dr. Snyder, the only white man now connected with that work, will be compelled to come home for rest very soon, in order to save his own life and that of his noble and devoted wife. [...] A full medical education is not essential, neither is it essential that one should have any seminary training, or be an ordained minister, though both of these are desirable. [Chester 1895b:446–447]

Chester's repeated references to "The State" appear to be an attempt to explain the APCM's racial policies as politically expedient rather than as a racist doctrine. Meanwhile, the church's strong desire to appease "The State," and its recognition that such appeasement had a racial dimension, reveal how the borders separating the mission and the colonial regime were bridged on the basis of white supremacy.

The pleas of the Committee for Foreign Missions were bolstered by a personal appeal that May Snyder, De Witt's "noble and devoted wife," wrote at around the same time: "My dear husband is now longing for at least one white male helper, but his constant reply to my question, 'Do you really think they mean to send any more white missionaries here?' is, 'This is the Lord's work. He knows our need. He will take care of it'" (Snyder 1896:78).

Between Snyder and Chester, such desperate pleas for white missionaries conflate the racial needs of "The State" with the "Lord's work." The results were often tragic. In November 1895, one month after Chester and Snyder's appeals, the Presbyterian Mission Board announced the appointment of Samuel Phillips Verner, who was ordained without any seminary education (three years typically were required for appointment) under the "extraordinary clause" emergency provision of the church's charter, and despite having suffered a nervous breakdown three years earlier (Crawford 1982:45).

Verner's disastrous tenure ended after two years, but not before he could purchase two African boys (Crawford 1982:57 n.54) who he "offered to rent" to the Smithsonian Institute in Washington (Bradford and Blume 1992:92). A few years later, his mission experience enabled him to sign a contract with the 1904 St. Louis Fair to bring Congolese people for public display. The group included Ota Benga, who Verner infamously displayed at the Bronx Zoo and the American Museum of Natural History in New York, and who committed suicide in Virginia in 1916 (Bradford and Blume 1992:218). After leaving the mission, Verner "faithfully allied himself with the Leopold regime," which raised the ire of his former colleagues (Morrison 1996c:245).

While Verner's emergency appointment was rooted in the pressing need to replace De Witt Snyder, the *Missionary*, interestingly enough, published May Snyder's plea in 1896, a few months after Verner had already been hired. The church, therefore, used Snyder's heartfelt letter to establish an ongoing racial hiring practice independent of the most immediate need for which she appeals. The church's white recruitment policy continued with explicit appeals in the *Missionary* even after the unceremonious end of Verner's tour in 1898 (*Missionary* 1898, 1902a, 1902b). This approach contrasts sharply to William Sheppard's recruitment of African Americans, many of whom had a longstanding interest in Africa, which Sheppard's writings and speeches were able to draw upon. During his 1893–1894 furlough, his first recruit was his fiancée, Lucy Gantt. The couple got engaged prior to his 1890 departure and were married in Jacksonville, Florida, in February 1894. Lucy, a graduate of Talladega College in Alabama, returned with William to Congo in 1894 along with two other Talladega graduates, Maria Fearing and Lillian Thomas, and a Stillman graduate, Henry Hawkins.

William Sheppard attracted a dedicated missionary contingent of talented men and women, such as Fearing, who was 56 years old in 1894. At Talladega, Fearing had been a dorm mother and roommate to Lucy Gantt, the school's youngest student when she entered at the age of 11. Fearing's "long cherished desire to be a missionary to Africa, was so deeply stirred and quickened by a visit and address from Mr. Sheppard, that she at once wrote to the Committee in Nashville, offering her services on the conditions named" (*Missionary* 1894:273). Her commitment was so strong that after being refused a salaried position, due to her age, she sold her house to Samuel Lapsley's father and used the proceeds to finance her passage to, and her work in, Congo.

> After she had been there about two years, our Executive Committee [of Foreign Missions], having heard how she had mastered the native language and of her ever-increasing efficiency in the work of the Mission, appointed her as a regular missionary under their care, at half the salary of a single worker. A few months later her salary was increased to the same amount as that paid to each individual missionary. [Edmiston 1937:18]

Fearing's sacrifices expose a gap between the enthusiasm of African Americans and their reluctant acceptance by the Executive Committee.

The influence of William Sheppard's speeches and publications, while not easily quantifiable, extended well beyond the influence of missionaries like Fearing, who sold their homes to join the mission. His work as a recruiter and lecturer at Historically Black Colleges and Universities (HBCUs), none of which, with the exception of Stillman, had any Presbyterian (US) affiliation, suggests that his missionary career in the African American community ran parallel to its official church career. For example, Sheppard collected hundreds of artifacts and textiles during his trip, which, according to an 1890 letter to the Hampton Principal Samuel Chapman Armstrong, he intended for the "Curiosity Room" at the school (Sheppard 1891:168). From the start, then, Sheppard intended for his mission work to directly serve Hampton as it did the church that appointed him.

In addition to the success of the Sheppards in recruiting black missionaries, William Sheppard's unique work in Congo was lauded by his white colleagues from the start. In an October 1890 letter to the *Missionary*, Lapsley writes that Sheppard:

> has won the esteem of all the missionaries as a true man and a gentleman, while with the natives he is, according to Dr. [Aaron] Sims [of the American Baptist Missionary Union], the most popular man that ever came to this station. He has the constitution needed, and the gift of getting on in Africa. While I was away he devoted much time to hunting on the river, and has actually brought home twelve "hippos," to the great delight of the blacks and admiration of Europeans. Dr. Sims, who has known and treated almost every important worker on the Upper Congo, says: "You have a treasure in him; the very best companion you could have on your trip." [Lapsley 1891:33–34]

One year later, Lapsley reported:

> Sheppard seems to have been as great a favorite there [at Wissmann Falls on the Kasai

> River] as at Kintame, for I find that numbers of the Bakuba trading here now, or a month ago at Kapunda, had learned to like "Shoppity," or "SHOPPIT MONINE," *the great Sheppard.* [Lapsley 1892:151]

Throughout his travels, Sheppard was continually well received and known for a litany of talents. The posthumously published *Life and Letters of Samuel Norvell Lapsley: Missionary to the Congo Valley, West Africa* describes Sheppard as "a most handy fellow," "a true river-man," and a skilled hunter (Lapsley 1893:55–58). Sheppard is consistently lauded for providing food for people, which suggests that he led a uniquely balanced mission that emphasized service and development, alongside of religion.

After the death of Lapsley, Sheppard's white colleagues continued to extol him in terms that consistently highlight his linguistic facility:

> Mr. Sheppard seems to have learned the language of the people rapidly. Mr. [George] Adamson [of Scotland] writes us that when Mr. Sheppard preaches to the people at Luebo, they listen with close attention and he says Mr. Sheppard is "gifted." [*Missionary* 1893:114]

A few months later, Arthur Rowbotham, a white missionary from England, wrote of his senior colleague: "Bro. Sheppard is just a whole team in himself. He has the natives well in hand, and they like him, too" (Rowbotham 1893:232). De Witt Snyder, who served from 1892 until 1901, noted the value of Sheppard's return from furlough in 1894: "Since the arrival of Mr. Sheppard we have acquired a deeper hold of the language, his knowledge of the Bakuba dialect being a wonderful assistance in getting at obscure meanings" (Snyder De Witt 1895:410). Like Lapsley, Rowbotham, Adamson, and Snyder,

William M. Morrison, the fifth white man appointed to the APCM, was taken with Sheppard's linguistic expertise: "Mr. Sheppard seemed providentially the man to go to open the mission. He has been there, is known along the road, and speaks the language" (1996b:109). Collectively, these communiqués suggest that Sheppard was perceived as having a unique relationship to Congo. As Morrison succinctly summarized, "There is no man in all this country who had the influence over this people that Sheppard has" (1899:30).

Sheppard's influence enabled him the access needed to document the brutality of Leopold's administrators and their agents. In September 1899, after witnessing the aftermath of a massacre by the Zappo Zaps, a reputedly warlike African people working for the Belgians, Sheppard interviewed Chief M'lumba N'kusa about what happened. Sheppard's (1996a:122) written account of the interview makes it clear that he blames the colonial government: "The state has sent you and you have to go by your instructions." The language of Sheppard's questions emphasizes where responsibility lies. In order to discern the extent of the violence, he asks, "To what villages did the state send you?" (Sheppard 1996a:122). In terms of ammunition, he reports that they have "8 state rifles" and a large box of state gunpowder (Sheppard 1996a:122–123). The most brutal and lasting image from his report was of a pile of 81 hands burning on a fire, which became the most prominent symbol of Leopold's depraved regime (Hochschild 1999:165). Sheppard writes, "M'lumba N'Cusa explained that they always cut off the right hand to give to the state on their return" (1996a:123). Sheppard's report does an excellent job of documenting the role of the state, something that may not have been visible to a more superficial observer. In the process, his report, which received media coverage in the US and in Europe (Benedetto 1996:126 n. 6), established the APCM as an important opponent of Leopold's regime.

Initial accounts in the US similarly echo Sheppard's criticism of the state. In the February 1900 edition of the *Missionary*, Morrison uses Sheppard's report to make a strong statement about responsibility for the atrocities:

> We do not blame the Zappo Zaps primarily, for they are only kept by the State to the number of several thousand and used as tools, but we do blame all the white Belgian officials from the highest to the lowest, who are implicated directly or indirectly in such outrages upon an innocent people, and we are praying that if they do not repent the Lord of justice will mete out to them swift and sure punishment. [Morrison 1900:66]

The *Southern Workman*, a journal which was published at Hampton Institute and closely followed Sheppard, promptly picked up the report, which "cannot fail to stir the hearts of the civilized nations of the world and cause them to demand a thorough investigation into the practices of the State authorities by whose orders, apparently, these bloody deeds are being committed" (Sheppard 1900:220). Sheppard's investigation was immediately recognized for its direct criticism of Leopold's Congo State and did not play into racial stereotypes that would have allowed the facile scapegoating of his African agents.

Sheppard's activist opposition to the state soon became the public face of the APCM. In 1903, when Liverpool shipping company employee E. D. Morel established the Congo Reform Association (CRA) to stir up opposition to Leopold's system of rule in Congo, Sheppard's report was central to the campaign, thanks in part to Morrison, who corresponded with Morel and other leading figures of the movement. Morrison sent Sheppard's 1899 report to Mark Twain

(Benedetto 1996:219). Morrison also quoted it in his address at the Boston Peace Conference where it was heard by dignitaries including Booker T. Washington, who had been Sheppard's teacher at Hampton (Vinson 1921:189). Both Twain and Washington became Vice Presidents of the American Congo Reform Association and cited Sheppard in their published writings on the Congo State (Twain 1992:672; Washington 1979:88–89). Sheppard's reports became emblematic not only of the mission, but also of the broader international campaign undertaken against Leopold's regime.

Around the time that Sheppard's activism was emerging, the APCM started printing its own magazine, the *Kassai Herald*, at Luebo Station in Congo.[2] In the January 1908 issue, Sheppard's article "From the Bakuba Country" reported:

> There are armed sentries of chartered trading companies, who force the men and women to spend most of their days and nights in the forests making rubber, and the price they receive is so meager that they cannot live upon it. [Sheppard 1996b:282]

His reference to "chartered trading companies," widely understood to be a reference to the Compagnie du Kasai, caused an international incident. Director Dreypondt of the Compagnie du Kasai complained that his company "does not use armed sentries at all, and is not a chartered C[ompan]y," and asked the *Kassai Herald* to publish a rebuttal to Sheppard's charges (Benedetto 1996:284). Morrison, then the editor, refused based on Sheppard's character and reputation:

> It would seem that if you had been desirous of really knowing the truth about the situation in this region, you would have instituted an impartial investigation, without presuming, as the tone of your letter implies, that Dr. Sheppard

> only ignorantly or maliciously maligned your company. If you were pained and astonished that Dr. Sheppard should write such things, I must say that I am equally astonished and pained that you should so hastily conclude that a man of Dr. Sheppard's long residence in Congo and his well-known integrity should write a serious article of this kind without knowing what he was doing. [Morrison 1996d:287]

When Sheppard's article appeared, the Compagnie du Kasai had already mounted a public relations campaign against its critics (Compagnie du Kasai 1906). In response to the *Kassai Herald* article, the company aggressively decided to file suit, arguing that Sheppard had mischaracterized its relationship to the state by characterising it as a concessionary company. While this may seem like a minor technical point, the company's hollow claim to autonomy demonstrates how deeply scrutinized its relationship with the state was, and, by extension, how private entities —whether businesses or missions— found themselves negotiating similar borders.

On February 23, 1909, a summons was issued suing Sheppard and Morrison for libel, but due to a technical mistake in the summons, the charges against Morrison were dropped. The trial was to be held before a court in Leopoldville (Kinshasa), hundreds of miles from the nearest APCM station across seasonably unnavigable waterways. Belgium had jurisdiction as a result of having taken control of Congo the previous year. Since the allegedly libelous article never named the Compagnie du Kasai, the case for the defence could have been made on narrow technical grounds. However, in preparing for the trial, Sheppard and the APCM made at least three crucial decisions. First Sheppard recruited 20 Congolese witnesses to travel with him to Leopoldville. Morrison was less keen on Congolese testimony, explaining to a white APCM colleague:

> Sheppard has been trying to persuade some Bakuba to go, but with no avail as yet. We shall try to take along a few Baluba. I was almost in favor of taking no witnesses at all; just telling them that when they had the trial in a place where we could get the witnesses, and all we wanted, we would be ready, and not before that time. Others thought that we might take what we could get. I am almost afraid that the few we shall get will do us no special amount of good, whereas if we went with none, and made no effort to prove anything under the circumstances, we would perhaps come out better. [Morrison 1996e:357–358]

Unfortunately, the witnesses who traveled to Kinshasa were not allowed to testify and their oral narratives never made it into the official record. Sheppard's insistent recognition of the importance of Congolese testimony affirmed his unique respect for the Congolese people. Here he distinguished his approach and attitude from that of Morrison, which is particularly notable given their shared criticism of the state. Sheppard was not alone in valuing the voices of African victims of European imperialism; another noted African American traveler, historian George Washington Williams (1985:252), is, according to Hochschild (1999:110), "of the hundreds of Europeans and Americans who traveled to the Congo in the state's early years [...] the only one on record as questioning Africans about their personal experience of [Henry Morton] Stanley." These examples suggest that African Americans were uniquely committed to documenting the voices of Africa victims of colonialism.

Second, the APCM retained Emile Vandervelde, a leading member of the Belgian Socialist Party and longtime critic of Leopold, as his attorney. In his opening speech to the court, Vandervelde made his priorities clear:

> In every circumstance, on every occasion, I have struggled for the rights of the natives of the Congo, and in doing so, I believe that I have defended the nation better than those who try to keep covered-up the mess, the existence of which is no longer contested. [Vandervelde 1996:388]

Vandervelde suggests that his defence of Sheppard is needed, at least in part, to preserve the integrity of the Belgian state in the colonial era. Still, by hiring a prominent leader of the Belgian opposition as counsel, the APCM chose to politicize the case in a manner that was explicitly critical of colonial rule.

Third, the church appealed to the US Consul for assistance, drawing the US Government into the conflict at the precise moment when the APCM's adversarial relationship with Belgium was at its peak. The Department of State advocated on Sheppard's behalf and both US Consul William Handley and Vice Consul Kirk attended the trial in Kinshasa (Phipps 2002:169; Kennedy 2002:182). In this moment, as fleeting as it may have been, the APCM forced the US Government to choose sides between its own citizens and the colonial regime of an allied European government. In choosing the former, the US declared its opposition, however modestly, to the old colonial infrastructure of the new Belgian Congo. The confidence of the US Government was affirmed on October 4, 1909, when Judge Charles Louis Gianpetri handed down his verdict of the case. Sheppard was acquitted and the Compagnie du Kasai was ordered to pay court costs of 42 francs (Gianpetri 1996:416). Despite Sheppard's legal vindication, with the support of his government, he still embodied the worst fears of the colonial authorities and their religious lackeys.

As a result of Sheppard's central role, these fears became increasingly racialized. In 1910, a few months after the acquittal, both William Sheppard and Lucy Gantt Sheppard retired from the APCM. Although the stated reason for William Sheppard's retirement was ill-health, Morrison had accused him of committing adultery while his wife was on leave. On his return to the United States, William Sheppard privately confessed to Presbyterian authorities and quietly served a one year suspension from the church (Benedetto 1996:423–425 n. 5; Kennedy 2002:189–191; Phipps 2002:177–178). Within a span of two years, Morrison levied similar charges against the three senior male missionaries at the time, all of them black. Joseph Phipps and Henry Hawkins, the only two black male missionaries who spent their entire tenures without wives in Congo, were forced to resign in 1908 and 1910 respectively, both based on Morrison's charges of sexual misconduct. When the Presbyterian Church appointed Hawkins (who was the *Kassai Herald's* only black editor, holding the position from 1904 to 1907), they refused to allow his wife to go to Congo, effectively ending his marriage. Sheppard's biographer, Pagan Kennedy, suggests the Hawkins's "sexual misconduct" was a long-term monogamous relationship: "After many years in the Congo, Hawkins took an African lover —whom he may have regarded as a wife— and fathered a baby" (Kennedy 2002:191). Such racially motivated charges by Morrison, which draw on a disturbing history of white attempts to control black sexuality, dramatically changed the complexion of the mission by silencing experienced and outspoken African Americans, whose criticism of the colonial regime Morrison ironically shared. While several black missionaries continued to serve on the APCM, there was only one new appointment in the 50 years following Sheppard's trial (and in that case it was a woman who married a recently-widowed missionary).

***

The careers of those who continued their missionary careers after Sheppard's retirement reveal other sources of tension regarding the relationship between the APCM and the state. Althea Brown Edmiston, who was born in Rolling Fork, Mississippi, joined the APCM in 1902 and married fellow missionary Alonzo Edmiston in 1905. She arrived in Congo a year after her graduation with a Bachelor of Arts from Fisk University, where she had been a campus leader and the only female graduation speaker. Her valedictory address was on the subject of "What Missionaries have Done for the World" (*Fisk Herald* 1901:4–6). She maintained close ties with Fisk, as Sheppard did with Hampton. Neither relationship ended with their travels to Africa; Sheppard delivered Hampton's prestigious Founder's Day Address in January 1915 after his retirement from the APCM (*Southern Workman* 1915:183) and Edmiston delivered Fisk's 1921 commencement address during a furlough (Jacobs 1982:167).

Edmiston spent her first 11 years on the APCM writing the 619 page *Grammar and Dictionary of Bushonga or Bukuba Language* and the next 20 years trying to publish it. She undertook this project at a time when the Congo State was promoting the regional use of the Tshiluba language at the expense of local languages like Bushong. Language policy, which was central to the colonial project, was becoming increasingly codified by the state in the 1920s in the Kasai region, as in Katanga, as Johannes Fabian (1986) has documented with regard to Kiswahili. The APCM supported the state initiative by publishing a *Dictionary of the Tshiluba Language* along with several religious parables in 1906 (Morrison

1939). By 1918, Morrison had translated the entire Bible into Tshiluba (Bedinger 1920:52). Meanwhile, Edmiston was unable to publish her Bushong dictionary even after spending two years rewriting the entire book "to conform to the State method" of Bantu orthography, which the APCM adopted in 1921 (Bedinger 1937:278). The APCM's adoption of the state orthography points to the increasingly problematic conformity of the mission to the dictates of the colonial government, which was promoting Tshiluba as a regional *lingua franca*. In the meantime, Edmiston was also involved, as early as 1912, in producing Tshiluba translations of Presbyterian hymns, an initiative which eventually expanded beyond standard issue Presbyterian songs to include African American spirituals. While her decision to translate songs into Tshiluba (rather than Bushong) represents, on some level, acceptance of Belgian colonial language policy, it was not hegemonic. Her Tshiluba work was mediated not only by her translations of African American spirituals and songs of liberation, but also by her continued devotion to preserving the language, against opposition from both the colonial state and the Presbyterian Church. The Bushong dictionary project would have codified a political system that predated colonialism and continued to exist, in some form, outside of it. Edmiston (1932:v) affirms this perspective in the preface to the dictionary that she eventually published, which gives careful attention to Bakuba Government traditions. Tshiluba, in contrast, was —before its adoption by the mission— a unique bi-national language, spoken by both Baluba and Lulua. As such, Tshiluba was less identified with a unified indigenous political tradition than Bushong.

Although Edmiston completed the Bushong dictionary in 1913, the church insisted that the reference book was unnecessary and refused to authorize its publication for nearly two decades. Edmiston's white colleague, Robert Dabney Bedinger, acknowledged her frustration: "It was this delay which tested her. It tested her faith in her fellow-missionaries.

It tested her loyalty to the Mission, and to the Executive Committee of Foreign Missions" (Bedinger 1937:277). When the Presbyterian Church finally agreed to print her *Grammar and Dictionary* in the late 1920s, they still refused to fund it. Edmiston needed to raise money for its publication from non-church sources. So, in 1929, she circulated a letter requesting funds on the basis of the complexity of the linguistic system rather than on its value as an instrument of proselytising:

> It is the language of the Bukuba tribe who are considered the most superior people of all central Africa. Their language is beautiful and highly inflected. The verb has a full conjugation with many shades of tenses. There are ten classes of nouns as well as all the other various parts of speech. [Bedinger 1937:279]

The final publication includes a grammar that is more than 200 pages long, suggesting that Edmiston emphasized systematic linguistic analysis rather than the kind of basic translation that could be accomplished with a dictionary alone. In 1932, two decades after its completion, the book was finally printed, thanks in large part to Fisk alumni who gave $400 toward its publication (Bedinger 1937:280). Even after 30 years of service as a Presbyterian missionary, Edmiston still relied on Fisk to see the value of work which the church did not. The dictionary's publication, which claimed, wishfully, that the mission was working "in two distinct languages," did not change the church's attitude toward the language (Edmiston 1932:v). As early as 1936, the APCM was using Tshiluba rather than Bushong as the language of instruction among Bushong speakers in Bakuba schools (Anderson 1936).

In 1933, one year following the publication of Edmiston's *Grammar and Dictionary*, an all-white APCM Dictionary Committee clearly explains the church's position on language, which sharply contrasts with Edmiston's letter, whose argument was based on the aesthetics and sophistication of the language:

> Possibly the material found between these covers may make some small contribution to that vast amount of data which is being accumulated by ethnographers and philologists concerning African languages and cultures, but our prime purpose in compiling this dictionary and our prayerful hope is that these pages, in a definite and far-reaching way, will be blessed and used of God to bring about a wider dissemination of the Gospel of Jesus Christ in Africa. [Morrison 1939: iii]

By contrast, Edmiston's (1932:vi) preface describes Bushong as a literary language, "full of many idioms, parables, fairy tales, lullabies and songs." Furthermore, she explains that the pre-colonial political formation that exists outside of, and in contrast to, the colonial state features a "highly organized government" and a democratic tradition that includes "many centuries" of female suffrage (1932:v). Additionally, Edmiston demonstrates an uncommon respect for Bushong linguistic culture by thanking her Congolese informants by name (1932:vii).

For the APCM in the 1930s, any use of its Tshiluba dictionary for purposes other than religious conversion was considered incidental. Here the church narrowly defines its mission in religious terms, which stands in contrast to the broader initiatives undertaken by Sheppard and the pioneers. Walter D. Shepard (who was unrelated and spelled his name with one p) served on the APCM from 1947 to 1960, and later as Area Secretary for the Presbyterian Church (US) Board of World Missions, insists that the mission prioritize religion above food, health, and education: "we must never lose sight of the fact that the most desperate need of men everywhere is a spiritual one" (Shepard 1968:18). This context reveals a gap between how the Presbyterian Church came to see the work of its missionaries and how its black pioneers defined their own labours, which also exposed the conflicting priorities of white churches and HBCUs. Edmiston and her Fisk backers saw her translation work more broadly as akin to that of an anthropologist or humanist. Despite the opposition of church leaders, Edmiston's linguistic achievements made the dictionary the standard for generations of scholars. When the Belgian anthropologist Jan Vansina was studying with the "famous Bantuist" Malcolm Guthrie at the School of Oriental and African Languages in England in the early 1950s, Edmiston's "missionary grammar" was the primary text for his language instruction (1994:11, 259 n. 13). Although Guthrie "did not know a word of Bushong" and Vansina learned little of the language, Edmiston's book, despite its limitations, and his studies with Guthrie, gave Vansina "an inkling of what a Bantu language was like" and impressed upon him the importance of linguistics as more than simply a tool for fieldwork (Vansina 1994:11).

***

While many African American missionaries like Edmiston developed and maintained a unique niche for themselves on the margins of the larger mission, these positions were increasingly contested. In *Black Americans and the Evangelization of Africa*, historian Walter L. Williams describes African Americans as targets of both mission boards and colonial governments:

> White mission boards feared that black Americans would spread racial ill feeling to the Africans. That fear was felt even more strongly by European colonial governments, which viewed Afro-American missionaries as potential troublemakers. As imperial control tightened over the continent, more restrictions were placed upon black missionaries. Even those churches which backed their black representatives, as the southern Presbyterians did William Sheppard, experienced much opposition from Europeans. [Williams 1982:42]

The decision of the Presbyterian governing body not to appoint black missionaries must have pleased Belgian officials, who considered African Americans to be agitators and bad examples for their colonial subjects. It would have been almost natural for the American Presbyterians to accommodate the colonial state by barring black Americans given US politics following the 1877 end of post-Civil War Reconstruction. This period in the US, which historian Rayford Logan (1965) famously termed the "nadir" due to economic repression, political disfranchisement, and racial violence, was characterized by systematic racial exclusion that was mirrored in Congo. Whereas 11 blacks were appointed to the APCM during its first 20 years, the Presbyterian Church only newly appointed one black person during the next half-century. Such exclusionary policies were consistent with those being codified in the US during the 1890s, a decade which saw the revision of state constitutions throughout the South and the Plessy v. Ferguson Supreme Court decision legalising segregation in public accommodations. For the Presbyterian Church, a policy of racial exclusion would have been consistent with trends in the US, while conveniently helping the church to more closely ally itself with the colonial government.

In the 1910s, despite some efforts to maintain autonomy and neutrality by, for example, refusing an offer of military protection for an expedition to the Bakuba (Washburn 1972:71), the increasingly white APCM was falling into line with the state at a time when the state was becoming more and more fixated on the perceived threat posed by African Americans. In the 1920s, the Belgian Government responded to the rising influence of Jamaican-born and US-based Marcus Garvey and the Universal Negro Improvement Association (UNIA) with particular paranoid vigilance. In particular, Simon Kimbangu's messianic activism in Congo was attributed to Garveyite agitation (Kodi 1993:275). Furthermore, in 1921, Belgium was a host to the Second Pan-African Congress, another cause for alarm. The correspondence of the Belgian Ambassador to the US from the time reveals not only the Belgian fear of Garvey, but its concern with the circulation of the UNIA newspaper *Negro World* (Kodi 1993:268, 270). In his essay *The 1921 Pan-African Congress at Brussels: A Background to Belgian Pressures*, M. W. Kodi (1993:267) details how the Belgian Minister of Colonies required the Ambassador to get his office's approval prior to issuing visas for African Americans, and mounted an extensive surveillance campaign against African Americans.

Over the course of the subsequent decades of the Belgian colonial era, the APCM became increasingly comfortable with the blurring of any borders separating the church from the state; their independence and autonomy were of diminishing importance. The APCM's alliance with Belgium reached full recognition in 1936, when white missionaries Hezekiah and Lillie Washburn were invited to visit the King and Queen of Belgium. Initially, Hezekiah feared that he was going to be put on trial, as Sheppard had been a few decades earlier (Washburn 1972:196). Instead the King hosted him at his luxurious suite at the Cosmopolitan Hotel and knighted him and his wife to the Royal Order for having "rendered a great service to us" (Washburn 1972:200). That service included donating corn produced on mission stations to mining concessions and, incredibly, to Brussels (Washburn 1972:200). The King's attempts to charm the Washburns had a lasting impact; nearly four decades later, Hezekiah titled his autobiography *A Knight in the Congo* in which he proudly included pictures of the awards the King had given him. Similarly, in 1959, on the eve of Congolese independence, C. Darby Fulton, the Executive Secretary of the Board of World Missions, writes exultantly that Vernon Anderson "has been decorated by the Government for services rendered the Colony" (Anderson 1959:iii). By allowing the colonial government to be the arbiter of a missionary's accomplishments, Fulton effectively erases the borders separating the mission and the state.

Belgium's fear of African Americans continued throughout this era and spiked again during World War II when the US military stationed African American servicemen in Matadi. In 1942, the Ministry of Colonies asked that the US Government redeploy its African American soldiers because they found it "a matter of the greatest importance not to raise any difficult problems of a social or an economic character among the native population" (Helmreich 1998:38). The US Government, which had defended William Sheppard before a Belgian court in 1909, agreed to withdraw its black soldiers from Matadi. Despite such accommodations, the Belgians considered African Americans, even in absentia, to be dangerous exemplars. A photo of African American officers that was found among *Force Publique* mutineers was blamed for an uprising in Kananga (Helmreich 1998:41); during World War II, Belgian authorities turned their attention to the potential threat posed by African American missionaries; and Belgian censors, who were monitoring mission correspondence, discovered that American protestant missions were considering bringing in black missionaries. The situation was considered serious enough that Governor General Pierre Ryckmans and

Foreign Minister Paul-Henri Spaak both approached US authorities on this subject (Helmreich 1998:150). Again, the US government and the churches responded favourably to the colonial authorities' requests.

Shortly after the end of the war, in 1948, in compliance with a Belgian requirement, the Presbyterian Board of World Missions began to require that all appointed missionaries spend a minimum of a year in Belgium studying, among other things, "Belgian and colonial history and government" (Anderson 1959:31). The APCM, among other denominations, complied without complaint and all of the new appointees and their families spent substantial time in colonial education programs in Brussels prior to traveling to Africa. At this same time, in 1948, the Presbyterian Church, for the first time, signed an agreement with the Ministry of Colonies for official recognition and financial subsidies from the state (Anderson 1959:37) in order to make its "training available to its people in a Christian atmosphere" (Wharton 1952:175). Fearing the loss of its religious foundation, the church debated the issue, but ultimately agreed to become an appendage to the state. Where Morrison and Sheppard found themselves embarrassed by Verner's close ties to the colonial regime, by the 1940s the APCM no longer saw the state as its adversary. The borders that separated the mission and the state so dramatically early in the century were largely eliminated. All the while, the colonial government had the continued support of the US Government. As late as 1957, the US State department had barred African Americans from traveling to Congo (Helmreich 1998:167), and it was not until 1958 that another African American was appointed to the APCM.

***

There is nothing especially surprising or unusual in the Presbyterian Church's complicity in Belgian colonialism; however, the shifting borders separating mission and state, and its concordance with US racial politics, make the transatlantic history of the APCM uniquely revealing. Its early years offer a glimpse of the possibility of an alternative model of missionary work in which a mission need not be an uncritical arm of the state. This history suggests that under black leadership, an activist missionary tradition —an admittedly problematic sort of imperial anti-colonialism— may have been possible.

Furthermore, these same shifting borders reveal something of colonialism's effective incorporation of non-state actors beginning in the 1920s and reaching its pinnacle in 1948. And, it appears that these relationships were facilitated, at least in part, by international opposition to black liberation —an alliance between the governments of the Belgian Congo and the United States, and supported by the Presbyterian Church. If nothing else, the Belgian Government's ongoing campaign against African American missionaries indicates a perceived threat to colonial rule that US churches and the US Government were altogether willing to accommodate.

From the mission's 1890 founding through the colonial era, American racial dynamics serve as a crucial backdrop for the changing dynamics of the relationship of the APCM to the colonial state. This process, whereby the Presbyterian Church became increasingly complicit with Belgian colonialism in Congo, can be understood, in part, through the lens of US racial politics. African Americans, who were increasingly marginalized on the APCM, created a lasting and influential legacy and, despite obstacles, helped to shape the mission and the state in the process. African American missionaries, who chose to live and work abroad, developed a critical perspective on the power of the colonial state, which reached back to the US through HBCUs and other channels. The efforts of figures like Sheppard and Edmiston, in fields ranging from direct political activism to linguistics, demonstrate a defiant willingness to exist on not only the borders of the mission but also on the borders of state power in ways that critically expose its racial dimensions.

ACKNOWLEDGEMENTS

I thank the Belgian Association for Africanists and the audience at its 2007 meeting in Tervuren for the opportunity to share this work. In addition, thanks to Hanan Sabea, John Schaefer, and Steven van Wolputte for insightful comments which helped me shape this essay.

NOTES

[1] All references to the Presbyterian Church (US), colloquially the "southern Presbyterian Church," refer to the southern branch, which was the result of a split with the Presbyterian Church (USA) during the Civil War. The northern and southern churches remained separate for more than a century, until reforming in 1983 under the Presbyterian Church (USA) name.

[2] 'Kassai' is elsewhere spelled 'Kasai.' I have followed the latter except in the cases of direct citations and titles.

REFERENCES

Anderson, V. 1959. Still Led in Triumph. [Nashville, TN]: Board of World Missions, Presbyterian Church U. S.

——— 1936. Annual Letter. 14 October 1936. Presbyterian Church in the U. S., Division of International Mission, Congo Mission, Records 1891-1980, Record Group 432, Box 40, Folder 21, Presbyterian Historical Society, Philadelphia.

Bedinger, R. D. 1937. Althea Brown Edmiston: A Congo Crusader. *In* Glorious Living: Informal Sketches of Seven Missionaries of the Presbyterian Church, U. S. S. L. Timmons, ed. Pp. 261–286. Atlanta, GA:

Committee on Women's Work, Presbyterian Church [U. S.].

——— 1920. Triumphs of the Gospel in the Belgian Congo. Richmond, VA: Presbyterian Committee of Publication.

Benedetto, R. (ed.). 1996. Presbyterian Reformers in Central Africa: A Documentary Account of the American Presbyterian Congo Mission and the Human Rights Struggle in the Congo, 1890–1918. Winifred K. Vass, trans. New York: E. J. Brill.

Bradford, P.V. and H. Blume. 1992. Ota Benga: The Pygmy in the Zoo. New York: St. Martin's Press.

Chester, S. H. 1895a. Help Needed for Africa. The Missionary 28(9, Sept.):398.

——— 1895b. A Man Needed at Once for Our African Work. The Missionary 28(10, Oct.):446–447.

Compagnie du Kasai. 1906. Question Congolaise: La Compagnie du Kasai à ses Actionnaires, Réponse à ses Détracteurs. Brussels: Imprimerie Tr. Rein for Compagnie du Kasai.

Crawford, J. R. 1982. Pioneer African Missionary: Samuel Phillips Verner. Journal of Presbyterian History 60(1):42–57.

Edmiston, A. B. 1937. Maria Fearing: A Mother to African Girls. Atlanta: Committee on Woman's Work, Presbyterian Church (U. S.).

——— 1932. Grammar and Dictionary of Bushonga or Bukuba Language as Spoken by the Bushonga or Bukuba Tribe who Dwell in the Upper Kasai District, Belgian Congo, Central Africa. Luebo, Belgian Congo: J. Leighton Wilson Press (APCM).

Fabian, J. 1986. Language and Colonial Power: The Appropriation of Swahili in the Former Belgian Congo, 1880–1938. New York: Cambridge University Press.

Fisk Herald. 1901. Commencement Day. 18(10, July):4–6.

Franklin, J. H. 1985. George Washington Williams: A Biography. Chicago: University of Chicago Press.

Gianpetri, C. L. 1996 [1909]. Verdict of the Tribunal of the First Instance at Léopoldville. 4 October 1909. *In* Presbyterian Reformers in Central Africa. R. Benedetto, ed. Pp. 411–417. New York: E. J. Brill.

Helmreich, J. E. 1998. United States Relations with Belgium and the Congo, 1940–1960. Newark: University of Delaware Press.

Hochschild, A. 1999 [1998]. King Leopold's Ghost: A Story of Greed, Terror, and Heroism in Colonial Africa. New York: Houghton Mifflin.

Jacobs, S. M. 1982. Their 'Special Mission': Afro-American Women as Missionaries to the Congo, 1894-1937. *In* Black Americans and the Missionary Movement in Africa. S. M. Jacobs, ed. Pp. 155–176. Westport, CT: Greenwood Press.

Kennedy, P. 2002. Black Livingstone: A True Tale of Adventure in the Nineteenth-Century Congo. New York: Viking.

Kodi, M. W. 1993. The 1921 Pan-African Congress at Brussels: A Background to Belgian Pressures. *In* Global Dimensions of the African Diaspora. 2nd edition. J. E. Harris, ed. Pp. 263–288. Washington: Howard University Press.

Lapsley, S. N. 1893. Life and Letters of Samuel Norvell Lapsley: Missionary to the Congo Valley, West Africa. Richmond, VA: Whittet and Shepperson Printers.

——— 1892. Letters from the Missions. 5 Oct. 1892 [sic]. The Missionary 25(4, Apr.):151–157.

——— 1891. Letters from the Missions. 2 Oct. 1890. The Missionary 24(1, January):33–34.

Logan, R. W. 1965 [1954]. The Betrayal of the Negro: From Rutherford B. Hayes to Woodrow Wilson. Revised and enlarged edition of The Negro in American Life and Thought: The Nadir, 1877-1901. New York: Collier.

Missionary, The. 1902b. Wanted–Another White Missionary for Africa." 35(10, October):461.

——— 1902a. The Congo Mission. 35(1, January):5.

——— 1900. Atrocities in the Congo Free State. 33(2, February):61–63.

——— 1898. Needs of the Congo Mission. 31(8, August):339.

——— 1894. A Remarkable Missionary. 27(7, July):272–273.

——— 1893. The Congo Boat Company. 26(3, March):113–114.

Morrison, W. M. 1996e [1909]. Letter to L. C. Vass. 3 April 1909. *In* Presbyterian Reformers in Central Africa. R. Benedetto, ed. Pp. 357–358. New York: E. J. Brill.

——— 1996d [1908]. Letter to Director Dreypondt. 27 April 1908. *In* Presbyterian Reformers in Central Africa. R. Benedetto, ed. Pp. 286–289. New York: E. J. Brill.

——— 1996c [1907]. Letter to "Whom it May Concern." 1 July 1907. *In* Presbyterian Reformers in Central Africa. R. Benedetto, ed. Pp. 244–248. New York: E. J. Brill.

——— 1996b [1898]. Letter. 7 Dec. 1897. The Missionary 31(4, Apr.). *In* Presbyterian Reformers in Central Africa. R. Benedetto, ed. Pp. 112–114. New York: E. J. Brill.

——— 1996a [1897]. Letter. [5 June 1897.] The Missionary 30(10, Oct.). *In* Presbyterian Reformers in Central Africa. Robert Benedetto, ed. Pp. 109–111. New York: E. J. Brill.

——— 1939 [1906]. Dictionary of the Tshiluba Language. Revised and enlarged edition by a Committee of the Mission. Luebo, Belgian Congo: J. Leighton Wilson Press (APCM).

——— 1900. Africa Between the Upper and Nether Millstones. The Missionary 33(2, Feb.):64–67.

——— 1899. The Late War as Reported on the Congo. The Missionary

32(1, Jan.):29–30.
Phipps, W. E. 2002. William Sheppard: Congo's African-American Livingstone. Louisville, KY: Geneva Press.
Rowbotham, A. 1893. Letters from the Missions. 17 Feb. 1893. The Missionary 26(6, June):230-232.
Shepard, W. D. 1968. Sent by the Sovereign. Nutley, NJ: Presbyterian and Reformed Publishing.
Sheppard, W. H. 1996b [1908]. From the Bakuba Country. Kassai Herald 8.1 (Jan.). *In* Presbyterian Reformers in Central Africa. R. Benedetto, ed. Pp. 281–283. New York: E. J. Brill.
——— 1996a [1899]. Interview with Chief M'lumba N'kusa Concerning the Zappo Zap Raid, 14 September 1899. *In* Presbyterian Reformers in Central Africa. R. Benedetto, ed. Pp. 121–126. New York: E. J. Brill.
——— 1900. In the Heart of Africa. Southern Workman 29(4, April):220–221.
——— 1891 [1890]. Letter. 1 Sept. 1890. Southern Workman 20(3, March):168.
Snyder, De Witt. 1895. Letters from the Field. 20 Apr. 1895. The Missionary 28(9, Sept.):410–411.
Snyder, Mrs. [May Heginbotham Thompson]. 1896. Letter from Luebo. 18 Oct. 1895. The Missionary 29(2, Feb.):78.
Southern Workman 1915. "At Home and Afield: Hampton Incidents." 44(3, March):182–185.
Twain, M. 1992 [1905]. King Leopold's Soliloquy: A Defense of his Congo Rule. *In* M. Twain: Collected Tales, Sketches, Speeches and Essays, 1891-1910. L. J. Budd, ed. Pp. 661–686. New York: Library of America.
Vandervelde, E. 1996 [1909]. Speech for the Defense (Court Proceedings). 20 September 1909. *In* Presbyterian Reformers in Central Africa. R. Benedetto, ed. Pp. 387–404. New York: E. J. Brill.
Vansina, J. 1994. Living With Africa. Madison: University of Wisconsin Press.
Vinson, T. C. 1921. William McCutchan Morrison: Twenty Years in Central Africa. Richmond, VA: Presbyterian Committee of Publication.
Washburn, H. 1972. A Knight in the Congo: God's Ambassador in Three Continents. Bassett, VA: Bassett Printing Corporation.
Washington, B. T. 1979 [1904]. Cruelty in the Congo Country. *In* The Booker T. Washington Papers, volume 8. L. R. Harlan and R. W. Smock, eds., Geraldine McTigue, associate ed. Pp. 85–90. Urbana: University of Illinois Press.
Wharton, E. T. 1952. Led in Triumph. Nashville, TN: Board of World Missions, Presbyterian Church (U. S.).
Williams, G. W. 1985 [1890]. An Open Letter to His Serene Majesty Leo-

pold II, King of the Belgians and Sovereign of the Independent State of Congo. *In* George Washington Williams: A Biography. By J. H. Franklin. Pp. 243–254. Chicago: University of Chicago Press.

Williams, W. L. 1982. Black Americans and the Evangelization of Africa. Madison: University of Wisconsin Press.

8
BORDERS OF THE PRESENT: MAASAI TRADITION, MODERNITY, AND FEMALE IDENTITY

Tammary Esho, Paul Enzlin and Steven Van Wolputte

INTRODUCTION

Female Circumcision (FC), variously known as Female Genital Cutting (FGC) and Female Genital Mutilation (FGM), is a traditional practice that incorporates bodily inscription as a signifier in girls' maturation into adult womanhood.[1] The practice has become a focus of eradication programs, courtesy of its associated and now universally infamous operative procedure that entails the partial or total removal of the female external genitalia (Abusharaf 2006).

This chapter takes issue with the paradigm that persists in predicating the present situation of African women upon age-old customs such as patriarchy and male ascendency. Taking Female Genital Cutting (FGC) among Maasai women in Kenya as an example, the analysis understands their position as being suspended in a borderland between frontiers of past and present, between customary constructions of femininity and identity and a constant pressure to capitulate to the contemporary maelstrom of modernity. Yet, neither the former nor the latter are able to provide a "compass" for these women to navigate and negotiate the uncertainties of daily life. The theme is explored through an analysis of ongoing discourses and practices (referred to as *emurata*) regarding Female Genital Cutting (FGC).[2]

The analysis emerged out of a broader critical exploration of the links between culture, femininity, identity and sexuality, especially in the context of female genital cutting among the Maasai (Esho 2012). The underlying question was why the practice of female genital cutting still persists there: despite the tremendous economical, social and political changes Maasai society went through over the past few decades, and despite a decades-long and dedicated eradication campaign, the Kenya Health Demographic Survey (KHDL 2003) estimates that about 94 per cent of Maasai women are circumcised. This number reflects either fundamental shortcomings of the prevailing eradication strategies, or the enduring or renewed meaning and importance of FGC for those who practice it. The research presented here hypothecates the latter, the premise being that the critical function of FGC relative to Maasai women's identity has not yet been fully appreciated.

STATUESQUE UNDER FIRE

Despite eradication efforts, many women submit themselves and their children to FGC. Many factors have been blamed for this but, predictably, religion and patriarchy in particular have been singled out. Critics see the practice as concealing an oppressive intent, in which men and a male-dominated society seek ascendency over women, especially in matters pertaining to femininity, feminine identity, and standing (Almroth et al. 2005; Dare et. al. 2004; Al-Krenawi and Wiesel-Lev 1999; Hosken 1994). However, an increasing body of literature takes the debate regarding FGC and its continued or renewed importance beyond what is perceived as the narrow confines of a mostly western feminist discourse (Njambi 2004; Gruenbaum 2001; Shell-Duncan and Herlund 2000; Obermeyer 1999).

Regardless of the well-intentioned strategies of FGC eradication, western feminist approaches justified their approach by claiming to rescue women from adverse health implications and from traditional, patriarchal, oppressive cultures (Wade 2009; Harding 2008; Mohanty 2003). It, however, failed to register significant success due to its unintended result of further marginalising indigenous women, their cultures, and their lives (Nnaemeka 2005). Also, recent scholarship questioned the universalistic approach towards the subject, arguing that the circumstances under which the practice is perpetuated are simply too diverse to warrant explication through a single discursive or theoretical lens (Shell-Duncan 2008; Obermeyer 2005). It points out that FGC plays an important role in facilitating culturally mediated processes of socialization, wherein it assists in the transfusion of gendered identities, and in addition to signifying the onset of pubescence and fertility, serves as a crucial element in legitimating the status of womanhood, opening the door to matrimony and motherhood (Van Rossem and Gage 2009; Shweder 2000; Ahlberg et al. 2000; Turner 1967; Gruenbaum 2001; Richards 1956).

Consequently, these critics argue that any attempt to dissociate these functions from its mediating ritual practice will almost certainly result in failure, as it amounts to a disposal of the very bases upon which such crucial elements are negotiated and established (Turner 1967; Richards 1956). Such attempts to eradicate practices of FGC may also be observed to be detrimental to critical aspects of society's fabric (Obermeyer 1999; Abusharaf 2006; Knudsen 1994). In particular, critics of the anti-FGC lobby deride the frequent portrayal of FGC subjects as passive victims in what is clearly a crucial and determinative aspect of their existence (Njambi

2004, 2005; Shell-Duncan 2008).

They argue, instead, that the ritual's perpetuation in the present has less to do with any male desire to superintend over societal matters pertaining to femininity, feminine identity and the status of women in society, but rather signifies women's own aspiration to carve out a niche within society by directly negotiating the cultural and social parameters upon which their daily life-worlds are mediated. Participation in the FGC maturation ritual is one avenue where women are able to achieve this aspiration (Njambi 2004; Shweder 2000; Gruenbaum 2001). This is a privilege they share with their male counterparts, for whom participation in the male circumcision ritual is, likewise, mandatory. In the same breath, the male rite provides the symbolic basis upon which male identities and social standing are instituted and established. Therefore, eradication would undermine the basis for negotiating a favourable position in society for those it claims to protect. Finally, in line with the prevailing postcolonial view of traditions as invented or imagined (Ranger 1993; Meyer and Geschiere 2003), some authors suggest that FGC is not a stubborn remainder of a petrified past. Its current prevalence should be understood as the outcome of a dynamic of social and political change. Susan Pedersen (2007), for instance, demonstrates how both the practice and its meaning changed as a result of the political tensions between British imperialism and emerging Kikuyu nationalism.

To understand the prevalence of FGC among the Kenyan Maasai, this chapter suggests to return to the practice itself, to its place and meaning for women in Maasai society. Female genital cutting, hence, is primarily approached as a rite of passage, from girl to womanhood. Such rites involve a state of being suspended between inclusion and exclusion, femininity and masculinity, tradition and modernity —a state of suspension which does not end with the conclusion of the ceremonial proceedings, but continues in lived experience and only gradually dissolves. These in-between spaces can also be referred to as borderlands created by boundaries of inclusion and exclusion. These boundaries, however, are shifting. Also, besides making and marking socially constructed differences, they connect and interrelate: boundaries, and the embodied borders discussed here, make negotiation possible. However, these boundaries and the marginal spaces that they create are unstable, unpredictable, precarious and always in transition (Anzaldua 2002). These borders represent the fault lines, conflicts, differences and fears which Chandra Mohanty (2003:2) suggests that the most expansive and inclusive visions of feminism need to be attentive to, whilst learning to transcend. Our research findings suggest that FGC is one such marginal space, used by Maasai women to negotiate gender, identity, and sexuality. Elsewhere, Esho (2012:66–67) demonstrates that women are best taken seriously as active agents in the invention and perpetuation of FGC, especially because of the perception that women are subjected to “traditional” and patriarchic authority —a view commonly held by governments and NGOs— has stood in the way of a more realistic understanding of the practice (also see Ahmadu 2000). Likewise, Esho (2012) also argues that the symbolic-cultural nexus plays an important role in the practice and experience of sexuality. Whilst it may be the case that this might sound obvious, for (most of) the Maasai women in our study this meant that they perceived of their circumcision not as an impediment to, but as a precondition to becoming female, sexualized beings (also see Esho et al. 2010). For these informants, circumcision is a woman’s right. As well as articulating Maasai belonging and identity, it also inscribes moral virtue, femininity (as opposed to masculinity) and womanhood (as opposed to girlhood).

Fig. 8.1. The village centre. Photo by T. Esho, July 2008.

THE RESEARCH

The material for this chapter was gathered during two field trips to Narok district in southwest Kenya during the summers of 2007 and 2008. Narok district is located in the Rift Valley of Kenya, and covers an area of about 15,000 square kilometres. It is home to the largest animal park in Kenya, and is situated in a highly forested highland area of the country known as Mau Forest, which is mostly evergreen as compared to the semi-arid southern regions of the district. Abundant rainfall makes the area suitable for livestock herding, subsistence farming and cash crops (such as wheat and barley). The good rainfall during the research visits meant that most people were busy ploughing or planting their crops. This, however, also meant that the research site was difficult to reach, if not completely inaccessible by car due to the muddy dirt roads.

Fig 8.2. Participants in one of the focus group discussions, August 2008. Photo: T. Esho.

This research site was a sparsely inhabited village that, except for the stores and school at its centre, mostly consisted of temporary, wooden, housing units alternating with mud and thatched-roof houses or more customary homesteads plastered with mud and *manyata* (cow dung).

The ethnographic study was carried out in two stages (one introductory and reconnoitring, one to conduct the actual interviews) and combined various research strategies, including participant observation and observation of a circumcision ceremony, in-depth interviews, and focus group discussions. One-on-one conversations offered the necessary privacy to allow for discussions of sensitive issues and personal experiences; the focus group discussions provided a more natural environment involving group interaction, everyday conversation, story-telling, jokes, and teasing. The interviews each lasted between 25 to 60 minutes; the group discussions took about one to three hours, including brief breaks. The main researcher (Esho) pretested the open-ended guiding questions used in the discussions on two female research assistants to make sure that they were appropriate within this context. This process informed changes to be made regarding some sensitive questions and how they should be phrased. Also, it allowed these assistants to familiarize themselves with the research topic and the used approach, and to receive training on how to conduct the interviews and group discussions. One of them also proved useful in translating the conversations into Swahili and English when necessary, and, later, in transcribing the data. The second research assistant was an older, well-known and respected woman from the village. She introduced the researchers to the interviewees and facilitated their access to the field throughout the two phases of the research.

Interviewees (women and men between 15 and 80 years of age) were selected through snowball sampling, informed about the purpose of the study, and asked to volunteer. With their informed consent, they were interviewed about their attitudes and perceptions with regard to Maasai customs in general and FGC in particular, and the relation of these practices to the construction of gender and identity. For the circumcision ceremony, permission was obtained for recording conversations and for photographing, but refused for videotaping. Later, these audio recordings were transcribed.

NAVIGATING THE BORDERLANDS

Far from being just a natural or material phenomenon, the human body is a product of a social process of construction and negotiation (Turner 1980) and it functions as the interface *par excellence* between the material and the symbolic (Moore 1994; Braidotti 1991). This is certainly true for the construction of femininity and female sexuality. This construction not only takes place in symbolic discourse: it is also enacted and experienced in gendered age-appropriate responsibilities and roles in the society. Young boys, for instance, are encouraged and expected to take up responsibilities outside of the homestead, such as accompanying an older animal caretaker in the fields to look after small stock, or, as they grow older, to take on the care of the cattle herd. Girls, in contrast, are encouraged to undertake responsibilities within the homestead. Their (future) tasks consist of housekeeping, cooking, washing, taking care of the children, milking and ploughing, planting and harvesting food crops in the fields.

This gendered division of labour does not mean that men cannot undertake female responsibilities. Men, too, take part in cooking (often on ritualized occasions) or work the fields. Women, too, are seen herding animals.

In general, women in Maasai are trained to be very self-sufficient from an early age, an attribute our interviewees related to the practice of polygamy: a man's resources and time need to be evenly spread between his wives and his children; hence, emotional and physical support is limited and shared. Also, polygamy implies long periods of separation between a wife and her husband. Therefore, women must be able to fend for themselves and their children, with little or no support from their husbands. They, for instance, have to make sure that their children attend school and get the formal education they can afford. Women are the household's main providers, as they engage in farming, or in running small businesses, such as selling clothes, groceries and other food stuffs, or in the burning and sale of charcoal. Some interviewees had professional careers such as primary and secondary school teachers, traditional birth attendants, or traditional circumcisers.

These gender and age responsibilities percolate into Maasai social structure, inform social discourse, and are embodied in everyday experiences and in ritual and symbolic activities by both women and men (Boddy 1989). Practices that play a role in constructing and inscribing gender identity amongst Maasai girls include rituals such as body markings

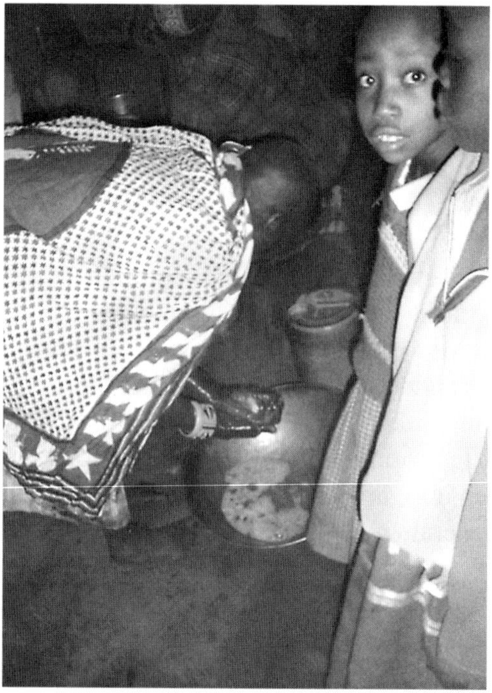

Fig. 8.3. A circumciser preparing for the procedure. Photo 8.3, August 2008. Photo: T.C. Esho.

and tattooing on various parts of the body such as thighs, arms, abdomen, and face. These are generally considered a sign of female beauty and, hence, are proudly worn and shown. In daily life, gender differences and signs of femininity take the form of body adornment (elaborate beaded necklaces, even though these, nowadays, have to compete with school uniforms and other forms of clothing), diet (women eat those parts associated with femininity, such as the liver, men eat the parts associated with masculinity, such as the heart), or the spatial organization of the homestead. For instance, women and children are usually expected to be somewhat aloof and, thus, mostly spend their time in the kitchen (a part of the house associated with femininity), while men would sit in the living room, regarded as a masculine section of the house.

It is tempting to regard these aspects of gender identity as a form of an ancient, received wisdom or ideology. Yet, gender identity involves a continuous struggle and adaptation to new challenges and situations. Also, for our Maasai interlocutors, the negotiation of the boundaries of female identity, and of self-regard and self-definition, poses a continuous challenge that is faced in different ways. One such often-practiced way is through becoming knowledgeable about, and aware of, the modernist discourse on traditional practices. For instance, the informants in this study were well informed about the ongoing modern female circumcision eradicationist discourse: on several occasions they attended seminars, meetings, and other community interventions organized by the government and non-governmental organizations geared towards eradicating the practice for both women and men. Women in particular expressed mixed emotions regarding eradication, with some arguing that continuing the practice is not necessary, others claiming that circumcision is crucial in the construction of gender and female identity, and still others taking up a position somewhere in between. This illustrates that our interviewees (for and as women) claim the right to themselves demarcate the boundaries of Maasai feminine identity.

Maasai believe that emurata (circumcision) has always been with them: it is generally regarded as an important stage in the lifecycle; a rite of passage in transforming an individual from child to adult, in transforming both boys and girls into responsible, sociable, adults in the community. For boys and men, circumcision allows them to be part of an age-set. Such age-sets have a specific name that refers to the men who underwent the ritual together or at the same period. Girls, in contrast, have two main age-grades; a first one consists of *intoyie* (sing. *Entito*, uncircumcised girls); a second one is referred to as *inkitok* (sing. *inkitok*) and comprises the circumcised women. The latter is further subdivided into the group of *isiankikin* (sing. *esiankiki*, "young women") and that of

Fig 8.4. The initiate leaves her mother's house for the ceremony. Photo T. Esho, August 2008.

intasati (sing. e*ntasat*): older, mostly postmenopausal women (Ndagala 1992). Finally, women take on the age-set of their husband when they marry and are accorded the same respect that comes with its membership. Women and men who do not undergo circumcision, in other words, who do not reach this stage of socially sanctioned adulthood, will hence be regarded as juniors. From this point of view, circumcision is a form of re-birth, the coming into the world of a new social and responsible member of society.

The female circumcision ritual is not the responsibility of the girl's mother alone, but of all the other adult (responsible) women in the community, and usually takes place after the onset of puberty. It is the outcome of a longer process that starts when the women notice that the girl's body is developing (for instance, growing breasts, her first menstruation, growing a fuller figure). Repeatedly bringing up the topic in conversation is seen as an important first step towards preparing the future *enkaibartani* ("initiate") for the event, one that ends when the girl agrees to undergo circumcision. The following section describes the transformation the initiate undergoes, and how it impacts on her identity and that of the women participating in the ritual. This description serves as a background to understand the role this body practice plays in the construction of femininity and Maasai identity.

Throughout the circumcision ritual and the implied transition from girlhood into womanhood, or from the non-social into the social domain, women (and, mutatis mutandis, men) receive recognition as social beings (Turner 1967; Butler 1993). Besides sociability, the ritual also inscribes femininity, sexuality, fertility and social identity on the body. This inscription is at once social and cognitive, emotional and physical: circumcision involves pain, bleeding, and the sacrifice of a part of the body.

The day before the circumcision takes place, the traditional blade (known as *olmurunya*) is used for shaving off all the hair on the girl's head. This act symbolizes leaving behind her old life as a child: new hair growth signifies a new beginning as a full, sexual member of society (see Turner 1980). The same blade is also used for the circumcision.

The girl is coached not to express pain during the cut. In order to ensure that a girl takes this seriously, several women spend the night at the girl's house the night before. The women also tease the girl by pretending to do the cutting act. During this time the girl is expected to keep her composure just as she will do during the real cutting process. The general consensus is that only cowards voice their pain.

During the night before the actual cut, the gathered women sing ritual songs that are supposed to encourage and inculcate to the girl the spiritual importance of the whole process. At the same time, the initiate (*enkaibartani*) undergoes a number of procedures said to numb the pain. She, for instance, is made to stay outside without clothes for about two hours before the moment of cutting, and just before the cut, she is washed with freezing cold water. The cold water is intentionally stored overnight in a clay cooking pot to further cool it down. While the cold numbs the girl's body, for the initiate it also signifies a process of being reborn into a social being. It is considered as a rite of passage signifying entry from childhood into adulthood. After the circumcision, the girl gains her status as an *i-sipolio* (lit. "the secluded one", a novice), a stage that ends when she leaves the seclusion of her mother's house to be metaphorically re-born from her mother's womb. Hereafter, society recognizes her as an *e-siankiki:* a young, marriageable, woman. Emurata is therefore not just a one day event but rather a long period of transformation as she embraces the physical, psychological, and social changes that confirm her status in society. Female circumcision is associated with becoming an ideal woman, feminine identity and inclusion into the network of adult responsible women in the community able to take part in rituals. The initiate, now a woman, will no longer play and dance with her former friends, until they too have undergone the cut. This symbolic goodbye is celebrated with a last cup of tea at the initiate's house, the day before the ritual.

Amongst the Maasai, the construction of gender identity (see for instance Moore 1994) is perceived as a continuous process. Throughout life, an individual moves from one social stage to the next as a result of marriage, motherhood and ritual. Thus gender identity can only be stabilized at a point in time but it is never complete (Moore 1999; Butler 1993). Hence, femininity and identity as Maasai women need to be continuously negotiated and maintained.

The initiate's mother plays a pivotal role in this process of negotiation. During the circumcision ritual, it is she who blesses her daughter and approves her going through this rite of passage. She takes out a special cowhide specifically intended for use during the circumcision, and she lays it on the ground for her daughter to sit on, thus showing that she fully supports her daughter to undergo the circumcision. After the cut, it is also the mother who takes up the hide, folds it together and carries it and its contents back into the house. The remnants of the cut (i.e. pieces of the external genitalia, blood, together with milk and the grease used immediately after the cut) and the blood shed during circumcision represent the bonding with the spiritual world of the ancestors. The skin and its contents are stored under the mother's bed. On this bed, the circumcised girl will rest and sleep until she fully recuperates, customarily until the third day when the girl is bathed for the first time on the hide. Then also the rotting remains will be buried under the soil behind the mother's house. This practice is a reminder of what happens to the placenta and blood from the womb after a woman gives birth. This symbolizes assured fertility and reproduction, not only in the physical but also in the social realm; not only for the individual or the family, but for Maasai society at large. This society also includes the world of the ancestors. Also in that sense, the bonding embodied when undergoing the cut ensures the continuation of Maasai culture, as it invokes the blessing by the ancestors.

Other women are also involved in ritual and its organization (see Hodgson 2005:235). After the cutting procedure, they welcome the initiate through a celebration. This celebration is much more elaborate than the goodbye party with the girl's former friends, as women from the wide vicinity meet at the initiate's house to receive a new woman into their midst, marking again the initiate's newly acquired status as an adult who now considers the women gathered in her house as her peers. The latter bring gifts (such as milk, potatoes, green vegetables, and livestock —in particular sheep— but also clothing and jewellery). In the days to come, they will make sure that the circumcised girl has enough food: she is put on a rich, fattening diet of soup, mutton fried in its own fat, fresh and sour milk, and local delicacies. Also, the initiate is made to bathe in a extract of particular herbs (*ilkitoloshwa*) soaked and boiled in water, said to relieve pain, stop bleeding, and facilitate the healing process. The wounds are properly taken care of by cleaning them once or twice a day, and by applying proper medicines such as honey and fresh ghee made from cow milk cream (*en'gorno*).

Once recovered, the real initiation begins. This period immediately following the cut may last from six months up to three years. During this time, the young woman receives arcane knowledge about family and social life, and about Maasai culture in general, on a much more fundamental level than before. This status is signified by the special ornaments she wears on her head and neck. These symbolize her transition into adulthood: the initiate has matured, and is ready for marriage. This borderland stage is ended when the initiate finally appears outside her mother's homestead (*enkang'*), a place she is expected leave soon as she is now ready to marry.

Important to note, however, is that circumcision has undergone important changes over the past few years, decades, or even century. First of all, it is naive (and even, as in the case of the Kikuyu, plainly wrong) to assume that circumcision is a mere remnant of a petrified past (see Pedersen 1991; for Maasai society, see Hodgson 2005:235–236). As Paul Rabinow (1975:1) already noted, "tradition is a moving image of the past [...] tradition is opposed not to modernity, but to alienation," and circumcision is no exception. Besides incorporating western practices (such as printed invitations) and borrowing elements from missionization among the Maasai (see Hodgson 2005:237), contemporary circumcision rituals have embraced modern ideas, such as sterility (new blades and surgical gloves for the circumciser); some families prefer to take their girls to the local health clinic, making use of the services of a qualified medical practitioner. As a result the severity of the cut has been reduced over the years, with Maasai women now practising what they refer to as "the modern way of cutting" (*ilkisili*), an evolution also found in other places (see El Guindi 2006). Nevertheless, circumcisions have taken on a semi-hidden character, out of fear for prosecution by government authorities.

CONCLUSION

This chapter's main aim was to elucidate the importance of bodily practices such as FGC in mediating the daily life worlds of Maasai women, and it regarded, in line with received wisdom in anthropology, circumcision as a rite of passage crucial in making Maasai women's identity. Hence circumcision appears as a borderland, where boundaries of identity and belonging (such as the distinction between immature girl and adult woman, between man and woman, or between non-Maasai and Maasai) are made and unmade by both initiate and society at large. In this, the ritual not only appears as a border zone; the body itself can be conceived as a borderland that demands continuous negotiation and (re-)drawing of boundaries.

One such process of negotiation concerns the often repeated dichotomy of so-called tradition versus modernity, and it is important to acknowledge that practices such as FGC among the Maasai are always an attempt to synergize and consolidate elements from what is imagined as "traditional" and from what is experienced as "new." Keeping in mind that both poles are a product of ideology and of the social imagination, it is important to acknowledge, too, that female agency is pivotal in re-inventing and continuing the practice of FGC. For the women in our sample, female circumcision is a crucial step in reaching adulthood, but also in morphing social identity, social competence, and female sexuality. For them, female circumcision is not viewed as a practice that demonstrates male domination; rather, it is a moment of transition crucial to themselves. Even though men are involved in dominant social discourse, among the Maasai it is women who are most intimately involved in organizing the events surrounding female circumcision. Therefore, the meaning and importance of FGC cannot be understood if this role of women as active agents is not taken into account. Also with regard to the often downplayed role of African women's agency, borrowing Gloria Anzaldua's (2002:2–3) words, the struggle of borders is still a reality. This is especially true for the Maasai women and girls in our study, as they strive to find ways in which they can experience and articulate their self-definition and female identity.

NOTES

[1] Today, this ritual practice is famously known by phrases such as Female Genital Mutilation or Female Genital Cutting, in reference to the associated bodily inscription.

[2] In local *Maa* language, *emurata* is an encompassing term referring to both female and male circumcision in local Maa language.

REFERENCES

Abusharaf, R. M. 2006. Introduction: The custom in question. *In* R. M. Abusharaf, ed. Female circumcision: multicultural perspectives. Pp. 1–24. Philadelphia: University of Pennsylvania Press.

Ahlberg, M. B., W. Njau, K. Kiiru, and I. Krantz. 2000. Gender masked or self-inflicted pain: Female circumcision, eradication and persistence in central Kenya. African Sociological Review 4:35–54.

Ahmadu F. 2000. Rites and wrongs: An Insiders/Outsider Reflects on Power and Excision. *In* B. Shell-Duncan and Y. Herlund Y., eds. Female "circumcision" in Africa: Culture, controversy and change. Pp. 283–312. Boulder: Lynne Reinner Publishers.

Almroth L., S. Elmusharaf, N. El Hadi, A. Obeid, M.A. El Sheikh M.A, S. M. Elfadil and S. Bergstrom. 2005. Primary infertility after genital mu-

tilation in girlhood in Sudan: a case control study. The Lancet 366:385–391.
Al-Krenawi, A. and Wiesel-Lev, R. 1999. Attitudes toward and perceived psychosocial impact of female circumcision as practised among the Bedouin-Arabs of the Negev. Family Process 38(4):431–443.
Anzaldua E. G. 2002. Preface : (Un)Natural bridges, (Un)Safe spaces. *In* Anzaldua G. and A. Keating, eds. This bridge we call home: radical visions for transformation. Pp. 1–6. London: Routledge Publishers.
Boddy, J. 1989. Wombs and alien spirits: Women, men and the Zar cult in Nothern Sudan. Madison: University of Wisconsin press.
Braidotti, R. 1991. Patterns of dissonance. Cambridge: Polity Press.
Butler J. P. 1993. Bodies that matter: On the discursive limits of sex. London: Routledge Publishers.
Dare F.O., Oboro V.O., Fadiora S.O., Sule-Odu A.O., Olabode T.O. (2004). Female genital mutilation: An analysis of 522 cases in South-Western Nigeria. Journal of Obstetrics and Gynaecology 24:281–283.
El Guindi F. 2006. "Had this been your face, would you leave it as is?" Female circumcision among Nubians of Egypt. *In* R. M. Abusharaf, ed. Female circumcision: multicultural perspectives. Pp. 27–46. Philadelphia: University of Pennsylvania Press.
Esho, T. C. 2012. An exploration of the psycho-social experiences of women who have undergone female genital cutting. A case of the Maasai in Kenya. Unpublished Ph.D. Dissertation, Faculty of medical sciences, University of Leuven.
Esho, T., P. Enzlin, S. Van Wolputte and M. Temmerman. 2010. Female genital cutting and sexual function: in search of an alternate theoretical model. African Identities 8(3):221–235.
Gruenbaum, E. 2001. The Female Circumcision Controversy. Philadelphia: University of Pennsylvania Press
Harding S. 2008. Sciences from below: Feminisms, postcolonialisms and modernities. Durham: Duke University Press.
Hodgson, D. 2005. The church of women: Gendered encounters between Maasai and missionaries. Bloomington: Indiana University Press.
Hosken, F. 1994 [4th rev. Ed]. The Hosken Report: Genital and Sexual Mutilation of Females. Lexington, MA: Women's International Network News.
Kenya Health Demographic Survey (KHDS). 2003. Magnitude of FGM in Kenya. Nairobi: National Focal Point.
Knudsen, O. 1994. The Falling Dawadawa Tree: Female Circumcision in Developing Ghana. Amherst: Smyrna Press.
Meyer, B. and P. Geschiere. 2003 [1999]. Globalization and identity: dialectics of flow and closure. Introduction. *In* B. Meyer and P. Geschiere, eds. Globalization and identity: dialectics of flow and closure. Pp. 1–

16. Oxford: Blackwell Publishing.
Mohamud A., S. Radeny and K. Ringheim. 2006. Community-Based efforts to end female circumcision in Kenya. Raising awareness and organizing alternative rites of passage. *In* R.M. Abusharaf, ed. Female Circumcision. Multicultural perspectives. Pp. 75–103. Philadelphia: University of Pennsylvania press.
Mohanty, C. T. 2003. Introduction: Decolonization; Anticapitalist critique, and feminist commitments. *In* C.T. Mohanty, ed. Feminism without borders: Decolonizing theory, practicing solidarity. Pp. 1–15. Durham: Duke Univerisity Press.
Moore H. L. 1999. Gender symbolism and praxis. *In* H.L. Moore, T. Sanders T. and B. Kaare B., eds. Those who play with fire: Gender, fertility and transformation in East and Southern Africa. London: Athlone Press.
——— 1994. 'Divided we stand': Sex, gender and sexual difference. Feminist Review 47 (Summer): 78–95.
Ndagala, D. K. 1992. Territory, pastoralists, and livestock: resource control among the Kisongo Maasai. Uppsala Studies in cultural anthropology 18. Stockholm: Almqvist och Wicksell.
Nnaemeka O. 2005. Introduction: The challenges of border-crossing: African women and transnational feminism. In N. Obioma, ed. Female circumcision and the politics of knowledge: African woman in imperialist discourse. Pp. 3–18. Westport: Greenwood Publishing Group.
Njambi, N. W. 2005. The consequences of female circumcision for health and sexuality: An update on the evidence. Culture Health and Sexuality 7(5):443–461.
——— 2004. Dualism and female bodies in representation of African female circumcision. Feminist Theory 5(3):281–303.
Obermeyer, C. M. 2005. The consequences of female circumcision for health and sexuality: an update on the evidence. Culture, Health and Sexuality 7(5):443–461.
——— 1999. Female genital surgeries: The known, the unknown and the unknowable. Medical Anthropology Quarterly 13(1): 79–106.
Pedersen, S. 2007. National bodies, unspeakable acts: the sexual politics of colonial policy-making. *In* M. Lock and J. Farquhar, eds. Beyond the body proper. Reading the anthropology of material life. Pp. 330–346. Durham: Duke University Press.
Rabinow, P. 1975. Symbolic Domination. Cultural Form and Historical Change in Morocco. Chicago: University of Chicago Press.
Ranger, T. 1993. The invention of tradition revisited. The case of colonial Africa. *In* T. Ranger and O. Vaughan, eds. Legitimacy and the state in twentieth-century Africa. Essays in honour of A.H.M. Kirk-Greene. Pp. 62–111. Houndsmill: MacMillan Press.
Richards A. I. (1956). *Chisungu*. London: Faber and Faber.

Shell-Duncan, B. 2008. From health to human rights: Female genital cutting and the politics of intervention. *American Anthropologist* 110(2): 225–236.

Shell-Duncan, B. and Hernlund, Y., eds. 2000. Female "Circumcision" in Africa. Culture, controversy and change. Boulder: Lynne Rienner, 2000.

Shweder, R. A. 2000. What about "female genital mutilation"? And why understanding culture matters in the first place. Daedalus 129:209.

Turner, T. S. 1980. The social skin. *In* J. Cherfas and R. Lewin, eds. Not work alone. A cross-cultural view of activities superfluous to survival. Pp. 112–140. London: Temple Smith.

Turner, V. 1967. A Forest Of Symbols: Aspects of Ndembu Ritual. Ithaca: Cornell University Press.

Van Rossem R. and J. A. Gage. 2009. The effects of female genital mutilation on the onset of sexual activity and marriage in Guinea. Archives of Sexual Behavior 38(2):178–185.

Wade L. 2009. Defining Gendered Oppression in US Newspapers: The strategic value of Female Genital Mutilation. Gender and Society, 23, (3):293–314.

INDEX

Afrikanische Studien/African Studies

Steven van Wolputte; Mattia Fumanti (Eds.)
Beer in Africa
Drinking spaces, states and selves
This volume on beer in Africa focuses on the making and unmaking of self in the inchoate, dark, exalted and sometimes upsetting context of bars, shebeens and other formal and informal drinking occasions. Beer in Africa takes the production and consumption of fermented drinks as its point of entry to investigate how local actors deal with the ambivalent and the hazy, and how this ambiguity stands as the sine qua non of social life and daily practice. *The book includes contributions by Gregor Dobler, Simon Heap, Mattia Fumanti, Sigrun Helmfrid, Detlev Krige, Patrick McAllister, Jonathan Roberts, Ute Röschenthaler & Steven Van Wolputte.*
Bd. 36, 2010, 336 S., 29,90 €, br., ISBN 978-3-8258-1257-7

Josephat Obi Oguejiofor, Tobias Wendl (Eds.)

EXPLORING THE OCCULT AND PARANORMAL IN WEST AFRICA

LIT

Josephat Obi Oguejiofor; Tobias Wendl (Eds.)
Exploring the Occult and Paranormal in West Africa
The point of departure of this book is a phenomenon which is often referred to as the "return of the religious", a recent but apparently ubiquitous phenomenon which does not fit the modernist axiom of secularisation, neither in the "developed" nor the "developing" worlds. In Africa, the last two decades have witnessed a remarkable and steady increase in the spread and reinforcement of occult and paranormal phenomena. The reports on these developments are not restricted to specific countries or areas; they cover the whole continent and surface in the most diverse images, media, stories and rumours. The credence accorded to them has become an important factor that shapes social relationships in everyday life, economic and political actions, medical decisions and religious adherence.
Bd. 47, 2012, 280 S., 29,90 €, br., ISBN 978-3-643-90183-5

LIT Verlag Berlin – Münster – Wien – Zürich – London
Auslieferung Deutschland / Österreich / Schweiz: siehe Impressumsseite